HAPPY DAYS ARE HERE AGAIN

HST: Memories of the Truman Years

Miracle of 48:
Harry Truman's Major Campaign Speeches

Eleanor and Harry:
The Correspondence of Eleanor Roosevelt and Harry S. Truman

Harry & Ike:
The Partnership That Remade the Post-War World

Rolling on the River:
The Best of Steve Neal

They Never Go Back to Pocatello:
Selected Essays of Richard Neuberger McNary of Oregon

Dark Horse: A Biography of Wendell Willkie

The Eisenhowers

Tom McCall: Maverick
(with Tom McCall)

HAPPY DAYS

ARE HERE

AGAIN

THE 1932 DEMOCRATIC CONVENTION,

THE EMERGENCE OF FDR—AND

HOW AMERICA WAS CHANGED FOREVER

STEVE NEAL

WILLIAM MORROW

An Imprint of HarperCollins*Publishers*

HarperCollins books may be purchased for educational, business, or sales promotional use. For information please write: Special Markets Department, HarperCollins Publishers Inc., 10 East 53rd Street, New York, NY 10022.

FIRST EDITION

Designed by Jo Anne Metsch

Printed on acid-free paper

Library of Congress Cataloging-in-Publication Data

Neal, Steve
    Happy days are here again: the 1932 Democratic convention, the emergence of FDR—and how America was changed forever / Steve Neal.— 1st ed.
        p. cm.
    ISBN 0-06-001376-1
    1. Roosevelt, Franklin D. (Franklin Delano), 1882–1945. 2. Presidents—United States—Election—1932. 3. Democratic National Convention (1932: Chicago, Ill.)   4. United States—Politics and government—1929–1933. I. Title.

E805.N43   2004   2003071060

04 05 06 07 08 wbc/qw 10 9 8 7 6 5 4 3 2 1

IN MEMORY OF

ROBERT J. DONOVAN

I pledge you, I pledge myself, to a new deal for the American people.
Let us all here assembled constitute ourselves prophets
of a new order of competence and courage.
This is more than a political campaign; it is a call to arms.

—FROM FRANKLIN DELANO ROOSEVELT'S ACCEPTANCE SPEECH,

DEMOCRATIC NATIONAL CONVENTION, CHICAGO, ILLINOIS,

JULY 2, 1932

CONTENTS

HAPPY DAYS ARE HERE AGAIN

1

THE MAN
WHO WASN'T THERE

F RANKLIN DELANO ROOSEVELT first visited Chicago in 1892, at
the age of ten, when he accompanied his father on a tour of the
site of the World's Fair celebrating the four-hundredth anniversary of
Christopher Columbus's discovery of America. For the rest of his life,
the prairie metropolis would be among his favorite cities. As the Democratic nominee for the vice presidency in 1920, he selected Chicago for
the kickoff of his campaign. "Tonight," he declared from the stage of
the auditorium, "we are firing the opening gun of a battle of far-reaching
importance, and once again the shots are going to be heard around the
world." In 1929, as the newly elected governor of New York, he made
his out-of-state political debut in Chicago, speaking before a luncheon
sponsored by the Democratic Party of Illinois. Although he would not
discuss his own future, FDR blamed Republicans for the Great Crash
and called for bold new leadership. This appearance in the heartland
marked the beginning of his quest for the White House.[1]

When the 1932 Democratic National Convention opened in Chicago,

Roosevelt was 836 miles away in his paneled office at the New York State Capitol in Albany. This marked only the second time in twenty years that he would not be in the convention hall for the presidential balloting. As the leading contender for the presidential nomination, FDR followed the tradition that front-runners did not engage the competition. Even though he was not on the scene, his name dominated every conversation. While a half dozen rivals courted delegates, Roosevelt had to protect his lead and find more votes. "Governor Roosevelt is as leading a candidate as one could find at the moment," a humorist wrote in *The New Yorker,* "bearing in mind that it is always difficult to tell just how leading any Democratic candidate is at any given moment."

To win the nomination, Roosevelt would need a combination of luck and savvy political management. Louis McHenry Howe, sixty-one years old, and James Aloysius Farley, forty-four, were in charge of the Roosevelt operation in Chicago. Their war room was Suite 1702 in the Congress Hotel. The sickly and frail Howe, who had been promoting Roosevelt for the presidency for twenty years, would not leave this suite for the duration of the convention. "Except that he threw his coat aside occasionally when he took a nap," FDR speechwriter Raymond Moley wrote of Howe, "I don't think that he had his clothes off the entire week."[2]

WORRIED ABOUT POSSIBLE subterfuge, Howe had one of his aides bribe officials at Chicago Stadium to obtain three adjacent rooms, with the center room to be used as Farley's convention hideaway. Howe ordered his aide to put locks on the side rooms and then spend the entire week night and day guarding this inner sanctum. Lela Stiles, one of Howe's assistants, recalled that her boss had a telephone booth installed in Farley's hideaway office "just to make doubly sure that no prying ears listened to any of the Farley conversations."

Among the reasons that Roosevelt, a polio survivor, had not gone to Chicago was that he would have had difficulty moving through crowds and standing in reception lines. "The other candidates had a certain advantage, of course, in being on the ground," Farley said.

But Howe improvised. A private switchboard was installed at the Congress Hotel with a direct line to Roosevelt's study in the Albany Executive Mansion. Howe had a voice amplifier attached with coils and wires to the switchboard for FDR's talks with delegates. "I would get on the phone first," Farley recalled, "and I'd say, 'Governor, we have in this room the delegate from Iowa. And the first man I'll introduce to you is that chap from Twin Falls, Ned Chapman, who knows you and you met him,' and then I'd mention the names of the other fellows who were there, and then Roosevelt would come on the loudspeaker and talk to these fellows, calling them by their first names, and thanking them for what they were doing.

"Those chats became so popular," Farley said, "that one or two delegations complained when they thought they were being left out."[3]

Even though Roosevelt was far ahead of his nearest rival, the nomination was in doubt. Of the 1,154 delegates, FDR had more than 600 votes. A majority was 578. But under the Democratic Party's rules, he needed a two-thirds majority of 770 votes to become the nominee. It took only 385 votes to deadlock the convention and that opposition had more than enough.

Roosevelt was strongest in the South and the West. Nearly half of his delegates (246) were from the Deep South and border states. He also had all sixty delegates from the Rocky Mountain states; twenty-six from the Pacific Northwest; eighty-one from the Great Plains; twenty-eight from New England; sixty-four from the Great Lakes states; and eighty-five from the Middle Atlantic region. The party's rural southern-western faction, which had once followed William Jennings Bryan and later William Gibbs McAdoo, had already chosen FDR as their new leader. What was most unusual about the Roosevelt coalition is that he did not have the support of his own region. The large industrial states of the Northeast were mostly against him, including his home base of New York.

As Farley noted, Roosevelt had delegates from thirty-one of the forty-eight states. But eight of the ten largest delegations were in the opposition camp. The Stop Roosevelt movement had a majority of the delegates in the Middle Atlantic states, New England, and on the Pacific Coast. If the opposition could unite behind a single candidate, the Democrats were headed for an epic battle. "There was to be no rival candidate before the convention," Farley said, "but all of the states not definitely committed to the Governor were to throw their favorite sons overboard and unite behind some mysterious candidate who would be trotted out at the last minute."

For Roosevelt to break a deadlock, something had to give. The states with favorite sons included Illinois with fifty-eight votes; Ohio with forty-eight; Missouri with thirty-six; Virginia with twenty-four delegates; and Maryland with sixteen votes. Perhaps the most coveted prize was Texas, which supported native son John Nance Garner and had forty-six votes divided among 184 delegates. In the war room, Howe had an extensive card file of delegations with background and analysis of key players. Ralph T. O'Neil, national commander of the American Legion and a delegate from Kansas, was listed as "friendly" and willing to help in other states. Amon G. Carter, publisher of the *Fort Worth Star-Telegram*, a Garner confidant, was referred to as "powerful, king-maker type," who "breaks with everyone." The entry on Houston banker Jesse H. Jones described him as a "double-crosser" and "for himself first, last and all the time." It also said that Jones "promises everybody everything." Senator Tom Connally, according to the Howe file, had "no conviction" but was a "key man" and had "tremendous influence."[4]

Howe and Farley had reason for concern. The Indiana delegation, whose thirty votes had been listed by Farley in Roosevelt's column, was flirting with the opposition. Meanwhile, the new leadership of the Minnesota Democratic Party announced plans to replace that state's pro-Roosevelt delegation. Twenty votes from Mississippi were also at risk. Under the unit rule, FDR held that delegation by a plurality of a single vote. If the Roosevelt lines broke at any point, his lead might not hold.

Powerful forces were out to stop him. The opposition included the leadership of the Democratic National Committee, the hard and ruthless bosses of the big-city machines, and the most influential members of the last Democratic administration. Three Democratic presidential nominees, including Alfred E. Smith, whose name Roosevelt had presented three times before national conventions, and James M. Cox, who had picked the young FDR as his running mate, were in Chicago working against his nomination.

"We were notably lacking in nationally known Democrats committed to our candidate," said Roosevelt strategist Edward J. Flynn, the Bronx Democratic leader. "Taking the Roosevelt organization from Jim Farley down, about 90 percent of them were newcomers and amateurs."[5]

In the era of the press lords, the largest newspaper chains opposed Roosevelt's nomination. "The times call for courage and action," the Scripps-Howard newspapers said in a front-page editorial. "We have those qualities in [Alfred E.] Smith. There are other men in the Democratic party who possess them. Judged by his performance Roosevelt does not." Only one of a half dozen New York daily newspapers supported Roosevelt. Of the five Chicago daily newspapers that would be read by delegates during convention week, none were friendly to FDR.

The popular and influential columnists Walter Lippmann, H. L. Mencken, Heywood Broun, and Will Rogers favored an alternative to Roosevelt in Chicago.

Organized labor was not aligned with Roosevelt or any of the Democratic contenders. William Green, president of the American Federation of Labor, and other influential union leaders were neutral in the 1932 Democratic presidential contest.

Big business openly worked against Roosevelt's nomination. The international bankers of Wall Street and the public-utility interests were determined to stop him. Roosevelt's advocacy of government intervention in the economy and federal development of hydroelectric power made him a threat to these special interests. "Howe had worked out an excellent system for keeping us informed, and for that reason we were seldom caught napping," Farley recalled. "A delegate from Iowa told us how he was called out of bed early in the morning by a gentleman who wanted to know on how many ballots he intended to stick by Roosevelt. A Southern delegate said his group were entertained all the way to Chicago by a couple of gentlemen who were extremely generous with food and drink but at the same time deeply distressed over their intentions to vote for the New York governor. We knew just where that pressure was being brought."[6]

As delegates arrived in Chicago, they were deluged with more than one hundred thousand telegrams urging them not to vote for FDR. But Howe had already written delegates: "A wish expressed by Governor Roosevelt that he could personally talk to the friends who have been selected by their various states to attend the Democratic National Convention, rather than to send a letter, brought out the suggestion that he take advantage of the newly devised paper phonographic records to convey his actual spoken words to those whom he wished to thank for their support."

Roosevelt also asked allies to hold their lines. "We are in a safe majority in the coming convention if we stand together," he said. "I hope history will point to your wise action at Chicago."

Before the presidential balloting, Howe and Farley would be facing contests over the seating of disputed delegations, the chairmanship of the convention, and the platform. A floor fight over the divisive Prohibition was regarded as such a potential threat that Roosevelt's camp discussed the possibility of delaying a vote on the platform until a presidential nominee had been chosen. If Roosevelt lost any of these preliminary fights, Farley knew that it could cost them in the main event.[7]

As the convention neared, the Roosevelt camp was caught by surprise when the *Chicago Herald Examiner*, published by William Randolph Hearst, reported that Senator Burton K. Wheeler of Montana had been chosen as FDR's running mate. This story broke at a time when Farley was using the vice presidency as a bargaining chip in discussions with more than one favorite-son presidential hopeful. Although Wheeler had been the first nationally prominent political figure to endorse Roosevelt for the presidency, his selection for the ticket would have sparked controversy. Many party regulars were still angry with Wheeler for abandoning the Democrats to run for the vice presidency on the Progressive ticket in 1924. Wheeler was now threatening to lead a third-party movement if Roosevelt failed to win the nomination. From Albany, Roosevelt dictated this message to Farley: "I understand the *Chicago Examiner* says that I have asked Senator Burt Wheeler to become the vice-presidential candidate. This story is not true. I have already made it clear to the press and the country that I have asked no one to be my running mate and that no one has been authorized to do so in my behalf."[8]

Frank R. Kent, political columnist for the *Baltimore Sun*, who had been covering presidential conventions for more than a generation, had

never seen it played this rough. "It is pretty hard to exaggerate the bitterness here," Kent wrote from Chicago. "Names are called, accusa-
tions made, treachery charged, and discreditable stories spread."

The most outrageous slander against Roosevelt was an allegation
linking him to the Ku Klux Klan. John M. Callahan, the Democratic
national committeeman from Wisconsin, sent all delegates copies of
letters purporting to show that the Klan had been involved in the Roosevelt campaign. "With such damaging information in circulation," he
asserted, "it will be impossible to win the election in November unless
another candidate is selected." All the documents showed is that orga-
nizers of an unauthorized Roosevelt club had enlisted the Klan's aid.
The Roosevelt campaign had long since severed ties with these dubi-
ous characters. In Albany, Roosevelt declined comment. "We must expect such violent attacks," FDR wrote privately. Howe had warned his
boss that the Roosevelt clubs were a nuisance that could come back to
haunt them. But nobody, including Callahan, believed that Roosevelt
was an ally of the Klan.

Another whispering campaign that disturbed Roosevelt and worried
his strategists involved the health issue. He had gained popular acclaim
for his brave comeback from the illness that left him crippled. But the
opposition questioned his fitness for the presidency, and even some
friends had doubts. When former New York governor Alfred E. Smith,
Roosevelt's major rival, departed for Chicago, it was reported from Albany that FDR might change his plans.

"There's one way I could get out to Chicago that you fellows haven't
guessed," Roosevelt said in response to this speculation. "It would not
be by airplane, train or automobile. I could simply drop out of sight,
nobody would have the slightest idea where I was, and eventually I'd
appear in Chicago. Of course, it would take quite a while," he added
with a laugh. "I could go by submarine."[9]

Roosevelt was having fun. "He actually seems to enjoy the experience," an Albany correspondent wrote, "of being between 100 and 150 votes away from the Democratic nomination for President of the United States—without, so far as the public is informed, being sure of those ballots."[10]

2

CHICAGO 1932

HICAGO MAYOR Anton J. Cermak fought hard for the right to host both the 1932 political conventions. Like the rest of the country, his city was reeling from the Great Depression. Three-quarters of a million residents were out of work and more than a hundred thousand families were on the dole. Half of the city's banks had failed, most of the Loop's great hotels were in receivership, and thousands of people had lost their homes. The city government was on the verge of bankruptcy. Schoolteachers and policemen were paid in scrip. If the Republicans and Democrats came to town, Cermak hoped that several million dollars would be pumped into the local economy. Few cities needed more help.

Cermak also wanted to improve his town's image. All over the world, Chicago was linked to gangland violence. Al Capone, the most notorious gangster of this era, knocked off a prominent Republican politician, an assistant state's attorney, a rogue newspaperman, and, in the infamous St. Valentine's Day Massacre of 1929, seven members of a rival gang. A month before the 1932 conventions, the Hollywood studio United Artists released *Scarface*, directed by Howard Hawks and based on Capone's brutal reign as king of the underworld. "This picture," it began, "is an indictment of gang violence in America and of the callous indifference of the government to this constantly increasing menace to our safety and liberty." The critically acclaimed film broke all attendance records in New York, San Francisco, and other major cities. But Cermak would not allow this movie to be shown on Chicago's silver screens.[1]

On January 8, 1932, the Democratic National Committee met in Washington, D.C., for the purpose of choosing a convention site. Cermak asserted that his town had been slandered. "I want to urge you not to believe one-half the lies they tell about Chicago," he declared. "Chicago is a wonderful city, and it is not deserving of the reputation it seems to have outside of the city of Chicago." Assuring the panel that Democrats would be safe, the mayor offered to provide bodyguards for delegates and other distinguished visitors.

San Francisco, Kansas City, and Atlantic City were also in the running. But Chicago had several advantages. It was the nation's convention center. Two-thirds of the delegates were within an overnight trip, and railroads offered special rates. With more than a hundred thousand rooms, Chicago's hotels had more and better accommodations. Even if the other cities had been equal in these areas, the convention hall was still the tiebreaker.

Both parties liked the new Chicago Stadium, which covered an entire city block on the Near West Side and dwarfed New York's Madison Square Garden. Twenty-five thousand people could be seated in the galleries and another six thousand on the floor. The indoor arena was the first to provide an unobstructed view from each seat and it was air-conditioned. For all of these reasons, the Greek temple on West Madison Street was the ideal convention hall.[2]

Chicago was also an exciting attraction, the town that the flamboyant evangelist Billy Sunday couldn't shut down. With a population of
nearly 3.4 million in 1932, it was the railroad capital of the world, the
nation's largest port and industrial center. The Loop was the nation's
busiest shopping district and also had more theaters and nightclubs
than anywhere west of the Hudson River. Though hard hit by the Depression, Chicago would not be broken. Grant Park, the lakefront park
that was being constructed on more than two hundred acres of landfill,
was nearing completion. With twenty-four miles of lakefront, Chicago
had a dazzling skyline. The gleaming clock tower of the Wrigley Building and the gothic spires of the Tribune Tower were the gateway to the
Near North Side. In the South Loop, Henry Ives Cobb's Federal Building, one of America's great public structures, had a three-hundred-foot-
high rotunda and a dome larger than the U.S. Capitol's. In the financial
district, the Chicago Board of Trade's forty-five-story limestone mono-
lith towered above LaSalle Street. On the north bank of the Chicago
River, the Merchandise Mart was among the wonders of the age as the
world's largest building.

Describing his city as a playground to the world, Mayor Cermak invited delegates to preview the 1933 Chicago World's Fair. By the time
the Democrats would come to town, most of the exhibits would be
built. The fairgrounds included homes of the future, a walled city from
China, a Japanese teahouse, an operating diamond mine, the streets of
Paris, the spectacular Fountain of Light designed by Joseph Urban,
and the "Sky Ride," a monorail that carried its passengers between
twin towers along the lakefront. More than forty million people would
attend the "Century of Progress" exhibition.[3]

At the Democratic site-selection meeting, Cermak outhustled the
competition. By tradition the convention city makes a substantial dona-
tion to the national committee. In his opening presentation, he offered

$150,000, which would be the equivalent of $1.5 million in today's currency. When Kansas City matched this amount, the Chicago mayor increased his bid by $50,000 "without any strings." The Democratic national committeeman from California, who had lobbied for San Francisco, glumly conceded.

In choosing the convention site, each of the states and territories had two votes. That meant Franklin Roosevelt, with his southern and western allies, would make the selection. On the eve of the site-selection meeting, FDR wrote a friend: "I take it that we shall be able to prevent the Convention from going to Atlantic City or San Francisco." But Frank Hague, New Jersey's Democratic boss, and newspaper mogul William Randolph Hearst, California's most influential Democrat, were opposing Roosevelt's nomination.

Cermak, who was still neutral in the presidential race, courted FDR's favor. "The Chicago Citizens Committee has raised a liberal fund to cover the total expenses of the Convention and has presented to the National Committeemen and Committeewoman of the Democratic Party the many superior advantages which make Chicago more convenient and economical for the delegates," the mayor wrote the New York governor.

"We have the political situation well in hand in our state and a very unusual condition exists. Some of the ambitious Republicans have hesitated so far to declare themselves as candidates for the April primaries on account of their chances for election being so uncertain. For this reason I am very anxious to secure the Democratic Convention for Chicago. It will materially strengthen our position and help us to carry the state next fall."

ROOSEVELT BOUGHT CERMAK'S argument. "The Roosevelt group was very anxious to have Chicago," recalled Frank C. Walker, FDR's fund-raiser. Arthur F. Mullen of Nebraska, who would later be chosen as Roosevelt's convention floor leader, FDR's ally Robert Jackson of New Hampshire, and Norman Mack, New York's national committee-man, voted for Chicago's selection. On the first roll call, Chicago led the other three cities with 51 out of 109 votes but fell 4 short of the re-quired majority. At this point, ten committee members changed their votes in Cermak's favor.[4]

What is surprising about Roosevelt's selection of Chicago is that he got nothing in return. As the chairman of the third-largest delegation, Cermak had more clout than the combined strength of California and Florida. It would be the mayor's strategy to hold these votes in an ef-fort to deadlock the convention. Cermak longed to be a kingmaker. Roosevelt viewed him as the key to the nomination. Few politicians could resist FDR's charm, and he confidently anticipated that Cermak would fall in line.

On his return from a western campaign swing, Roosevelt stopped in Chicago, and the two men conferred in FDR's private railroad car. Their session did not go well. Roosevelt consented to stay out of the Illinois primary in which Cermak was running Senator J. Hamilton Lewis as a favorite son. "I think things are going well and I hope, of course, that Illinois will come my way at the earliest possible moment," Roosevelt wrote a friend after this meeting. "I understand the desire of many to give a complimentary vote to the Senator."[5]

Anton Joseph Cermak was in no hurry to release those delegates. If Roosevelt could be stopped short of a two-thirds vote, the mayor could very well determine the next president of the United States. He was the most cunning of big-city politicians. Broad-shouldered, stocky, and muscular, Cermak talked like a tough guy, and, at the age of fifty-nine, he still had a dark head of hair. A native of Bohemia, he ran Chicago like an Old World autocrat. He had just led Democrats to their most sweeping triumph in Illinois since the Civil War and had built what was already recognized as the nation's most formidable political organization. Until he took command of the Cook County Democratic Central Committee, Republicans had dominated the local political scene. After Cermak took over at City Hall, the GOP never recaptured the mayor's office.

A former coal miner, mule driver, and street peddler, Cermak had the shrewdness of a self-made man. For more than half of his life, he had held elective office. In his rise to power he used political connections to make a fortune in banking, insurance, and real estate. His net worth was about $7 million. Untroubled by the appearance of impropriety, he lobbied for the liquor interests while serving in the Illinois legislature and the Chicago City Council. Cermak used his influence to fight closing laws and protect gambling houses. Early in his career he challenged several rivals to fistfights. Another politician recalled, "He was like a powerful animal with other animals."[6]

As an immigrant in a city where two-thirds of the residents were foreign-born or first-generation Americans, Cermak smoothed away his rough edges to become a coalition builder. There were more Czechs in Chicago than in Prague, and this ethnic group became his political base. Joining forces with Italians, Jews, Germans, and Poles, he broke up the Irish monopoly on Democratic Party leadership. In the 1920s, as president of the Cook County Board of Commissioners, he became Chicago's most important Democratic officeholder. He expanded roads, improved services, and took care of his friends by building the county hospital and criminal courts building in his own neighborhood. He was the first ward boss to provide free garbage cans for the residents of his ward. Cermak made himself into a skillful administrator and revived his party's political fortunes. "He had the biggest Democratic patronage office," recalled longtime associate Henry Sonnenschein. "He knew where everybody in the party stood; which were friends and enemies of each other, and he played them off, one against the other. He had ways of getting information, so he always knew what was going on in politics."

Sonnenschein, who spent a quarter century as Cermak's top aide, said years later, "Never once did Cermak say 'please' or 'thank you' to me, or 'well done.' He was all business, cold and efficient, but fair, understanding, and tolerant."[7]

Cermak knew what he was doing. "It has fallen to my lot," he told FDR in 1929, "to direct the operations of our party in this section and I might add that we have just completed a most successful judicial election."

At the same time that Roosevelt sought to make Democrats more competitive in upstate New York, Cermak reported about his efforts to make inroads into Cook County's Republican-dominated townships: "When I became president of the County, I decided to work about a change of this situation. I began distributing what patronage I could in these country towns and the result this year was that the votes in these towns was two to one as against eight to one four years ago. We have worked on the theory that if we get our count we can at least strike at victory, and with additional work whereby we hold down the plurality in the country towns we gain victory for much of our ticket.

"Let's fill up the holes in our organization, not alone in Illinois," he added, "but let us have a national survey made and build a solid national organization whose power is felt in off years as well as in the quadrennial period when we trot out our thoroughbreds."[8]

In 1931 he challenged the corrupt William Hale Thompson, Chicago's three-term Republican mayor. A flamboyant rogue, Big Bill had once accepted a $250,000 contribution from Capone and allowed the crime syndicate to do whatever it wanted. Thompson looted the city treasury and damaged the public school system. Cermak vowed to "sweep City Hall clean" and "restore Chicago's standing before the world." The independent Harold L. Ickes observed that Cermak was a good executive who knew "everything there was to know about the city and he is an indefatigable worker. Of course what will go on behind the scenes will perhaps not bear close examination, but even if he gives us an administration that is only good on the surface it will be a gain over [Republican mayor William Hale] Thompson."

Cermak rolled up a plurality of more than two hundred thousand votes and won by twenty percentage points. Dr. Shailer Matthews, dean of the Divinity School of the University of Chicago, proclaimed, "I believe that this is the greatest opportunity that ever came to the city." Even the new mayor's critics acknowledged that he was a force to be reckoned with. "To the practical and unprejudiced observer it appears that Chicago has simply swapped one evil for another," *The Nation* editorialized. "Indeed, it is clear that the great crusade has had one net result: the people of Chicago, by electing Tony Cermak, have made him the most powerful boss in the United States today. The power that lies in his hands is greater than that possessed by any other boss anywhere in this country; it may eventually prove greater than that of any other boss in American history."[9]

He did what had to be done. The city was in worse shape than Cermak had imagined. The new mayor slashed expenditures, reduced the city's payroll, and improved the efficiency of tax collection. Civic leaders credited him with rescuing Chicago from financial collapse. In dealing with the mob, he was just as tough. Soon after taking office, he called in gangland leaders and told them to fold their tents. In the spring of 1931 Capone was also indicted by a federal grand jury for tax evasion and was convicted that fall on five counts and sentenced to eleven years in prison. After the mobster's fall, Cermak went after his gang. "I am against this Mafia business," he declared. "The Capone bums have gotta go." Frank Nitti, Capone's successor, refused to leave town. Not long afterward, he was shot in the back by Cermak's bodyguard.

As the leader of the Democratic Party, Cermak controlled forty thousand patronage jobs and had absolute power. He chose the U.S. senator, governor, state's attorney, and aldermen. The city council became his rubber stamp. "I want your cooperation, and if I cannot have it, I will go ahead anyway," he told the aldermen. Cermak was often ruthless, using his police department to gather intelligence on other public officials, employees, and political enemies. He opened letters of associates without their knowledge and wiretapped friend and foe alike. The police became Cermak's political enforcers. In an attempt to break the GOP's hold on the black vote, he ordered police to crack down on the South Side's policy games. When African American politicians quit the Republican Party to become Democrats, the police raids stopped. Cermak had his own police captain at the Lawndale station for twenty-eight years. Captain John Ptacek never interfered with the speakeasies and gambling establishments in the ward. But in 1932 when he refused to approve a new handbook, Cermak abruptly had him transferred out of the ward.[10]

At the national level, he focused on a single issue: the repeal of the Eighteenth Amendment that outlawed alcoholic beverages. This was an ambitious undertaking, for no amendment to the Constitution had ever been repealed, and yet the mayor sensed that it could be done. When Prohibition became law in January 1920, small-time hoodlums cornered the liquor market, and organized crime became big business. In a single year, 1927, Capone netted $105 million from bootlegging and rum running. As a social issue, Prohibition sparked bitter debate and a cultural divide. Roosevelt, who had once been an ally of the

Prohibition movement but now favored repeal, thought that the Democrats had nothing to gain by taking a stand on this emotional issue. Cermak, a founder of the National Association Against Prohibition, argued that the Democrats could have "a mighty future on the national discontent with prohibition."[11]

Before the Democratic convention, Cermak went to New York for meetings with Democratic National Committee chairman John J. Raskob, Mayor James J. Walker, and Jersey City's Frank Hague. If Prohibition ended, these men would be empowered to grant liquor licenses and stood to make millions. Cermak and his allies plotted strategy to press for a floor vote at Chicago Stadium on a repeal amendment. In an attempt to have it both ways, Roosevelt had tentatively endorsed a new constitutional amendment that would allow dry states to retain Prohibition with federal aid, and wet states to permit liquor, with local option and with state stores replacing the saloon. But Cermak's group would not settle for this compromise. Roosevelt had given the impression to southern allies that he was not all that opposed to the Eighteenth Amendment. By forcing him to declare himself on an up or down vote on repeal, Cermak's group hoped to put him on the spot. Cermak was so doubtful about Roosevelt's commitment to repeal that he was ready to publicly denounce him after their meeting. "I had to keep kicking his heels to keep him quiet," said Edward J. Kelly, president of Chicago's South Park Board.

FDR believed that Al Smith had doomed his chances in 1928 when a New York newspaper goaded him into "sending that fool telegram . . . telling how wet he was. Al had every wet vote in the country but he needed a good many millions of the middle of the road votes to elect him President."

By now, Roosevelt knew that he would be going into a hostile arena. Cermak controlled access to the convention floor and could pack the galleries. The mayor would also decide when the lights went down and whether demonstrations got "psychological accompaniment" from the mighty pipe organ a hundred feet above the delegates. Though FDR had made him the ringmaster, Cermak had a short memory. "I'd vote for Lewis on the first ballot," the mayor declared, "even if Roosevelt gets 90 percent of the vote."[12]

3

FRONT-RUNNER

ROM NEW HAMPSHIRE to California, Franklin D. Roosevelt
would be running against the field in the Democratic presidential primaries. There were seventeen of these contests in 1932 and he
welcomed the opportunity to compete on the national stage. With the
party's Old Guard opposed to his candidacy, the primaries gave him a
chance to demonstrate popularity with ordinary people. His goal was
to win so many primary votes that his nomination could not be denied.
But only about a third of the delegates would be chosen in primaries.
Most of the delegates would be selected by party leaders and state conventions.

Since Roosevelt had been reelected to New York's governor's seat in
1930 by a three-quarters-of-a-million plurality, he had been the favorite for the Democratic presidential nomination. It was his good fortune to be in this position when his party's prospects seemed the
brightest in two decades. Roosevelt had once noted that "conservatives
find it nearly always easy to control government at least two-thirds of

the time because they are united on the perfectly simple proposition of 'doing nothing' and 'leaving well enough alone.' " In late 1931, he wrote privately: "I am fully convinced that the cycle has swung again after twelve years and that it is our turn next."[1]

Roosevelt's lead for the 1932 Democratic presidential nomination was based on two decades of political activity. He had already waged a national campaign as the 1920 Democratic nominee for the vice presidency. In this losing effort, the young FDR barnstormed in forty-two states, delivered more than four hundred speeches, and got to know the country. Roosevelt also established friendships with elected officials and party activists who would expand his political network. After he was crippled by polio in 1921, he maintained a wide correspondence with politicians throughout America. At the low point of the Democratic Party's fortunes, Roosevelt wrote thousands of state and county leaders seeking their advice about the party's future. Many of them replied that he should lead their party back to power. "I am now only anxious to have the opportunity to urge your nomination for the Presidency," James F. Byrnes, soon to be elected to the U.S. Senate from South Carolina, wrote FDR in November 1928. "If you take care of your health you are certain to be re-elected in the off-year election and you offer the only hope for democracy to again get control of the government."[2]

OTHER HOPEFULS INCLUDED former New York governor Alfred E. Smith, the 1928 presidential nominee, who wanted a rematch with President Hoover. Smith had been the most progressive governor of his era but had run for the presidency in 1928 on a conservative platform and had moved farther to the right. Though he still wore his brown derby, smoked cigars, and talked with the thick accent of the Lower

East Side, he now lived on Fifth Avenue overlooking Central Park and earned five times his gubernatorial salary.

John Nance Garner, the white-haired, rough-hewn Speaker of the U.S. House, was the first Texan to gain serious consideration for the presidency. Senate minority leader Joseph T. Robinson of Arkansas, the 1928 vice-presidential nominee, was also regarded as a possible contender.

Former secretary of war Newton D. Baker, viewed by many Democrats as the most likely nominee if Roosevelt faltered, was receptive to a possible draft. As mayor of Cleveland, Baker had been among the great figures of the Progressive Era and President Woodrow Wilson's administration. What made Baker threatening to Roosevelt was that he appealed to the Democratic Party's rural and urban factions.

Albert Cabell Ritchie, Maryland's four-term governor, emerged in the 1920s as a leader of his party's conservative wing and in 1932 hoped to win the presidency. Bernard Baruch, former chairman of the War Industries Board, hailed him as a man of destiny. At the national Governors' Conference, Roosevelt was asked by a newsreel reporter to stand next to Ritchie. "We'd like to get a shot of the next President of the United States," said Steve Early, who would later work for Roosevelt, "and I think we'll have it if you two pose together."[3]

Melvin Alvah Traylor, president of the First National Bank of Chicago, a native of Kentucky who spent his early career in the Texas hill country, was touted by Democratic National Committee chairman John J. Raskob as a potential contender for the presidency and had some support in all three of his home states.

Owen D. Young, chairman of the General Electric Company and the founding chairman of the Radio Corporation of America, took himself out of the running, but influential friends were promoting a draft. Smith and Roosevelt held him in high regard, and there was speculation that both men might support Young in the event of a dead-locked convention.

A 1931 poll of delegates and alternates to the 1928 Democratic National Convention showed that Roosevelt was the undisputed front-runner. Jesse Isador Straus, president of the R. H. Macy & Company department stores, who had long been active in the Democratic Party, did not include New York State in his survey because he presumed that the governor would have the support of his own state. Roosevelt led the Democratic pack in thirty-nine out of forty-four states. He was ahead in every western state that responded to the poll and in every southern state but Arkansas, where he trailed favorite son Robinson. Al Smith led by two to one in Massachusetts while running even with FDR in Connecticut and Delaware, and Albert C. Ritchie was strongly favored in Maryland. Roosevelt was ahead in the megastates of Illinois, Michigan, Ohio, Pennsylvania, California, and Texas. There were no replies from Oregon, Wisconsin, or Wyoming. Of the 844 delegates or alternates who expressed a preference, Roosevelt was favored by 478; Smith, 125; Owen Young, 75; Ritchie, 39; Joseph T. Robinson, 38; and Newton D. Baker, 35.

In another survey, Straus polled twelve hundred Democratic businessmen and professionals about the 1932 presidential election. Roosevelt led Young by two to one and Smith by five to one. The results of this second Straus poll were more surprising than the first because FDR was viewed with skepticism and hostility by many in the business community.[4]

The Roosevelt campaign was directed by Louis McHenry Howe, who had spent more than twenty years in the making of a president. As a legislative correspondent for the old *New York Herald*, he met Roosevelt, a freshman state senator, in 1911 and became his political mentor. When FDR was up for reelection in 1912 and incapacitated with typhoid fever, Howe took over the campaign. By targeting the rural and farm vote, he expanded FDR's political base and enabled him to win reelection in the Republican district. From then on Howe was his most trusted adviser, best friend, and confidant. "After 1912 it would be impossible to think of Roosevelt or Howe without the other," the historian Alfred B. Rollins later wrote. "They operated as parts of one political personality. They complemented each other in strengths and weaknesses." When FDR joined the Wilson administration in 1913 as assistant secretary of the navy, Howe went along as top aide, speechwriter, troubleshooter, and patronage chief. In 1920 Howe opposed his friend's acceptance of the vice-presidential nomination because the Democratic ticket was certain to lose. However, when Roosevelt was nominated, Howe ran the campaign. It had been his plan to go into private business. But when FDR was stricken with polio, Howe rushed to his side, reinforced his protégé's will to recover, moved into the Roosevelt household, and kept alive the once and future contender's public career. He never lost faith in FDR's candidacy for the White House and gave up a normal family life and independent career for this cause. In the 1932 Democratic presidential race, Roosevelt and Howe were running ahead of schedule. Howe had been against FDR's bid for governor in 1928, which was expected to be a Republican year. Under his timetable, Howe wanted Roosevelt to run for the governorship in 1932 and the presidency in 1936. This was Howe's strategy for Roosevelt, as governor, to advocate programs for farm relief and public power that would advance his presidential candidacy in the South, Midwest, and Pacific Coast states.

A frail little man with a chronic cough, Howe was sixty-one years old in 1932. He wore ill-fitting suits, shirts with high stiff collars, and chain-smoked Sweet Caporal cigarettes. During the presidential campaign, he worked out of an office at 331 Madison Avenue across the street from the Biltmore Hotel. He did not suffer fools and could be blunt to the point of rudeness. When Joseph P. Kennedy, the Wall Street financier, dropped in to see him at Roosevelt headquarters, Howe treated him with disdain. Kennedy, who had already met Roosevelt, was the biggest contributor to the preconvention campaign. "Howe had no personality, no charm," remembered former navy secretary Josephus Daniels, "but he knew politics and forgot himself."[5]

Edward J. Flynn, New York's secretary of state in 1932 and Democratic leader of the Bronx, played a key behind-the-scenes role in the Roosevelt campaign as fund-raiser and adviser. "Roosevelt suggested that I should go out through the country, making contacts with these friends and acquaintances, and begin to line up delegates," he recalled. "I did not agree with this suggestion, for I realized my own limitations. I was not an easy mixer, found it quite difficult to move about with facility among strange people."[6]

On Flynn's recommendation, the energetic James Aloysius Farley became Roosevelt's traveling salesman and delegate hunter, and there could not have been a better choice. If it was difficult for most people to warm up to Howe or Flynn, it was impossible not to like Farley. An Irish American who had grown up in the Hudson River Valley, Big Jim was fondly remembered in his hometown as the best first baseman that the village of Haverstraw had ever produced. Along with baseball, Democratic politics was his lifelong passion. At the age of eight, he led a torchlight parade for William Jennings Bryan in the 1896 presidential campaign. In 1912, at twenty-four, Farley won his first elective office as town clerk of Stony Point. Elected Democratic chairman of Rockland County in 1918, he was appointed port warden of New York City as his reward for helping Al Smith win the governorship. From 1923 to 1925 he served in the New York State Assembly but was defeated for reelection in a district that traditionally voted Republican. Farley, who had worked for fifteen years as a salesman and bookkeeper, formed his own building supply company in the middle 1920s and did so well that he merged it with five other firms. Smith also appointed him to the New York State Athletic Commission, of which he served as chairman from 1925 through 1933. "Big Jim Farley was the only political figure who ever used the chairmanship of the boxing commission as the launching pad for a flight to national prominence," sportswriter Red Smith later noted. "For small men with small talents, it turned out to be a small job. It worked for Jim because he was a big man and a master of his art. He could make a free ringside ticket or a job as a boxing judge or deputy inspector go farther than any commissioner before or since his time."

In a sport tainted with corruption, he stood out as a public official of fairness and integrity. Farley penalized managers who attempted to take an excessive share of their fighter's earnings, banned mismatches between boxers from different weight classes, and, in an era when other professional sports were lily white, upheld the right of an African American to get a title shot. Harry Wills, a black heavyweight from New York, had been the number one contender in the first half of the 1920s. When heavyweight champion Jack Dempsey signed to defend his title against the lower-ranked Gene Tunney in 1926, Big Jim ruled that Dempsey had an obligation to fight Wills and refused to sanction the Tunney bout. The fight went to Philadelphia where Tunney outpointed Dempsey for the title. "He's as pigheaded as they come, once he gets his mind set on something," a fight manager said of the boxing commissioner, "but there ain't no doubt that he's as honest as any guy in the state or in the world, for that matter."

In 1928, with Smith's support, Farley became secretary of the New York State Democratic Committee and found party headquarters in such disarray that there was not even an accurate list of county chairmen. Smith declined to help when he sought to build up the party beyond

New York City. But after Roosevelt moved into the governorship, Farley traveled throughout the state, making new allies and replacing weak
chairmen with fresh talent. In some upstate counties, for the first time,
he organized full central committees, signed up precinct workers, and
cleaned up voter rolls. He also recruited strong candidates in districts
where Republicans had often been elected without opposition. He did
his job so well that in 1930, as Roosevelt prepared to run for reelection
as governor, Farley was promoted to state Democratic chairman. Sending out thousands of letters to party workers and candidates, he signed
them all in an Irish green ink that would become his trademark. "Farley possessed and cultivated, more than any man of his generation, the
primary talent of a politician mentally to catalogue names and faces, to
learn and retain the facts of association among people, to know who is
related to whom by blood, business or politics, to labor with meticu-
lous diligence by mail or otherwise to make and retain contacts," Roosevelt adviser Raymond Moley recalled years later. "He astonished and
needled the egos of countless humble people by remembering their
names, their habitats, their days of happiness or sorrow, their needs and
the needs of their friends."[7]

    In the summer of 1931, Farley embarked on a whirlwind tour of
eighteen states in the Great Plains, Rocky Mountain, Pacific Coast,
and Great Lakes regions. As the national president of the Benevolent
and Protective Order of Elks, he was already scheduled to attend the
Grand Lodge Convention in Seattle. It was at Howe's suggestion that
Farley extended a brief trip into a three-week tour for the larger purpose of organizing Roosevelt's national campaign.

    Before Farley left New York, Roosevelt summoned him to Spring-
wood, his Hyde Park estate. "At his suggestion I was equipped with a
Rand-McNally map of the United States, a flock of train schedules, and
the latest available list of Democratic National Committee members and

state chairmen," Farley remembered. "We ate lunch and then adjourned to his tiny office, off in a wing of the house, where we spread out the documents and went to work. . . . The itinerary was decided upon in large measure by the Governor, who had a keen sense of selection in determining what states it was wise to visit and what states it was wise to shun."

In large and small groups, Farley conferred with more than eleven hundred Democratic leaders and would keep in touch with many of them up to and beyond the Chicago convention. Years later, he would look back on the western trip "as a sort of graduation from the political minor league." His approach was diplomatic and considerate. "I was extremely careful to get first and last names correctly and of course never disputed the views of others if it was at all possible to agree," he recalled. "It always creates a bad impression to start off with an argument. By carefully observing those simple and essential rules, I managed to strike up the kind of informal, easygoing friendships that make future understandings a great deal easier to arrive at."

At these luncheons, dinners, and meetings, he was introduced as the Democratic chairman of New York State. In opening remarks, Farley would get a sense of his audience and then suggest that his state had three potential contenders for the White House in Smith, Young, and Roosevelt. "I never talked to individuals about the presidential nomination unless I was certain of the other fellow's position," he recalled. If the politician was receptive to his candidate, Farley stated that "the name of Roosevelt is magic." W. W. Howes, the Democratic national committeeman for South Dakota, told Farley that he supported Roosevelt because he was "damned tired of backing losers." After their luncheon meeting, Howes wrote Farley: "Our boys all liked you very much. If you make as good an impression everywhere as here there will be no question that Roosevelt will be nominated."[8]

Farley, who was well received at every stop, forged alliances with key politicians and made lasting friendships. By telegram and special delivery letters, he kept Roosevelt informed. "Since I left New York I have visited Indiana, Wisconsin, Minnesota, North and South Dakota, Montana, and am now in Seattle," he reported to FDR. "There apparently is an unanimity of sentiment for you in every one of these states and the organization in every instance is for you wholeheartedly. Here and there, and not very frequently, is sentiment for Smith. To be frank with you, that comes mostly from ardent Catholic admirers and in some cases from strong wet advocates. On one or two occasions I have had Baker's name mentioned but that is all.

"In my talks with the different leaders they indicated that there occasionally crops up a boost for Ritchie or Young and in nearly every instance it comes from the Power crowd who apparently are trying to get in back of either one or the other, or both, in the hope that they might be able to tie up some votes for Young or Ritchie to be used later on when they decide what candidate they are going to support to try and keep you from getting the nomination. In the states I have visited it doesn't appear that at the moment they are going to get anywhere, but that is something we will have to watch very carefully. . . . I am satisfied, Governor, that they are feeling around with the hope that they may be able to develop some strength for these other candidates, not with the idea of expecting that they will be able to put anyone over, but to try and keep a sufficient number of delegates away from you to prevent your nomination on the first ballot, with the hope they may be able to bring about a situation to eliminate you from consideration, assuming of course that you are not named on the first ballot."[9]

The Pacific Northwest was perhaps Roosevelt's strongest region. Seattle lawyer Scott Bullitt, Democratic national committeeman for Washington State, assured Farley that his state would be solidly for

FDR. "Your trip here was certainly a success," Bullitt wrote Big Jim. "You did a lot of good in crystallizing the Roosevelt sentiment, even when you were unconscious of it." Former governor Oswald West, Oregon's Democratic national committeeman, told Farley: "You need not lose any sleep over this state sending a Roosevelt delegation to the next convention. There is nothing you could do to stop it. So don't let any of our local parasites try to shake you down for any money for promotion purposes. Keep it for the national campaign."[10]

In San Francisco, Farley locked in the support of California's Democratic national committeeman Isidore Dockweiler and of Justus Wardell, chairman of the Democratic state executive committee. Both predicted an easy victory for Roosevelt in the California presidential primary, yet Farley did not share this optimism. "I think this is almost too much to hope for," he told Howe. "There is, among a lot of the voters, strong sentiment for Governor Smith, and more so than in any other state in which I have traveled."

What Roosevelt worried about more than a Smith comeback was the growing threat of favorite-son candidacies. From Reno, Farley wrote FDR: "Have indicated that they must all get away from the favorite son idea, on the theory that it is only used for the purpose of tying up blocks of delegates to be manipulated.

"I have told the different people along the line that we do hope that they will not in any case instruct for their governors or United States senators, who hope that lightning might strike.

"It has been brought to my attention that the reason a number of these senators and governors want their names presented to the convention as presidential candidates is because they feel it is the only way that they can be considered as a vice-presidential nominee, believing that if their names get before the convention in such a manner, they might have some luck...."

"Governor, the presidential job must be a great one, judging from the way they are all anxious to have it."[11]

In Kansas City, Farley was tactful in dealing with former senator James Reed, who would be Missouri's favorite son at the Chicago convention. When a Reed ally protested the New Yorker's visit and the former senator vowed to have nothing to do with Farley's appearance, Howe wanted Farley to cancel the luncheon and take Kansas City off his schedule. "We argued over it but I was determined to go," Farley said. He suggested that local party officials extend an invitation to Reed, a tough old campaigner notorious for making vitriolic personal attacks. When the former senator showed up at the luncheon, Farley did not know what to expect. Reed volunteered to address the gathering and graciously introduced Farley as "an Elk on tour." Farley was generous in his comments about Reed and refrained from making a pitch for Roosevelt. Later, Reed came up to Farley's hotel room and thanked him. Even though Reed would be among Roosevelt's challengers, he would not be hostile. Howe cited Farley's Kansas City diplomacy as proof that he was "winning his spurs" as a politician.[12]

It was unnecessary for Farley to make a similar journey to the South. Roosevelt, who described himself as an honorary southerner, owned a cottage and a center for the treatment of polio victims in Warm Springs, Georgia, where he had first gone in 1924 seeking recovery from the paralysis inflicted by polio. Just as Farley cultivated support in the Midwest and the West, FDR took care of business in Dixie. In October of 1931, he hosted Democratic leaders from Alabama, Georgia, Mississippi, and Tennessee at his southern home. "As far as the South goes," declared Senator William J. Harris of Georgia, "it is all for Roosevelt." By the fall of 1931, Roosevelt had picked up the support of Senators Pat Harrison of Mississippi, Cordell Hull of Tennessee, and James Byrnes of South Carolina. "The situation is very odd and my friends in both the South and the West strongly advise me to let things drift as they are going for the present," Roosevelt wrote privately in September, "as the great majority of these states through their regular organizations are showing in every way friendliness towards me."

Indeed, Roosevelt was so upbeat about his chances for the presidential nomination that he began developing, at Hull's suggestion, the 1932 Democratic platform. "I am more than ever convinced that if the general impression that Franklin is to be the nominee continues," Howe wrote Hull, "it will be quite possible to agree on a platform beforehand. . . . Of course, real doubt as to the candidate has always made it impossible to conduct quiet conferences of this kind in the past as the platform depended more or less on which faction of the convention won out." FDR sent out a memorandum to political allies seeking "a confidential interchange of tentative views relating to the platform, and not in any way to candidates." Former attorney general A. Mitchell Palmer, Roosevelt's neighbor during the Wilson administration, was asked by FDR to write the first draft of the proposed planks.[13]

As the year 1932 began, Roosevelt looked unstoppable. "Roosevelt is way out in front again," Breckinridge Long, former assistant secretary of state in the Wilson administration, told former Treasury secretary William G. McAdoo. "When I saw you it was my impression that he had lost some ground, but when the men met here from all over the United States at the Jackson Day dinner, I talked to a good many of them from everywhere and almost every one of them were for Franklin Roosevelt. I was quite astonished at the unanimity of opinion. New England, the Northwest, North Central, Middle West, South, and Atlantic Seaboard—were practically every one of them for Roosevelt."

Congressman Sam Rayburn of Texas, who would be a major player at the Chicago convention, had a similar analysis. "It appears to me that Franklin Roosevelt is far and away in the lead of all probable Democratic nominees," he reported to a Texas friend. "There is quite a movement throughout the country, however, designated to be a 'Stop-Roosevelt' campaign. Roosevelt, with his position in New York, has appealed to the popular imagination of the American people as no other man does at this particular time. However, within the next two months there will be developments that will show us all, I think, a clear road, whether it leads to Roosevelt or another direction."

Robert W. Woolley, Roosevelt's old friend from the Wilson era, thought that FDR might be peaking too soon. "If the nomination were held tomorrow we would have nothing to fear," he told Roosevelt adviser Colonel Edward M. House, "but there are strong undercurrents running against our man and I am fearful of what may happen."[14]

4

PRIMARY COLORS

O N JANUARY 22, 1932, Franklin D. Roosevelt formally declared his candidacy in a letter entering his name in the North Dakota primary. "If it is the desire of our party leaders in your state that my name be presented at your coming primaries as a candidate for the Democratic nomination for the presidency," he stated, "I willingly give my consent, with full appreciation of the honor that has been done me.

"It is the simple duty of any American to serve in public position if called upon," he added. But he would not be campaigning in North Dakota or other primary states because as governor of New York, "I am, especially at this time, obligated to a still higher duty. These people when they re-elected me in 1930 gave to me a great confidence that I would continue the task of helping to solve the serious problems which confront us.

"I know that you will understand the good faith in which I tell you this," FDR concluded, "and also my hope that our party will place before the nation candidates who stand for progressive ideals of government, who represent no mere section, no narrow partisanship and no special class."[1]

Ending months of speculation, former New York governor Alfred E. Smith launched his comeback on February 6. In 1928 he had received 15 million votes, which almost doubled the 1924 Democratic presidential vote and came close to matching the combined vote of Wilson's two national victories. Even though he had carried only eight states and lost to Hoover by a plurality of six million votes, Smith felt that the Depression had given him another chance and thought that he deserved the 1932 Democratic presidential nomination. But if this prize was beyond his reach, Smith had another motivation for running. More than any other Democratic contender, he had the ability to rally the opposition to Roosevelt and prevent him from winning the required two-thirds vote in Chicago. "He has stiffened the anti-Roosevelt forces in the important states," Frank R. Kent of the *Baltimore Sun* reported, "and the drive to stop Roosevelt has been given renewed impetus."

Smith, who had waged a coast-to-coast campaign in 1928, would not go on the road in primary states. In this era it would have been unusual for a politician of his stature to personally campaign in primary or caucus states. "If the Democratic National Convention," he said, "after careful consideration, should decide it wants me to lead I will make the fight; but I will not make a pre-convention campaign to secure the support of delegates." The former governor insisted that there was no hidden agenda in his declaration. "By action of the Democratic National Convention in 1928, I am the leader of my party in the nation," Smith asserted. "With a full sense of the responsibility thereby imposed, I shall not in advance of the convention either support or oppose the candidacy of any aspirant for the nomination."[2]

Then as now, the presidential primaries began in the deep snows of New Hampshire. The unusually early vote was scheduled to coincide

with Town Meeting Day, the second Tuesday in March, to save the state
the cost of an extra election. Roosevelt's camp, gunning for a knockout,
spent more money in New Hampshire than in any other primary. The
candidate's son James Roosevelt, a twenty-four-year-old Harvard graduate and Boston insurance broker, campaigned across the Granite State
in behalf of his father. Wealthy Concord lawyer Robert Jackson, New
Hampshire's Democratic national committeeman, had been among
Smith's top financial contributors in 1928 but organized the state for
Roosevelt. Before entering the New Hampshire primary, Smith met
with Jackson and asked about his prospects. Jackson told him that Roosevelt was headed for a decisive victory. "He became angry and questioned the accuracy of my prediction," Jackson later wrote. "I suggested
that if he was in doubt" that a mutual friend "could substantiate my ap-
praisal of the situation in a two-day visit to New Hampshire."

Smith should have listened.

In future presidential seasons, New Hampshire's voters would make
a sport out of humbling front-runners. But they liked Roosevelt, who
won an overwhelming victory with 61.7 percent of the vote, took eight
of the state's eleven cities, all but 5 of the 224 towns, and swept the
eight delegates. Smith, who ran strongest among Catholics, narrowly
carried Manchester. Roosevelt might have won by an even larger margin, but a blizzard in the northern part of the state reduced voter turnout in one of his strongest areas. "I want you to know that the entire
United States was looking for the results from New Hampshire," Farley told Jackson. "I do not know of anything that will happen that will
have a more wholesome effect than did the results in your state."[3]

In North Dakota, Smith failed to get on the ballot. Heavy snows
blocked the roads between Minot and Bismarck, preventing Smith's
campaign manager from filing petitions. But this did not mean Roosevelt would win the March 15 primary by default.

Oklahoma governor William Henry "Alfalfa Bill" Murray, a rustic champion of the downtrodden, would campaign in North Dakota and eighteen other states in pursuit of the Democratic presidential nomination. The tall, craggy-faced, stoop-shouldered Murray had a walrus mustache, smoked long black cigars, wore unmatched coat and trousers, and sipped coffee from a saucer. His campaign slogan was "Bread, Butter, Bacon, and Beans." Appearing before a Jamestown farm audience, he declared, "I'm running for president because I think the people want me, that is the plain people."

Murray, sixty-three in 1932, was a veteran of the Populist movement of the 1890s and had been the lawyer for the Chicksaw Nation when Oklahoma was Indian Territory. As a legislator, he had drafted the state's constitution and helped to create colleges and universities. As governor of Oklahoma, he increased the gasoline tax to provide relief for the unemployed, distributed $300,000 in seeds to needy farmers, and called for tax reform. When a gas company cut off five hundred families, the governor put the state militia on alert to make certain that the heat was turned back on. When Oklahoma City police arrested river-bottom squatters on vagrancy charges and hauled them from their shacks, an angry Murray granted instant pardons. At his urging the governments of Oklahoma and Texas built free bridges to replace toll bridges across the Red River. When the toll-bridge owners obtained a federal court injunction to prevent the opening of the new bridges, Murray called out the state militia, who opened the free bridges and kept them open. "I learned my politics out there in the country," he said. "Don't know as I'm much of a politician, but I do know people and people make a government."[4]

Murray expected to do well in North Dakota, where farmers drove through snowstorms to hear him speak, and audiences cheered his populist rhetoric. Openly hostile to Roosevelt, he depicted his rival as out of touch with the problems of the farm belt. It would be folly, the Oklahoma governor claimed, for the Democrats to nominate a candidate from New York. Earlier in the year, Murray asserted that FDR lacked courage and did not measure up to presidential standards. "Roosevelt may have the politicians," Murray told his brother George, a North Dakota farmer, "but I will have the people."

Roosevelt, who had the support of the regular Democratic organization, was warned that Murray should not be underestimated. "I am wholly willing to trust things to a real expression by the voters," he wrote privately, "even if this means I will lose a few delegates to Governor Murray of Oklahoma and some others." But he was playing to win. On the eve of the primary, he vowed, if elected to the presidency, to provide emergency relief for western farmers. Senator Burton K. Wheeler of Montana, Roosevelt's surrogate in North Dakota, said in a radio address that Murray was a good public official but was being used by "a corrupt gang in the East, which, for want of a better name might be called the 'Wall Street crowd.' "[5]

On March 15, Roosevelt captured 62.1 percent of North Dakota's vote and won nine out of the ten delegates. Murray's brother was elected to the other slot. The biggest surprise was the 84,670 turnout for the Roosevelt-Murray contest, which was more than twice the combined vote of North Dakota's three most recent Democratic presidential primaries. More than half of the '32 Democratic voters were Republican crossovers, a clear indication that the farm belt was breaking from the GOP.

Roosevelt defeated Murray by even more lopsided margins in the Nebraska, West Virginia, Oregon, and Florida primaries. Murray won twenty-two delegates from his home state but none elsewhere. He would later win Ohio's nonbinding presidential preference primary in which he ran without opposition. When Murray missed the filing deadline for the

Georgia primary, FDR asked the state executive committee to bend the rules and put the Oklahoma governor on the ballot. Roosevelt, who did not regard Murray as serious competition, wanted to get credit for winning another contested primary. The state executive committee denied Roosevelt's request and kept Murray out of the primary. FDR won Georgia by eight to one over Judge G. H. Howard of Atlanta, a Garner supporter who ran in defiance of the House Speaker's request that he withdraw.

Near the end of March, FDR faced difficult tests at state conventions in Iowa and Maine, where the Stop Roosevelt forces had substantial support for the election of uncommitted delegations. At FDR's urging, Farley headed for Davenport and saved the day. "It would have been absolutely impossible to have gotten an instructed delegation if Mr. James A. Farley had not come to Davenport," Iowa Democrat John F. Sullivan told Roosevelt. "As soon as Mr. Farley arrived in Davenport the opposition to an instructed delegation melted away."

On the same day, Jackson hustled for votes at the Maine Democratic convention in Portland. "The tendency among the Maine leaders was not to press for instructions and they managed to raise a doubt in Louis's mind as well as in FDR's as to whether we could obtain them," Jackson later recalled. "In fact, Louis instructed me not to try for them as he feared defeat would be construed as a serious reverse for the Roosevelt candidacy." But Jackson, who wanted to make the fight, appealed to Farley in Iowa. "He finally told me to go ahead and use my best judgment," Jackson remembered. "Jimmy Roosevelt was rooming with me and I remember that he was considerably alarmed when I told him I was going to take a chance but was reassured when I told him that Jim favored this action." His gamble almost failed. By a standing vote, the Maine convention rejected Jackson's resolution to send an instructed delegation to Chicago. But Jackson pressed for a roll call vote and bluntly

told a Roosevelt floor manager to quit making excuses and start round-
ing up votes. In a close vote, FDR's forces won the roll call to send a
delegation to Chicago pledged to their candidate. "We always looked
back upon March 29 as a red-letter day for the Roosevelt candidacy, if
not the turning point of the entire campaign," Farley said. "Iowa gave
us twenty-six votes and Maine twelve. Those two states are far apart on
the map—their people have little in common politically. When they
took similar action on the same day, it demonstrated to us and to the
country that Roosevelt had nationwide political appeal."[6]

Wisconsin, the state that invented the presidential primary in 1903,
was Roosevelt's next battleground. Smith's allies were running as uncommitted delegates in the state's independent tradition. In the 1928
general election, Smith had garnered 450,000 votes in Wisconsin and
had been the state's choice at the two previous Democratic national conventions. More than a third of Wisconsin's Democratic primary voters
were Roman Catholics, Smith's most reliable constituency. But it was
also a farm state and Roosevelt had dominated the rural vote throughout the primaries. On April 5, with a record Democratic turnout that included crossover voters from "Fighting Bob" La Follette's Progressive
Party, Roosevelt swept Wisconsin's twenty-six delegates.

In the wake of Wisconsin's verdict, a longtime Smith friend urged
him to reassess his comeback. "There are times for all things and for all
men," Senator Key Pittman of Nevada told the *New York Times*. "Sometimes the man and the issue meet, as they did in Governor Smith in 1928.
Another time the junction does not seem to be made, as in Governor
Smith's candidacy this year, but that does not reflect on the man. . . .
The whole matter is in the hands of his friends. They should no longer
expect this great leader, who will always have a powerful influence in
our party, to further contest when he is not a candidate for nomination
and will make no campaign."[7]

Roosevelt's camp shared this view. After the New Hampshire primary, Howe privately wrote that Smith's campaign "is largely a fake movement." This may explain why Roosevelt made the questionable decision to challenge Smith in the April 26 Massachusetts primary. James Michael Curley, Boston's flamboyant and controversial mayor, urged FDR to run in the Bay State and assured him a victory. Jimmy Roosevelt, who was close to Curley, seconded the mayor's recommendation and took over the state campaign. "The whole Massachusetts mess could have been avoided but for him," observed Robert W. Woolley. Governor Joseph B. Ely, Senator David Walsh, and former Boston mayor John F. "Honey Fitz" Fitzgerald were Smith's most prominent supporters in Massachusetts. Roosevelt and Howe knew, from the Straus poll, that Smith remained the state's favorite Democrat. "As matters stand today," Jackson told Roosevelt, "it is better to lose every delegate from this state with a generous gesture of refraining from a contest than to risk a contretemps which might exert an unfavorable psychological influence in the other New England states."

Another problem for Roosevelt was that Curley and Ely were political enemies, and their feud overshadowed the presidential contest. "It is almost impossible for one not steeped in this particular Boston environment to realize the bitterness and intensity of the internecine hatreds which cloud the Democratic political sky. The presidency is an unimportant, almost valueless, pawn in a game where the principal stake is control of the state organization," Jackson reported to FDR. "Your fortunes are incidental. There is no true loyalty to Smith but his name possesses value as a shibboleth. Privately the real leaders would like to declare for you if such a declaration did not involve an appearance of surrender to the Mayor. They are convinced Smith cannot secure the nomination; they want to be on the bandwagon; but more they want to carry the election of their state ticket and above all they appear to wish to strip the Mayor of all power and influence. If you will recall the personal physical assaults which figured in the 1930 campaign you can gain some idea of the passions which underlie this problem.

"It must be confessed that a cold analysis of the present distribution of power in the party here leaves one wondering just how the Mayor can secure delegates for the candidate he favors. West of the Charles River he has no discoverable personal support. On the contrary, he is a distinct handicap. Outside of Boston, the hostility toward him is well-nigh incredible and in Boston, where can he elect his candidates for delegates? . . . There is great Roosevelt strength among the voters but I am convinced it has a better chance of expression at the polls without any leadership whatever than with the wrong management."[8]

Boston lawyer La Rue Brown, who attended Harvard with Roosevelt, also advised FDR that Curley was a liability and warned that he was headed for certain defeat. With Roosevelt's approval, Jackson and Brown began talks with Smith's allies about a possible compromise. FDR would pull out of the primary if the Smith delegation included slots for several members committed to FDR as a second choice. Ely and Walsh were receptive but Curley killed the deal when he publicly called on Smith to withdraw "for the promotion of harmony." In several public telegrams to Smith, Curley gratuitously accused the former governor of trickery and deceit.

Smith, who had held back, became an active candidate in the face of Curley's insults. In the feud of Irish American political heavyweights, Smith had far more appeal among their ethnic brethren. The young Thomas P. "Tip" O'Neill, future congressman and House Speaker, was among the Boston Irish who jeered Curley for leading the opposition to their hero. While marching in a St. Patrick's Day parade in South Boston, Curley and Jimmy Roosevelt were pelted with snowballs.

On April 26, Smith carried Massachusetts by three to one, won two to one in Boston, and swept all of the thirty-six delegates. Smith received 73.1 percent of the vote and rolled up a plurality of a hundred thousand votes. "Massachusetts returns teach a lesson which should profit us much," Woolley wrote privately. "If a man like Homer Cummings [Connecticut's Democratic national committeeman] had been sent in there at the outset, harmonious action could have been attained. . . . Instead, the hands off policy, of which Farley and Howe have been so proud, gave Curley ample opportunity to demonstrate to the country how big a jackass he can be—and, thank God, to hang himself politically."

Roosevelt's camp reacted defensively to the crushing loss. "We felt we had to contest because if we didn't contest in Massachusetts, it would look as if we were afraid," Farley said. "But we went in with our eyes open, knowing what the consequences would be." Howe added that "it was necessary to make that fight in order to keep Pennsylvania from feeling that we were so weak in the East as to not make it worthwhile. In my judgment we never would have won Pennsylvania if we refused to contest Smith in Massachusetts."[9]

The problem for Roosevelt was that his narrow victory in Pennsylvania fell short of the grand expectations raised by campaign manager Joseph F. Guffey, a former state Democratic chairman. Guffey had predicted a near-sweep of the state's seventy-six delegates. But Hague, Jersey City's political boss, and Jouett Shouse, the Democratic national committee's top political operative, covertly launched a get-out-the-vote effort for Smith in urban and Catholic precincts. Smith held Roosevelt to forty-four and a half delegates and showed surprising strength in the popular vote. The erosion of Roosevelt's Pennsylvania support was more jolting to his partisans than the anticipated loss in Massachusetts.

Suddenly and almost overnight, Roosevelt was no longer invincible.

Hull worried that the nomination was slipping away. Woolley predicted that Roosevelt's lackluster showing in Pennsylvania would embolden Cermak to throw his support to Smith. The usually pessimistic Howe assured allies that Roosevelt would quickly recover. "If we have any luck in California," he told Josephus Daniels, "I do not think that the Massachusetts result will do us any great harm. If in addition, we have a little luck in Connecticut, the Smith-stop-Roosevelt movement will collapse.

"Of course, the only way to prevent Smith from getting a block is to put him out of business as early and as expeditiously as possible by instructed delegations," Howe added. "Every uninstructed delegation from now on will be claimed by the Smith forces and will be a constant source of worry to us all."[10]

Smith, though, was coming on strong in the Northeast. Connecticut governor Wilbur Cross, who supported Smith, had offered Roosevelt an even split of his state's sixteen delegates. But Roosevelt's forces blundered away those eight votes by rejecting the governor's proposal and seeking to capture the entire delegation. Smith won them all. In Rhode Island, Smith defeated Roosevelt by more than eight to one at the state convention. Roosevelt was also dealt a setback in his home state of New York when all of the district delegates selected in the primary and the at-large delegates chosen by Tammany Hall boss John F. Curry were uninstructed.

The May 3 California primary was critical to Roosevelt's western and southern strategy. If he could win the Golden State's forty-four delegates, FDR would be within striking distance of the two-thirds majority required for nomination. "I am convinced we won't even have a contest," former California Democratic gubernatorial nominee Wardell had told Roosevelt months earlier, "but if we do, the result will be so overwhelmingly in our favor it will indicate most impressively what the sentiment is among the Democrats of the state."

Roosevelt was misinformed. Garner chose California as the only place outside of Texas where he would allow his name on the ballot. His candidacy was the invention of California's media tycoon William Randolph Hearst, and Garner would be relentlessly promoted in Hearst-owned newspapers, magazines, and newsreels. Smith, who got a larger vote in California in 1928 than any previous Democratic presidential nominee, made it a three-way battle. McAdoo, Wilson's son-in-law and a former presidential contender, was the state's most nationally prominent Democrat and a Los Angeles lawyer. Still ambitious at the age of sixty-nine, McAdoo endorsed Garner as a fellow westerner and attacked Smith and Roosevelt as "Tammany candidates from New York." California, whose population had more than tripled from 1.49 million in 1900 to 5.5 million in 1930, was the fastest-growing state in the nation and its politics were changing. It helped Garner that the Texas State Society of California, which had a membership of one hundred thousand former Texans, became active in his campaign. Jimmy Roosevelt and Senator Wheeler of Montana, the great western progressive, made appearances in behalf of FDR. Wheeler, who sensed that Garner was gaining momentum, attacked him as a conservative. Smith's partisans ridiculed Roosevelt's efforts to dodge the Prohibition issue by taunting: "If you are wet, vote for Smith; if you are dry, vote for Garner; if you don't know what you are, vote for Roosevelt!"[11]

Despite this competition and his recent setbacks, Roosevelt was viewed as the probable winner when California voters went to the polls on the first Tuesday in May. The backing of the regular Democratic organization was expected to give Roosevelt the edge. In San Francisco, bookmakers rated FDR a two-to-one favorite and even money to win a majority over his two rivals.

In the most sensational upset of the 1932 primaries, Garner won

California with 41.3 percent of the vote, followed by Roosevelt with 32.5 percent, and Smith with 26.3 percent. Roosevelt carried thirty-five of the state's fifty-eight counties and did best in rural and farm areas. Smith was strongest in San Francisco, where he got more votes than both opponents combined, and he also ran ahead of Roosevelt in Los Angeles. Garner nearly tripled Roosevelt's vote in Los Angeles County and won eight out of ten counties in Southern California. The House Speaker's winning margin in Los Angeles County wiped out Roosevelt's plurality in the rest of the state.

ROOSEVELT'S CAMP BLAMED this loss on Hearst and Smith. "We were terribly disappointed to be frank with you over the results in California because all the information we had indicated we would win," Farley privately acknowledged. "We are just not going to have the forty-four votes we counted on."

FDR, in Warm Springs, was less than candid in a letter to Daniels. "The California result I had rather expected," he wrote. "The main point is now to persuade Garner to take no part in any mere 'block movement.' I think Garner is big enough to see this. The Texas delegation and the California delegation would cinch the matter."[12]

Colonel Edward M. House, Wilson's confidant and Roosevelt's adviser, thought that FDR was suffering from front-runner's syndrome. "Things have been going the Governor's way and he has let them, more or less slide," House observed after California's verdict. "If he seriously wants the nomination he had best take stock of conditions and change the tactics."

Roosevelt won 44.5 percent of the national Democratic primary vote in 1932 and carried eleven of the thirteen states where his name was on the ballot. Even though he was closing in on a majority of Democratic delegates, he was well short of the required two-thirds vote. "I am wondering what will come out of Chicago," Felix Frankfurter, a Harvard Law School professor, wrote privately. "If FDR is nominated, it will certainly prove there is no limit to the amount of fumbling one can do and still win a game."[13]

5

CITIZEN HEARST

H E WAS A force of nature. Everything about him was bold and flamboyant. In 1932 William Randolph Hearst owned more newspapers and had the largest readership of any publisher in American history. A tall, horse-faced man with a high-pitched voice, he once pursued the White House and now lived in a Spanish Renaissance castle on a California hilltop overlooking a private ocean frontage of more than fifty miles. This presidential election year would mark the first time since the turn of the century that he would not be attending either of the major political conventions. But from his magnificent estate at San Simeon, where he owned more than 265,000 acres, he would be among the key players in the unfolding drama at Chicago Stadium. At the age of sixty-nine he had long since abandoned his own quest for the presidency. Yet he was at the peak of his influence because more than thirty million Americans read his newspapers and magazines.

Hearst had long mixed politics and journalism. It was no accident that he wanted to be a player in both fields. He was the son of the late

California senator George Hearst, who bought the *San Francisco Examiner* in 1880 and ran it as a Democratic propaganda sheet. Before going into politics, the elder Hearst built one of the great western mining fortunes. The silver baron's only son inherited a passion for Democratic politics and was suspended from Harvard in 1884 for staging a loud and out-of-control celebration of Grover Cleveland's election to the presidency. Two years later the elder Hearst was appointed to the U.S. Senate and in 1887 reluctantly allowed his son to take over the ownership and management of the *Examiner*. The younger Hearst increased the size of the *Examiner*, which he called "The Monarch of the Dailies," hired talented writers, boosted circulation, and made it into the best newspaper of this era on the Pacific Coast. In his first editorial crusade, he challenged the Southern Pacific Railroad's domination of California politics and thwarted the railroad's attempt to avoid repayment of a federal loan. When his father died, he inherited the equivalent of $100 million in today's currency and began looking for ways to expand his influence.[1]

In 1895 he purchased the *New York Morning Journal* and took on Joseph Pulitzer's mighty *New York World*. Hearst raided Pulitzer's staff and doubled and tripled their salaries. He cut the price of the *Journal* from two cents to a penny and Pulitzer was forced to do the same thing. Hearst compelled public attention with huge headlines, innovative layouts, and the first color presses and all-color Sunday comic sections. In his first year in the big city, he boosted circulation from twenty thousand to four hundred thousand copies a day.

Just selling papers would never be enough for Hearst, who wanted to make history on a grand scale. Instead of limiting himself to covering the news, the Chief was determined to shape events. The Spanish-American War might never have happened if he had cared more about fair and honest reporting. But his personal agenda dominated the front pages of his newspapers. By publishing inflammatory articles about Spanish atrocities in Cuba, he led the campaign for American military intervention. When one of his artists, Frederick Remington, reported from Cuba that all was quiet, the publisher replied: "You furnish the pictures, and I'll furnish the war." In the winter of 1898 the sinking of the battleship *Maine* gave Hearst his opportunity to demand war. After President William McKinley declared war in April, Hearst got himself commissioned as an ensign and embarked for Cuba as a war correspondent. At the Battle of Santiago, he swam ashore and accepted the surrender of twenty-nine Spanish prisoners. The Chief, who often referred to the Spanish-American conflict as his war, ordered his London correspondent to sink a steamer in the Suez Canal and stop the Spanish fleet. It was fortunate that the fleet turned back before Hearst created a world war. "A blackguard boy with several millions of dollars at his disposal," lamented the progressive editor E. L. Godkin, "has more influence on the use a great nation may make of its credit, of its army and navy, of its name and traditions, than all the statesmen and philosophers in the country."[2]

The more he accomplished, the more he wanted. Hearst was politically ambitious. It bothered him that Colonel Theodore Roosevelt emerged as the hero of the Spanish-American War and captured the New York governorship in 1898. The Chief detested Roosevelt for stealing his thunder. In the spring of 1900, he made his first move toward a future political career by getting elected president of the National Association of Democratic Clubs, which under his leadership grew to more than three million members. He got this party leadership position after agreeing to open a newspaper in Chicago at the request of Democratic national chairman James K. Jones. On July 4, the first edition of the *Chicago American* was published for the opening of the Democratic National Convention in Kansas City after William Jennings Bryan wired the publisher to "Start the Presses."

"The fact that your newspaper was established not merely to make money, but because of your desire to aid the Democratic leaders that you should duplicate in Chicago the splendid work done by the *Journal* and the *Examiner* in '96," Bryan told Hearst, "ought to commend the paper to the friends of democracy. And I am confident that a large circulation awaits the *Chicago American*."[3]

He pushed to become Bryan's running mate at the Kansas City convention but was passed over in favor of the old warhorse Adlai E. Stevenson of Illinois. A larger disappointment for the ambitious publisher was Theodore Roosevelt's surprise selection as the Republican McKinley's vice-presidential nominee. The Hearst press attacked both Republicans without restraint, and two of these assaults came back to haunt him. In the winter of 1901 Ambrose Bierce wrote after the assassination of the Democratic governor-elect of Kentucky that the bullet "is speeding here to stretch McKinley on his bier." Several months later, in an attack on McKinley, the *Evening Journal* editorialized: "If bad intentions and bad men can be got rid of only by killing, then killing must be done." So when the president was assassinated in September 1901, Hearst was widely depicted as a force of evil. Numerous threats were made on his life, boycotts were launched against his newspapers, and he was hung in effigy.[4]

The controversial publisher may have been down but he was far from out. His newspapers exposed corruption, advocated voting rights for women, direct election of U.S. senators, and public ownership of utilities. He championed organized labor and took on big business. "Mr. Hearst has waged as many good fights as any reformer I know. There isn't room even for a list of the good things Mr. Hearst has done or tried to do," the muckraking journalist Lincoln Steffens wrote. But he added, "There isn't room either for a list of the bad, the small things he has done, the scandals he has published, the individuals he has made to suffer beyond their desserts."[5]

In his first run for office, W. R. got elected to Congress in 1902 from midtown Manhattan. To have a national political future, he understood the importance of shedding his playboy image. One day before his fortieth birthday, he married the Broadway dancer Millicent Willson. His congressional record was undistinguished. The brash freshman lobbied unsuccessfully for a slot on the Ways and Means Committee, then alienated more senior colleagues by maneuvering himself onto the Labor Committee. Long accustomed to running his own show, he lacked the patience and discipline to become a serious legislator. His voting record was progressive, but W. R. showed up for few roll calls. Bored and frustrated in the role of junior legislator, he became notorious for chronic absenteeism.

In 1904, Hearst spent lavishly and made a credible run for the Democratic presidential nomination. His platform called for breaking up "criminal trusts," a graduated income tax, and comprehensive school reform. Old Guard Democrats on the national committee were so worried about the political newcomer that they rejected New York City and Chicago as convention sites out of concern that his newspapers in those cities could sway delegates. When St. Louis landed the convention, the national committee reserved the right to change the site if W. R. should open a newspaper there. Organized labor and western progressives provided his strongest support. The Chicago lawyer Clarence Darrow, who was gaining fame as an advocate for working people, gave a seconding speech. Hearst, who had been among Bryan's staunchest allies, felt betrayed when the two-time presidential nominee declined to return the favor. In the presidential balloting, W. R. placed a respectable second among ten candidates. On the first roll call, he received 263 votes from twenty-one states, including unanimous support from the California and Illinois delegations. This would be as close as he ever got to the presidency. The conservative Judge Alton B. Parker of New York won the nomination and was overwhelmed that fall by the Republican Roosevelt. In that same election, Hearst easily won a second congressional term.

The master showman of American newspapers was a mediocre performer on the stump and the most unlikely of politicians. He did not enjoy public speaking, hated small talk, and did not like most politicians. W. R., though, was shrewd in choosing issues that struck a responsive chord with the voting public. Franklin Lane, the California Democratic leader, said that the wealthy newspaperman "knows public sentiment and how to develop it very well, and will be a danger in the United States, I am afraid, for many years to come. . . . He feels with the people, but he has no conscience."[6]

In 1905, he ran for mayor of New York on a third-party reform ticket and attracted wide support for his campaign to end the corrupt Democratic machine's dominance of City Hall. The insurgent candidate vilified Democratic boss Charles F. Murphy as a thief and the *Journal* published a cartoon of Murphy in prison stripes with the caption: "Every honest voter in New York wants to see you in this costume!" The publisher attracted huge crowds and won crossover support from both major political parties. If there had been an honest count, he would have been elected. Tammany Hall, which controlled the election machinery, stole just enough votes to win. Out of 590,000 ballots in the official tabulation, W. R. lost to incumbent George B. McClellan by 3,485 votes.

On the basis of this strong showing, Hearst won the 1906 Democratic nomination for governor of New York. By holding out the threat of running as an independent, he forced party bosses to put him at the top of the ticket. Though it had been fifteen years since a Democrat had last won a gubernatorial election in the Empire State, the maverick publisher was taken seriously because his appeal transcended party lines. Upton Sinclair, whose novel *The Jungle* was just published and creating a sensation, predicted that W. R. was on his way to the presidency and would put an end to "wage slavery" as Lincoln had ended "chattel slavery." From the White House, Teddy Roosevelt viewed Hearst as a menacing threat but also recognized his popular appeal. "He preaches the gospel of envy, hatred, and unrest. His actions so far go to show that he is entirely willing to sanction any mob violence if he thinks that for the moment votes are to be gained by so doing," the Republican president wrote a British editor. "He is the most potent single influence for evil we have in our life." Roosevelt sent Secretary of State Elihu Root into the campaign to state that the president considered the publisher unfit to govern and partly to blame for the assassination of McKinley. Hearst came close again but lost to Republican reformer Charles Evans Hughes. Roosevelt's intervention made the difference. It could not have gone unnoticed at the White House that W. R. got more votes in losing than the Rough Rider did eight years previously in winning the governorship.[7]

This defeat eliminated Hearst from contention for the presidency. In 1912, his newspapers strongly supported House Speaker Champ Clark for the Democratic presidential nomination and were a large factor in his crushing victories over New Jersey governor Woodrow Wilson in the Illinois and California primaries. Clark, who went into the Baltimore convention with a majority of delegates, failed to get the required two-thirds majority and the convention deadlocked. Wilson prevailed on the forty-sixth ballot and went on to become only the second Democratic president since the Civil War.

An outspoken critic of Wilson's foreign policy, W. R. opposed American intervention in the Great War. His newspapers accused Wilson of favoring the British and predicted victory for Germany. Even after the United States joined the war, a Hearst editorial alleged that the

Allies "are beyond any effective help of ours, and we are simply wasting sorely needed men and supplies by sending them abroad." Once again, he was burned in effigy, denounced as a traitor, and entwined in controversy. When the war ended, the isolationist publisher fought Wilson's effort to bring the United States into the League of Nations.[8]

With a large German American and Irish American readership, Hearst was still a force in New York politics. In 1917, he helped elect Brooklyn judge John F. Hylan as mayor of New York. A year later, W. R. sought another chance at the governorship in 1918 but lost the nomination to Alfred E. Smith, president of the New York City Board of Aldermen, who narrowly won the general election. Hearst supported Smith in that race. Then, in a mistake that would end his public career, the publisher turned on the new governor by unfairly blaming him for a milk famine in New York City caused by a price increase by milk companies. Smith was viciously depicted in the Hearst press as a baby killer and stooge of the Milk Trust.

W. R. had bullied lesser political figures with impunity. But Smith, who grew up in a neighborhood of tenements on the Lower East Side and throughout his political career had given voice to the powerless, would not allow Hearst to get away with this reckless slander. He challenged Hearst to a public debate and rented Carnegie Hall. W. R. replied in a signed editorial that since he was not running for office and did not enjoy "the company of crooked politicians" he would not share the stage with the governor. Hearst also publicly apologized for having supported Smith.

In an extraordinary performance, Governor Smith demolished Hearst on the stage of Carnegie Hall. "Of course, I am alone," he declared with contempt. "I know the man to whom I issued the challenge, and I know that he has not got a drop of good, clean, pure red blood in his whole body. And I know the color of his liver, and it is whiter, if that could be, than the driven snow." He accused W. R. of publishing "deliberate lies," and for "the gravest abuse of the power of the press in the history of this country." In conclusion, Smith urged the people of "this city, this state, and this country . . . to get rid of this pestilence that walks in the darkness."⁹

Before this night at Carnegie Hall, only Theodore Roosevelt had gone after Hearst with such ferocity. If T. R. prevented W. R. from winning the governorship, Smith ultimately drove him out of New York. His attack on the controversial publisher enhanced Smith's national reputation, and politicians in other parts of the country began pointing to him as presidential timber.

In the Republican landslide of 1920, Smith was defeated for a second gubernatorial term. Eager to make a comeback and still interested in the presidency, W. R. lined up substantial support to run for governor in 1922. Smith, who was earning five times his gubernatorial salary as the president of the United States Trucking Corporation, had doubts about returning to politics. Franklin D. Roosevelt, in his first political activity since the crippling polio attack, led the movement to draft Smith. FDR, who viewed Hearst as a probable loser in the general election, had not forgotten the publisher's endorsement of Republican Warren G. Harding over the Cox-Roosevelt ticket, and regarded Smith as the only Democrat who could thwart the Chief. "We realize that years of public service make it most desirable that you think now for a while of your family's needs," FDR wrote Smith in a public letter. "I am in the same boat yet this call for further service must come first."

As the Smith boom gained momentum, W. R. told party leaders that he would drop his gubernatorial bid and run for the U.S. Senate. Murphy and Brooklyn Democratic boss John H. McCooey agreed to back Smith for governor and Hearst for senator. "I will not run on a ticket with Hearst," Smith told delegates to the state convention in Syracuse.

"I'm damned if I will." By playing it tough, the former governor settled an old score and killed his rival's attempted comeback. The Chief,
who was fifty-nine years old in 1922, would never make another run
for public office. FDR was not bashful about taking some of the credit
for the newspaper titan's political demise. "I had quite a tussle in New
York to keep our friend Hearst off the ticket and to get Al Smith to run,"
Roosevelt reported to Joseph E. Davies, "but the thing went through in
fine shape."

From then on, W. R. hated Smith more than any other politician.
Even though Roosevelt was also connected with these events, the publisher did not begrudge his involvement. FDR turned down the senatorial nomination offered by Smith after his elimination of Hearst. When
party leaders, as a concession to the maverick publisher, nominated
Hearst ally Royal Copeland for senator, Roosevelt agreed to become
the honorary chairman of the campaign.[10]

Following Roosevelt's election as governor of New York in 1928,
Hearst sought to advance his political fortunes. "As Roosevelt is a probable presidential nominee and the one we are most likely to support," the
Chief wrote *New York American* editor Edmond D. Coblentz in early
1931, "we should keep him and his policies before the nation. There has
been no adequate promotion of him in our papers. We should begin now
to see that there is." W. R. dispatched his editor to meet with Roosevelt
"and tell him of our desire to publicize him nationally."

Hearst editorially supported FDR's advocacy of the development of
public power, forest conservation, prison reform, and streamlining state
and local government. "Of course we will handle all of Roosevelt's
important utterances in a conspicuous way not only in New York but
throughout the country," he told Coblentz.[11]

As Roosevelt broke into a decisive lead over the Democratic pack,
W. R. had second thoughts. His disillusionment began when Wilson's

closest adviser, Colonel Edward M. House, announced his return to presidential politics as Roosevelt's adviser. The isolationist publisher supported Harding over the Cox-Roosevelt ticket in 1920 when the Democratic candidates embraced Wilsonian internationalism. Hearst's anxiety about Roosevelt's foreign policy views gave him a reason to look for another presidential contender.

In December of 1931, when Garner became Speaker of the House, Hearst dispatched national political correspondent George Rothwell Brown to interview the Texas Democrat. Garner had first been elected to the House with Hearst in 1902 and they had been friendly. Since 1924 W. R. had owned a newspaper in Garner's congressional district, the *San Antonio Light*. But it had been decades since the former colleagues had spoken. "I received a request from Mr. Hearst to inform him how Mr. Garner stood on certain vital political questions then agitating the country," Brown remembered. ". . . Among these were retrenchment of government expenditures, the League of Nations, and the cancellation or reconsideration of the European war debts."

After meeting with the Speaker, Brown reported to the publisher that Garner "opposed all foreign entanglements," favored repayment of European war debts, and "believed in thrift, prudence, and economy in government." Brown had known Garner for three decades and shared his thoughts with Hearst. "I said that Mr. Garner had a deep sense of obligation first of all to his own country, that he was an old-fashioned, patriotic American and a rugged Democrat of the Andrew Jackson school," the veteran correspondent recalled years later.[12]

Hearst had found his man. On the first Saturday night of 1932, he spoke over the NBC radio network and blamed Wilson for the decline of the Democratic Party and for what he termed a catastrophic change in American foreign policy. "It is about time that the Democratic party got back upon the high road of Americanism," he asserted.

"Unless conditions change radically in the next few months the next President of the United States is likely to be a Democrat.

"The Democratic candidates—Mr. Roosevelt, Mr. Baker, Mr. Ritchie, Mr. Smith, and Mr. Young are all good men in their way, but all internationalists—all, like Mr. Hoover, disciples of Woodrow Wilson, inheriting and fatuously following his visionary policies of intermeddling in European conflicts and complications."

Then he endorsed Garner as "a loyal American citizen, a plain man of the plain people, a sound and sincere Democrat; in fact another Champ Clark.

"His heart is with his own people. His interest is in his own country," the publisher concluded. "Unless we American citizens are willing to go on laboring indefinitely merely to provide loot for Europe, we should personally see to it that a man is elected to the Presidency this year whose guiding motto is 'America First.' "[13]

In the wake of this broadcast Garner was a contender to be reckoned with. Roosevelt's camp had counted on winning the forty-six votes of the Texas delegation. Once the Speaker allowed his name to be entered as a favorite son, FDR withdrew from Texas. Hearst, who owned twenty-six newspapers in nineteen cities, a features syndicate, two wire services, thirteen magazines, eight radio stations, and two film companies, had the resources to make or break a national candidate.

Hearst used his newspapers to build up Garner and find fault with FDR. "It is very important to get Governor Roosevelt's statements on the Wilson policies. Please put men on this work who are accustomed to going through library files," he instructed Coblentz. There was abundant material, for Roosevelt had made the League a central issue in his campaign for the vice presidency. "Today we are offered a seat at the table of a family of nations to the end that smaller peoples may work out their own destiny," FDR said at Hyde Park in his vice-presidential nomination acceptance speech. "We shall take that place." Roosevelt's old speeches were reprinted in editorials attacking the governor's internationalism.

Seeking to minimize the damage, Roosevelt reached out to Hearst through third parties, including House and Joseph P. Kennedy. House advised W. R. that Roosevelt had outgrown his youthful internationalism and would be willing to talk about his foreign policy views in a private conversation. "I beg leave to say that if Mr. Roosevelt has any statement to make about his not now being an internationalist, he should make it to the public publicly and not to me privately," the publisher shot back in a signed editorial. "He has made his numerous declarations publicly when he said that he WAS an internationalist and was in favor of our country joining the League of Nations. . . . He should make his declaration publicly that he has changed his mind and that he is now in favor of keeping the national independence which our forefathers won for us, that he is now in favor of not joining the League."

Then Hearst made it personal. "My experience has proved that a man who is running for office and is not willing to make his honest opinions known to the public either has no honest opinions or is not honest about them. If a man is hiding his opinions from the public and only expressing them privately to people whose support he wants I would consider him either cowardly or untrustworthy."[14]

From an individual newspaper or columnist, FDR might ignore such criticism. But W. R., whose publications were read by thirty million Americans, was in a league of his own. Howe advised Roosevelt "to be sure and telephone Hearst. . . . You may have to make a public statement before we get through, if this thing gets any more violent." The governor made the phone call to the Lord of San Simeon.

Then, two days after W. R. issued his public challenge, FDR publicly declared that he no longer favored American participation in the

League of Nations because the organization "is not the League conceived by Woodrow Wilson." Instead of working to promote world
peace, he asserted that the League had become "a mere meeting place
for the political discussion of strictly European political difficulties. In
these the United States should have no part."

Politically he did the right thing. The Hearst newspapers, though
still propaganda sheets for Garner, quit bashing Roosevelt. It was also
a politically defensible position. The League of Nations, for reasons
cited by the governor, was an ideal that had failed. As early as 1923, he
had drafted a proposal "to kill the existing League and set up something in its place" that would be more acceptable to the American
people. But since this document had never been published, Roosevelt
was accused of bowing to expediency. "It will be generally regretted,
we think," the *New York Times* editorialized, "that Governor Roosevelt
should have been so plainly swayed by political motives in this public
recantation."[15]

If Hearst pressured him, Roosevelt had discussed with advisers the
possibility of ending his support for the World Court. "In view of your
attitude on the League of Nations," Colonel House told FDR, "I do
not think such a reply would satisfy many of your most ardent and influential friends. What you said about the League has already strained
their loyalty, and many of them have told me that if you take the same
position on the World Court they cannot support you. This has come
from some of those close to you."

Robert W. Woolley, FDR's friend from the Wilson years, attended a
meeting in Senator Hull's office and reported to House: "Every man
there looked as if he might be attending his own funeral . . . I don't
suppose the Governor of New York will ever realize the extent of the
tragedy which he wrought in that entirely unnecessary statement . . .
Hearst's cohorts here are having the time of their lives raucously

laughing at the manner in which their chief brought the Governor of New York to his knees. They boast that from now on Roosevelt is at Hearst's mercy."

FDR privately assured his pro-League supporters that he still shared their commitment to internationalism but was being pragmatic. "Can't you see that loyalty to the ideals of Woodrow Wilson is just as strong in my heart as it is in yours," he told Woolley, "but have you ever stopped to consider that there is a difference between ideals and the means of attaining them? Ideals do not change, but methods do change with every generation and world circumstance.

"Here is the difference between me and some of my faint-hearted friends: I am looking for the best modern vehicle to reach the goal of an ideal while they insist on a vehicle which was brand new and in good running order twelve years ago. Think this over! And for heaven's sake have a little faith!"[16]

At about this same time, Hearst was putting together the Garner campaign for the California primary. "I could get nothing but evasion from the Democratic party leaders," W. R. recalled, "and was finally compelled to run a separate Garner ticket." Former Treasury secretary William Gibbs McAdoo of Los Angeles, who had been supported by Hearst for the presidency in 1924, took over the Garner campaign at the urging of the publisher. This formidable alliance put Garner over the top in the May primary and thwarted FDR's hopes of winning on the first ballot.[17]

On at least one issue, Hearst was in agreement with Roosevelt. W. R. blamed the two-thirds rule for the destruction of Clark in 1912 and McAdoo in 1924. As Democrats gathered in Chicago, W. R. was asked by another news organization whether he favored elimination of the rule. "Yes," he wired back from his California hilltop, "it is at variance with every Democratic principle."

Hearst was also asked his second choice if Garner fell short of the nomination. "Garner," he replied.

Would he support Roosevelt if nominated?

"I will support any genuine Democrat," W. R. said, "but I will not support any candidate of Wall Street and the international bankers nominated to perpetuate the Hoover policies and make the interests of the United States subservient to the interests of foreign countries."[18]

Of all the contenders, Hearst was most determined to stop former secretary of war Newton D. Baker, the Democratic Party's leading spokesman for liberal internationalism.

6

BUGLE CALL

N EWTON D. BAKER hated war yet organized the greatest fighting
force in American history. As secretary of war in the administration of Woodrow Wilson, this small man of great eloquence raised
an army of four million men, removed politics from his department,
chose General John J. Pershing as commander of the American Expe-
ditionary Force, and helped to turn the tide of the Great War. "He made
it possible," Black Jack said, "to do what I have done."

On the Western Front, Baker saw the dying and the dead. "As much
as I deplore the taking of human life," he told a friend, "I am convinced that now we are in, there is but one thing to do—and that is to
kill Germans and kill Germans and kill Germans until their numbers are
sufficiently reduced to make the rest listen." In contrast with other distinguished visitors, he would not be content to watch the fighting from
a safe distance. Baker went where the action was. On at least one occasion, he narrowly escaped three exploding German shells. His coolness
under fire became part of the Baker legend.[1]

So did his standing up for his men. In the face of pressure from British prime minister David Lloyd George and French premier Georges Clemenceau, he resisted their efforts to consolidate the Americans into their armies. "In military operations against the Imperial German Government you are directed to cooperate with the forces of the other countries employed against that enemy," the secretary of war ordered Pershing; "but in so doing the underlying idea must be kept in view that the forces of the United States are a separate and distinct component of the combined forces, the identity of which must be preserved."

It was America's intervention, Baker noted years later, that made the Allies a winning coalition and forced Germany to sign the Armistice. "It seems to me that the German collapse came when the Germans had used up their last reserves, and that Pershing used these reserves up for them in the Argonne," he observed.

After leaving office, he made a fortune in private law practice. His clients included the Van Sweringen real estate and railroad interests, public utility holding companies, the J. P. Morgan Company, and the Scripps-Howard newspaper chain. Baker also stayed active in politics as the leading advocate of American membership in the League of Nations. There was even speculation at one point that he might be named secretary general of the international organization.[2]

Baker was the son that Wilson never had. They had first met at Johns Hopkins University where Baker took Wilson's course in political science and the two men roomed for two years in the same boardinghouse. Wilson later observed that his protégé had a mind like chain lightning. A year after Wilson's election as governor of New Jersey, Baker was elected mayor of Cleveland on a platform of progressive reform. When Baker helped him win the presidency, Wilson offered to make him his chief assistant or a member of the cabinet. Baker felt obligated to serve out his term as mayor. After his former pupil's term expired, the president asked him to take over the War Department. Wilson regarded Baker as his intellectual peer and the most valuable member of his cabinet.

At the 1924 Democratic National Convention, four months after Wilson's death, Baker delivered a powerful and moving tribute, urging his party to continue the late president's legacy. "I served Woodrow Wilson for five years. He is standing at the throne of a God whose approval he has won and has received," Baker asserted. "As he looks down from there I say to him: 'I did my best. I am doing it now. You are still the captain of my soul.'" The young Adlai E. Stevenson II, a future Illinois governor and two-time Democratic presidential nominee, said it was the greatest speech he ever heard. Oswald Garrison Villard of *The Nation*, who had no great love for the departed president, said years later that Baker's speech was among the few times that he had seen grown men weep in response to spoken words.[3]

In foreign policy, Baker remained the voice of Wilsonian idealism. Following the Japanese invasion of Manchuria in 1931, he joined the presidents of Harvard and Columbia universities in calling for an economic boycott of Japan. But President Hoover declined to impose economic sanctions. "I think it is of the highest importance that nations which start on aggressive programs should know in advance that the United States will make common cause with the League," Baker wrote Walter Lippmann, "in discouraging aggressive military adventures."[4]

Baker came gradually to a decision that he would seek the 1932 Democratic presidential nomination. Even though he had been out of office for a dozen years, he was the perceived heir to the most popular Democratic president since Andrew Jackson. He also had a political base in the critical state of Ohio and a national constituency of World War I veterans and the American Legion, which was emerging as a major political force. The publication of a two-volume biography, written by Colonel Frederick Palmer with Baker's cooperation, was timed to boost the cause. "I should think that a thousand copies of the book, well distributed among the men who had influence at conventions," Palmer wrote a Baker strategist, "would have a surprisingly good effect."

By the late spring of 1931, Baker was gaining momentum as an undeclared contender for the Democratic presidential nomination. His strategy was to avoid the primaries and position himself to be the Chicago convention's compromise choice in the event of a deadlock. "Your boom for my presidency seems to be making some headway," Baker told campaign manager Ralph Hayes. A poll of newspaper editors in thirty-four states indicated that he was their first choice. If Roosevelt failed to win on an early ballot, there were hints that the convention might turn to Baker. The theory was that Smith and Roosevelt would eliminate each other, setting the stage for Baker's nomination. Before the convention, thirteen state delegations asked their members to list a second choice for the presidential nomination. Eleven of these states and 220 delegates selected Baker.[5]

"One hears a good deal of talk here about Roosevelt not measuring up intellectually to Grover Cleveland and Woodrow Wilson," FDR supporter Robert Woolley reported to Colonel House. "I am constantly being surprised and worried by the manner in which people who have been talking for Roosevelt readily fall in with the idea that Baker is a second Cleveland or Wilson—if not even bigger than either."

It was Wilson himself who had first touted his former student for the presidency. In the summer of 1918 the last Democratic president of the United States confided that Baker should be his successor. "The next President will have to be able to think in terms of the whole world," Wilson said. "He must be internationally minded."[6]

In 1932, Edith Bolling Wilson, the president's widow, former U.S.

Supreme Court Justice John H. Clarke, former Treasury secretary Carter Glass, former Agriculture secretary David Houston, former war propaganda director George Creel, former War Industries board chairman Bernard M. Baruch, and Admiral Cary Grayson, Wilson's physician, were looking to Baker to pick up the fallen standard of Wilsonian liberalism and complete the late president's unfinished work.

Franklin D. Roosevelt had long regarded Baker as presidential timber. Robert W. Bingham, president and publisher of the *Louisville Courier-Journal*, recalled a discussion with FDR in the fall of 1931. "He told me at the time that he felt that Newton Baker was, in a sense, the heir of Wilson's spirit more than anyone else," Bingham remembered, "and that if Newton Baker should consent to be a candidate he not only would not oppose him, but would do all in his power to aid him in bringing about his nomination and election." But Roosevelt had already committed himself to the race and was doubtful that the former war secretary would be a candidate. "Baker would be the only dangerous competitor," the historian and Democratic activist Claude G. Bowers told Roosevelt, "and he will not be an open candidate. His only chance would be to openly announce and take the stump and that he will not do." After discussing the presidency with Baker, Bowers added, "I was impressed with the feeling that he would like the nomination, provided it fell into his lap, but that he would make no aggressive contest for it."[7]

When Baker emerged as a real threat, Roosevelt privately suggested that his nomination would be a disaster. "I don't need to tell you how much I admire and respect Newton Baker," he wrote Josephus Daniels, "and what a wonderful asset he can be to the Party during the next four years if we win. The trouble is that he labors under very definite political handicaps. Because of, or rather in spite of, his perfectly legitimate law practice he is labeled by many progressives as the attorney for J. P.

Morgan and the Van Schweringens [*sic*]; he is opposed by Labor; he would be opposed by the German-Americans; and also by the bulk of the Irish because of his consistent League of Nations attitude up to this year. As they say, 'them are the sad facts.' All of this seems a pity because Newton would make a better President than I would!"[8]

Being human, Baker also believed that he would be a better president than Roosevelt. "My personal contacts with him have not been extensive," he wrote in the winter of 1932. "I think he has a fine academic training, great personal charm, and a real desire to serve uprightly in any situation where the public interest is involved. It seems to me wholly likely that he will receive the Democratic nomination and I can think of nobody in the Democratic party at the moment whose nomination would seem to me better. The two reservations I have about Frank are an overemphasis on the mechanics of politics, leading to statements and silences born of expediency, and as I see it, constituting a surrender of leadership, and two, what seems to me a naïve attempt at intellectual isolation so far as international affairs are concerned."

Baker, a deep thinker, believed that Roosevelt lacked political courage and intellectual curiosity. "My deepest disappointment about him," he wrote Lippmann, "has come from his silence ever since 1921 about things which matter ultimately in the composition of our modern world. So far as I know he has never said a word about America's duty as a member of the family of nations and I have now lived long enough to know that our welfare has to be sought in this world along the lines of the performance of duty and cannot be safely allowed to arise out of mere chance or good fortune. Until we moderns acquire again some resoluteness in accepting the burdens which modern civilization imposes, we can have no feeling of safety that the thing we call civilization will last long enough to be enjoyed by our children."[9]

As governor of New York and presidential contender, Roosevelt was more focused on domestic issues than on foreign policy. But Baker underestimated FDR's knowledge of the world. Since his youth Roosevelt had traveled widely in Europe and knew its history, culture, and politics. As assistant secretary of the navy, Roosevelt had been among the first officials in the Wilson administration to perceive the threat of German militarism. During the twenties, Roosevelt began developing plans for an international organization that could replace the League of Nations. Appearing before the 1930 New York State convention of the American Legion, FDR talked about the importance of a strong national defense. "We should all work against war," he said, "but if it should come we should be better prepared than we were before. . . . I am not militaristic by any means. I do not believe in a large standing army, as you know, nor in a large navy, but I am 100 percent for having this country ready for an emergency."[10]

During the winter of 1932, Baker made the first policy flip on the League. At a January meeting of the League of Nations Association, advocates confidently predicted that Baker, if elected president, would bring the United States into the League. In his endorsement of Garner, Hearst put candidates on notice that his newspapers would show no mercy to candidates aligned with Wilsonian internationalism. Smith, through his strategist Belle Moskowitz, advised Baker that his identification with the League was a potential liability. A Democratic national convention had not endorsed U.S. membership in the League since Wilson was in the White House and the lopsided defeats of Cox and Davis convinced Smith that it would be folly for Baker to champion this lost cause.

Hayes, who had worked for Baker at the War Department and then devoted more than a decade to this presidential bid, urged Baker to cut his losses. "I don't like to think of the number of people who had gradually shed fantastic notions about you in the past ten years and who are now seized again with a fixed idea that hell and hot water may not thaw out of them—namely that your chief political concern and title is that of a kleagle in an evil international hierarchy engaged in preying on honest Americans.

"I just don't want to see you hand over to the other side on a silver platter the one issue that will save them from defeat," Hayes concluded, "and permit them to wrap themselves in the flag while they coast again to victory."[11]

Baker was persuaded. His friend Roy Howard, publisher of the Scripps-Howard newspaper group, broke the story. Howard boarded a ship in Lower Manhattan and met Baker, who was about to embark with his wife on a vacation in Mexico. Speaking as "a private citizen," Baker reversed himself on the policy that linked him to Wilson.

"I am not in favor of a plank in the Democratic national platform urging our joining the League. I think it would be a great mistake to make a partisan issue of the matter," he declared. ". . . I would not take the United States into the League, if I had the power to do so until there is an informed and convinced majority sentiment in favor of that action."

By distancing himself from the League, Baker removed all doubt that he wanted the presidential nomination. "Let me know what people in Washington say about Newton Baker coming out against our entry into the League," Roosevelt wrote a friend. "He has, of course, said the right thing, but I wonder if a lot of people will not regard it as going back on his previous declarations."

The columnist Heywood Broun wrote that Baker's retreat proved that he "would rather be candidate than candid." Oswald Villard, recalling Baker's tribute to Wilson at the 1924 convention, wrote acidly that "the man at the throne of God is no longer captain of his soul!" After Roosevelt dropped his advocacy of the League, Henry Suydan of the *Brooklyn Eagle* lamented: "Newton D. Baker's shelving of the

League was more of a shock than Mr. Roosevelt's because the former has stuck to the League issue through good times and bad, and this steadfast conviction was one of the admirable things about him."

Baker would not respond to this public criticism and declined when Hayes urged him to clarify his position in the wake of Roosevelt's abandonment of the League. "If there is one thing which the course of my life has taught me," Baker replied, "it is that explanations simply entail more explanations."[12]

Lippmann, who had worked for Baker at the War Department and was among Wilson's advisers who drafted the Fourteen Points at the Versailles Peace Conference, began writing a political column for the *New York Herald Tribune* in September of 1931. He used this forum to advance a not-so-hidden agenda. "Franklin D. Roosevelt is a highly impressionable person, without a firm grasp of public affairs and without very strong convictions," Lippmann wrote in the winter of 1932. "He is no tribune of the people. He is no enemy of entrenched privilege. He is a pleasant man who, without any important qualifications for the office, would very much like to be President."

"The strength of Baker," Lippmann wrote later in the year, "derives from an almost universal confidence in his ability and in his character. He is profoundly trusted. As to other men, it is necessary to guess whether they have the qualities of mind and heart needed in a world crisis. But Baker has been tested in a world crisis. He has piloted a ship in a great storm. It is not necessary to ask whether he can organize men for action. He has organized more men for action than any other living American. It is not necessary to ask whether he has the mind to grasp quickly the truth hidden in great complex problems. Every year the testimony has grown more compelling as to the effectiveness with which he improvised a great army. . . . No one has to ask himself whether Baker has the power to make decisions amidst danger and confusion.

No one has to ask whether he is brave. No one can doubt that he has calm judgment, and that in the fevers of a crisis he has shown himself to be cool, serene, patient and resolute."[13]

What his readers did not know was that the journalist was advising Baker on issues and strategy. He was also writing speeches and position papers for his candidate. As chief editorial writer for the *New York World*, Lippmann had supported the failed Democratic presidential campaigns of John W. Davis in 1924 and Alfred E. Smith in 1928. Neither of them, he confided to Baker, did enough homework on issues. "I believe more and more firmly that you're destined to be nominated," he told Baker in December, "and I am writing to say that I hope you can find a way to reduce the amount of your activity in your law practice so as to have ample time for reading and reflection, and perhaps even to have careful studies made, under your direction, matters that will be discussed in the campaign."

Baker replied that he kept informed "in a general way" but was not ready to undertake more comprehensive studies. "I am now almost daily instructed by you in a way which nobody was doing for Davis and Smith at the time to which you refer," he told Lippmann.[14]

"I hope that you will not hesitate to speak at fairly frequent intervals on important public questions quite regardless of the political implications," Lippmann wrote Baker. "I don't think you should be silenced for fear that you might be considered a candidate for President any more than an active candidate like Roosevelt ought to be silent because it's politically expedient for him to commit himself."

Since the presidential election would be a referendum on the economic policies of the Hoover administration, Lippmann urged Baker to show leadership in offering bold alternatives. Lippmann wanted Baker to raise taxes on the wealthy "because it's morally necessary to begin with the rich." He would then have Baker roll back the Republican tax cuts of the 1920s and restore taxes that were imposed during the Great War. Lippmann said that Baker could connect with people hurting from the Depression by proposing direct relief. "I have been wondering whether a good way to go about the matter wouldn't be to revive the War Finance Corporation," he told Baker, "and give it authority to make loans to states as to the nature of their plans for relief."

These were issues that voters cared about in 1932 and, if he had followed Lippmann's advice, Baker could have related to ordinary people hungry for new leadership. But he preferred talking about foreign policy. In his next speech, rather than talk about the Depression, he proposed a constitutional amendment to eliminate the two-thirds Senate majority required for the ratification of treaties.[15]

While his rivals focused on the economy, Baker painted himself into a corner. "More people are hungry in this country today than ever before in my lifetime or yours. More workmen have no work. More farmers are smothered and impoverished under mountains of unmarketable crops. Industry languishes and dies behind a barrier designed to stop imports, which, instead prevents exports. The country's distress carries it to the brink of destruction," Hayes told Baker. "You are the one person who could give inspiration to a people who cry for a leader. And yet instead of addressing yourself to the issues that so urgently weigh upon the mind and conscience of the country, you spend your strength in expounding upon a possible Twenty-first Amendment to the Constitution designed to realize the apportionment of power between the Executive and the Senate."

Baker did not disagree with this criticism. "Quite clearly the Philadelphia speech is wholly out of focus," he acknowledged to Hayes, "if one considers it as an attempt to address one's self to the present practical and urgent situation." Yet when Baker began drafting a speech about the Depression with an aide, he admitted that "neither of us knew what to say."

So his next speech, at Wilson's tomb, was another tribute to the late president. "Again we have fallen upon days of doubt and disillusionment," Baker said. "Again we need the scholar's detachment and the leader's voice. For the moment we can but say to this great soldier, 'Sleep on. The army which you led is still advancing.' "

Bruce F. Barton, spokesman for the United War Work Agencies during the Great War, wanted Baker to step out of Wilson's shadow. "The people are in a hell of a mess," Barton wrote Hayes, "and they do not think the spirit of either Abraham Lincoln or Woodrow Wilson will pull them out."[16]

Baker, who had given serious thought to these issues, showed the crusading zeal of his youth when he privately outlined what had to be done to lift the nation out of the Depression. "If the captains of industry in the United States have not sense enough to organize industry upon a plan which will prevent the disastrous and cruel unemployment which we have at this time," he wrote Hayes, "then they ought not to be permitted to organize it at all.

"This does not mean that I believe that industry can always be kept at the flood tide of peak production, but it does very definitely mean that industry has no right to impose upon labor the vicarious suffering caused by making it bear all the consequences of maladjustments and peaks and valleys in the industrial system. I am sure that I have no patent medicine remedy for the existing situation, but I do know that the responsibility for finding a remedy rests upon the employer class and is at this moment not being met or even considered with any genuine concern.

"If this sounds a bit radical to you, I assure you it is the most conservative thing I have ever said in my life, for he is, after all the true conservative who best realizes the extent to which the preservation of an economic system depends upon the justice with which it distributes rewards and imposes burdens. If I may counterweight this piece of wisdom with the definition of a radical, I would say a radical is one who realizes that there are injustices and is willing to cure them by imposing the opposite injustice."[17]

When Baker finally made a speech about the economic crisis, he spoke in bland platitudes about the need for a leader to mobilize the "character and intellectual reserve" of the country to fight the Depression.

At such forums, he was reluctant to criticize the efforts of the Hoover administration or his rivals for the Democratic nomination. With his strategy pegged to a convention deadlock, the undeclared hopeful could not afford to make enemies.

Baker, who publicly maintained that he was not a candidate, might have waged a more active campaign if he had been in better health. He had suffered a heart attack while campaigning for Smith in 1928 and another heart ailment in 1930 kept him bedridden for six weeks. Shouse, who had urged Baker to make an all-out bid for the nomination, said that the former cabinet secretary "was warned by his physicians of an almost certain recurrence if he subjected himself to any undue exertion." To promote a Baker draft, Shouse encouraged Smith into the race in hopes of deadlocking the convention.

As his nomination became a real possibility, Baker submitted to a physical examination by his cardiologist, Dr. R. W. Scott of Western Reserve University's School of Medicine, and obtained a second opinion from Dr. E. P. Carter of Johns Hopkins University. "I have observed that Mr. Baker can do an extraordinary amount of mental work without apparent mental or bodily fatigue," Dr. Scott said in his report. "Public appearances and important decisions made in the course of his work appear to cause him no worry either at the time or afterwards. However, in the event a political campaign should force Mr. Baker to undertake considerable physical exertion—a two-month tour of the land with several speeches each day, shaking the hands of multitudes, etc.—I would advise him, as I would many men of his age, not to do it."[18]

At sixty years old, Baker was willing to take that risk if the convention nominated him. When there was speculation in published reports about Baker's health, Roosevelt's camp was the probable source. "I have information which I regard as entirely reliable that those who are very close to Governor Roosevelt, and probably the Governor himself are spreading the report that Newton Baker is disqualified because of his health," Lippmann wrote Colonel House. "It seems to be particularly distressing that the Governor, or people close to him, should inject into the discussion the question of physical fitness. That is a subject that they had better not discuss at all. . . . For of course if this propaganda persists someone is sure to bring it out into the open and ask for a general showdown on the question of physical fitness."

Roosevelt, who had been the target of whispering campaigns about his polio that would continue into the Chicago convention, was unmoved by Lippmann's threat. Baker had told FDR in 1928 that his heart ailment was the reason why he had not run for public office. Roosevelt denied to House that he had been the source of published reports about Baker's health. "Many of those close to the Governor feel about Newton Baker as I do," House replied to Lippmann, "that if the nomination does not go to our man it should go to him. However, I have cautioned all of them to keep off the subject of Newton Baker's health."

Unsatisfied by this response, Lippmann shot back, "The very assurances you quote are not very reassuring. If I want to create the impression that a man is in bad health all I need to do is to keep inquiring solicitously about his health."[19]

As the convention approached, Baker speculated about his prospects. "If that comes, it can only come and ought to only come," he told a friend, "if there is nothing else for the convention to do."

To help make this happen, Hayes planned to flood delegates in Chicago with pro-Baker telegrams and plotted with Lippmann and Roy Howard to generate popular support for their candidate. "If, at the end of say, the second or third ballot, the convention has not named a candidate and if the anti-Roosevelt groups show signs of holding veto strength or better, a large group of papers, not including the Scripps-Howard chain, should publish an urgent editorial plea, with as prominent display as possible, calling on the convention to avoid the danger of falling into a factional debacle similar to that of 1924 and to turn to Mr. Baker as obviously the most desirable leader in the coming campaign."[20]

7

LONE STAR

AS SPEAKER OF the House, John Nance Garner was the nation's highest-ranking Democratic officeholder in 1932 and insisted that his ambitions had been fulfilled. "There are no presidential bees buzzing around my office. My duties as speaker have kept me so busy I have given this matter no consideration," the white-haired Texan stated in a public letter, "and I expect to be kept equally busy until the House adjourns."

Garner, a congressman for three decades, felt comfortable in this role and never talked about running for governor or senator. Even before he took over the leadership of the House of Representatives in December 1931, a group of Houston businessmen launched a movement to draft him for the presidency. He regarded this movement as nothing more than home-state boosterism and had few illusions about his chances. "No Democrat from Texas is going to have availability for his party's presidential nomination except under extraordinary circumstances," he told Bascom Timmons, a longtime confidant and Texas newspaperman based in Washington.

"I am Speaker of the House and devoting my time to its duties," Garner added. "This is the first time the Democrats have controlled any branch of government for ten years. If we do not function properly between now and the Democratic National Convention the Democratic presidential nomination won't be worth two whoops in hell to anybody."[1]

When Hearst endorsed him for the presidency, Garner declined comment. House majority leader John McDuffie of Alabama, who urged Garner to seek the nomination, said that when he brought up the subject, "John growls like an old bear. If he is not interested, why should his friends be?"

Texas congressman Sam Rayburn took a similar attitude. "I think the best thing for Garner's friends to do is to adopt a little bit of watchful waiting for the next two months," he wrote a former colleague in January. "Garner is a little embarrassed right now by the talk as he desired to become reasonably well seated in the Speakership before small jealousies are created by his being talked about for a higher position."

After cutting off questions on the subject at a press conference, Garner pulled aside his friend Timmons and opened up. "I have been Speaker for less than sixty days. I have got a tender majority of three," Cactus Jack wryly observed. "If I can stay close to the gavel I can get along all right. The biggest single bloc of votes in there is controlled by Tammany. It's more than a tenth of all the Democratic votes in the House. They have got a Roosevelt-Smith split among themselves already. Smith has got support among congressmen from other states. The Maryland fellows are lined up for Ritchie. There are Roosevelt people in nearly all the delegations. I don't want to jeopardize our cohesion and the legislative program by a presidential candidacy program of my own."[2]

No legislator enjoyed more goodwill among colleagues of both parties. On George Washington's two-hundredth birthday, House

Republicans joined the Democrats in cheering their new Speaker. "It will interest you to know that Jack Garner's ovation was three times as hearty as that accorded to the President," Woolley wrote. "Nearly every newspaper correspondent you talk with here will tell you that Roosevelt is stopped and that Garner will be the nominee."

With a magnetic and engaging personality, Garner spoke in the clipped cadence of the Old West, minced few words, and was known as a straight shooter. He drank whiskey, played cards, and had a robust laugh. Born in a log cabin in Red River County only three years after the Civil War, Garner was the son of a former Confederate soldier. The Indian wars were a recent memory when the future House Speaker settled in Rio Grande country. In his youth, he herded cattle, rode the range, and for the rest of his life would have the squint of a cowboy. Among his close friends and gambling cronies was Sheriff Pat Garrett, the lawman who shot Billy the Kid. As a young lawyer who made court appearances in nine counties, Garner rode on horseback and carried a single-action Colt .45. Since he accepted in-kind payment for his legal services, Garner accumulated thousands of acres, livestock, and commodities.

"He takes a frontiersman's pride in being very much on the level, and in having a reputation for self-reliance and guts," Paul Y. Anderson reported in *The Nation*. Garner was not a large man. But he was a distinctive presence with white hair, long shaggy eyebrows, and the most expressive blue eyes in American politics.[3]

"His smile is a golden glow," Claude Bowers observed. "It not only lights a room but warms a visitor. His voice and manner have all the heartiness of the West and South. But no student of faces will fail to note the keen intelligence of those blue-grey eyes or to realize that they are the eyes of a fighter, capable of the reflections of cold steel. No pretense. No pose. No illusions here. Just a two-fisted, upstanding human being who has grown very wise in the many years he has dealt with men and politics."

While attending a state Democratic convention in the early 1890s, Garner decided to go into politics. "I looked things over and saw all the big men," he recalled. "I said to myself: 'Well, now I have nearly as much sense as these people. I think I will just look around and see if I can't take one of these jobs myself.'"[4]

In 1893 he began his public career with his appointment as judge of Uvalde County. A year later, he was elected to a full term. Mariette Elizabeth Rheiner, a young woman who lived on one of the largest ranches in the area, campaigned against him on the grounds that Garner's reputed exploits at poker disqualified him for the bench. After the judge won retention, he sought out his critic and began courting her. In November of 1895 they were married.

Elected to the Texas House of Representatives in 1898, he served two terms in Austin. Garner made his mark as an advocate of tighter regulations on corporations and also sought to reduce the influence of the railroad lobby in state government. One bill that he sponsored, citing terms of the treaty of annexation, would have divided Texas into five states. His argument for this change, noting that Texas was 213 times larger than Rhode Island, was that smaller states on the Atlantic seaboard had more influence on national legislation than the Lone Star State. Under his proposed change, the region would gain eight seats in the U.S. Senate and about twenty electoral votes. His resolution was passed by the Texas House but vetoed by the governor. He also lost his battle to call a new state constitutional convention to replace the outdated document that had been drafted before the Civil War.

In his second term, Garner got himself named chairman of the redistricting committee that created a new congressional district, which was larger than the state of New York, and ran more than four hundred miles along the Rio Grande. The King and Kenedy ranches, which made up more than 1.5 million acres, were also part of the new 15th congressional district. Of seventeen Texas legislators who sought congressional seats in 1902, Garner alone prevailed.[5]

It was said of Garner that his guns were notched with more victories over formidable adversaries than any other member of Congress. "If a person wronged me," he said years later, "I never rested easy until I got even."

Roosevelt's camp did not want Garner as an enemy. James A. Farley, who met Garner shortly after he became Speaker, later wrote that he felt intimidated when the Texan stepped back and gave him the once-over. "It was apparent that he recognized the name and knew why I was there, and for a moment I was afraid that he was going to let go with a few explosive remarks about individuals who used the lobbies of Congress to promote presidential politics," Farley recalled. "He said nothing more, however, and continued on down the stairs. . . . His steady gaze and rather stern manner were a little too sharp for an easygoing fellow like me, and I felt as a result of this first encounter that he was hardly the kind of man with whom I could get acquainted on affable and friendly terms." Farley, who came to admire Garner, said that his first impression was "about as far wrong as any judgment could be."[6]

When he first arrived in Washington in 1903, Garner quipped that he was taken for "just another cattle thief from Texas." But he impressed colleagues in both parties with his hard work, attention to detail, and political savvy. He soon gained renown as among the best poker players in Washington and during several congressional sessions made most of his annual income at the card table. Garner's biographer Marquis James noted that Henry Clay, Daniel Webster, and Sam Houston were among the more skilled poker players of an earlier congressional era. House Speaker Joseph G. Cannon, the hard-bitten and autocratic Illinois

Republican, was so impressed with the young Texan that he made him a member of his poker club at a K Street hideaway.

Garner and his wife, Ettie, lived simply. When they first arrived in the capital city, the Garners lived in a boardinghouse on Franklin Square, where he had his office and she worked as his secretary. "I rode the streetcar a mile or more from the boardinghouse," he recalled. "If you wanted to attend to business, you stayed all day at the Capitol." After the first House Office building opened in 1908, she performed all his secretarial duties. Later, he had a gas range installed in the office and she would cook his lunch.

By the time he rose to the Speakership, the Garners had an apartment in a hotel near the White House. They were not active in Washington society. On becoming House Speaker, he was persuaded by his wife to order formal evening clothes, including striped pants and what he referred to as "one of those coats with half the stuff cut off." Garner also bought several new suits. "I never had that many clothes before in my life," he said.

In keeping with his philosophy of holding the line on federal spending, Garner gave up his official limousine and chauffeur. "I just couldn't do it," he told a friend. "It was costing the government five dollars a day to haul me from my hotel to the Capitol and back. I can get there in a taxi for twenty cents." He and his wife often walked a mile to work.

At a press conference, he scoffed when asked if turning back the car had diminished the dignity of the office. "It doesn't take an automobile to make the office dignified," the Texan replied. "I'll lend the dignity."[7]

A well-informed and productive legislator, Garner seldom spoke on the House floor. It offended him that colleagues would insert undelivered speeches into the *Congressional Record*. When he obtained an editor's proof for revision of his remarks, Garner would delete his comments or reduce them to a few words. "It was a good many years before any remarks of mine got in the *Record,*" he told another Texas congressman, "and I hope you won't be making a damn fool of yourself either."

Garner was the first Texan to head any branch of the federal government and throughout his public career he delivered for his home state. He obtained funding to improve the harbor at Corpus Christi, construct a canal on the Gulf Coast, establish a weather bureau at Del Rio, and build a new federal courthouse. "Every time one of those Yankees gets a ham," he once said, "I'm going to do my best to get a hog."

When he was about to become chairman of the Foreign Affairs Committee, he gave up his seniority for a junior slot on the Ways and Means Committee. An advocate of tax fairness, he used his influence on this committee to pass the first graduated income tax in 1913 and to defeat tax breaks for the rich in the 1920s. In 1931 he forced the Hoover administration to disclose huge tax refunds to corporations.[8]

Once his name was mentioned in connection with the presidency, Garner preempted the field in Texas. By the middle of February, Senators Tom Connally and Morris Sheppard endorsed him as "a rugged and militant champion of the American people." Former lieutenant governor T. W. Davidson, Roosevelt's Texas coordinator, suspended the campaign. "It would be impossible to overcome the state pride in instructing for Garner," Thomas W. Gregory of Austin, a former U.S. attorney general, advised Roosevelt's camp.

"John Garner occupies the highest position of any other Democrat in public life in America today and is doing the job of Speaker and leader of the Democrats in the House in a masterly way," Rayburn wrote a friend in Texas. "He is catching the imagination of the country and it is not far from probable that quite a myth may be built up around him before the next convention meets.

"At this particular time," Rayburn added, "when Mr. Hoover and the Republican Party have so utterly failed to meet the expectation of the country, we need a man of the two-fisted variety, such as Garner, and who has his splendid intelligence, courage and statesmanship. I am of the opinion that at this time the movement in his behalf in Texas is not offensive to him and whether he makes a statement now or later is entirely a matter which he alone will decide."

Shouse, a former House colleague, regarded Garner as among the few contenders with the potential to stop Roosevelt. "He is a man of great ability, who would fill with credit, any office within the gift of the people," stated the chairman of the Democratic National Committee's Executive Committee.

Colonel House, a native of Houston, had known Garner since early in his congressional career and did not take him lightly. "I have had a feeling for sometime that John Garner was the man to give Roosevelt the most trouble," he wrote Woolley. "If he gets actively into the race, and if our friend does not watch his step, he will find for the first time a formidable opponent."[9]

Following a meeting with President Hoover, Garner joked with reporters that this visit reminded him why he would not want to trade places with Hoover. "I always thought of the White House as a prison," he quipped, "but I never noticed until today how much the shiny latch on the Executive office door looks like the handle on a casket."

Despite comments like this, Garner wanted the presidency and maneuvered behind the scenes to get the nomination. "Early in 1932 Garner had quietly come to Sam Rayburn and me and asked us to take an active part in organizing his campaign," Senator Connally recalled. "Although I didn't have much hope that John would get the nomination, I agreed to line up delegations for him. To my way of thinking Garner was an able and vigilant public official who had grown a great deal in office."

Connally, a freshman U.S. senator in 1932, owed much to Garner with whom he had served in the Texas legislature and the U.S. House of Representatives. It was with Garner's help that he got a slot on the House Foreign Affairs Committee as the United States was about to enter the Great War. Connally would later become a major influence on American foreign policy as among the creators of the United Nations and the North Atlantic Treaty Organization. He would never forget that the isolationist Garner made all this possible.

Another enduring bond that Garner and Connally shared was their opposition to the Ku Klux Klan when the hooded order was a force in Texas politics. In 1922, as some of the state's more prominent Democrats embraced the Klan, Garner denounced the group and a fiery cross was burned on the hill behind his home. "Most of these people who belonged to the Ku Klux not only had hatred, but they were cowards," Garner recalled. That same year, Earle B. Mayfield was elected to the U.S. Senate with Klan support. In 1928, Connally made the Klan an issue when he successfully challenged Mayfield. Except for their opposition to the Klan, Garner and Connally were conservatives on racial issues. Both supported states' rights and opposed federal civil rights legislation.

Even without these personal ties, Connally would have supported Garner out of home state loyalty. As the first Texan to gain serious consideration for the presidency, Garner was endorsed by Governor Ross Sterling, the entire Texas congressional delegation, and every major newspaper in the state. "All the citizenry of Texas take pride in him," said Sterling.[10]

Rayburn, at fifty, had been a congressman since 1913 and was Garner's closest ally in the Texas delegation. Under the sponsorship of the older man, Rayburn was named early in his career to the House Interstate and Foreign Commerce Committee. As Garner ascended to the Democratic floor leadership, Rayburn was among his chief lieutenants. It bothered him at first that Garner would not take him into his confidence about the Democratic presidential race. "I do not know whether Mr. Garner takes very seriously the movement to make him a candidate or not," Rayburn wrote privately in January. But Garner knew what he was doing and that he could count on Rayburn.

At Garner's request, McDuffie, the House majority whip, stayed in contact with Hearst. "This liaison arrangement enabled him to maintain that he personally was doing nothing to further his own prospects," wrote the historian Earland I. Carlson, "while at the same time remaining fully informed as to what his admirers were doing for him."[11]

The Hearst endorsement caught Garner by surprise. "I never did know why Mr. Hearst supported me," he said years later. "It stopped me from breathing for a while. . . . I always thought that maybe the Hearst support went back to a small favor I did for him in the House in the early days when we served together there." Garner never provided further details about what this favor might have been.

In gratitude for the publisher's support, Garner abandoned his long-time opposition to a general sales tax. When Secretary of the Treasury Andrew Mellon proposed such an idea, Garner attacked him for seeking to increase the tax burden on working people. But the wealthy Hearst, seeking relief from his personal income taxes, in 1932 launched an editorial campaign for a federal sales tax "to replace the income tax which has degenerated into a racket."

"The economic crisis emphasizes the hazard of relying on the unstable factor of profits for taxation," a Hearst editorial stated, "instead of on the more durable foundation of business transactions."

Garner, with some reluctance, endorsed the sales tax and pushed the measure through the Ways and Means Committee. This concession to Hearst was the Texan's most controversial action as Speaker. When the sales tax was rejected by the full House with two-thirds of the Democrats in opposition, Garner's leadership was criticized by the Hoover administration. "It wouldn't have done any good," he said, "for me to have taken the floor in an endeavor to induce the Democrats to vote in favor of the sales tax. The majority of them do not approve of that kind of a levy and that settles it. Nor is it correct to say that insurgency among the Democrats had anything to do with the action of the House on the sales tax. . . . The Revenue Bill is a bipartisan measure, brought to the floor under the most liberal rules designed to allow members to express their individual views and offer such amendments as they deem advisable, and therefore the mere fact that the majority of the Democrats do not agree with me in regard to one feature of it cannot be construed to indicate that my prestige, if I have any, has been materially diminished, or that I have suffered any loss of control."[12]

Just two days after this setback, Garner handed off his gavel, descended from the rostrum, and then from the floor asked recognition to join the debate. He spoke about the national crisis and the need to balance the federal budget. "I think more of my country than I do of any theory of taxation," he declared, "and the country is in a condition where the worst taxes you could possibly levy would be better than no taxes at all.

"You have expressed yourselves. You have arrived at a conclusion that you will not have a sales tax. I have no quarrel with you because of it. I appeal to you not only in the name of my party but my country that in view of the fact that there has been stricken from this bill more than 500 million dollars of taxation, it is your duty, your paramount duty, to restore some taxes to this bill in order that the country's financial integrity may be maintained. . . . I believe that if this Congress today should decline to levy a tax bill there would not be a bank in the United States in existence in sixty days that could meet its depositors."

Then Garner called for "every man and every woman in this House" who favored a balanced budget to "rise in their seats." An overwhelming majority stood and cheered the Speaker's remarks. That same day, in response to the Speaker's challenge, the House approved a tax bill. "In the national government," Bowers reported, "Garner has given us a leadership that has been lamentably and tragically absent."

"Rarely in the annals of parliaments," Arthur Krock wrote in the *New York Times*, "has the intervention of one member in a crisis dispelled it so promptly and so effectively as did Speaker John N. Garner's address to the House."[13]

Hoover welcomed Garner's aid. Earlier in 1932, the Democratic Speaker had supported the Republican president in the creation of the Reconstruction Finance Corporation to make loans to banks and railroads. Garner also backed the administration in expanding the lending powers of the Federal Reserve System and farm loans. But as Garner became more serious about the Democratic nomination, he broke with Hoover on the issue of unemployment relief.

In the wake of his California primary victory, Garner came forward with a massive $2.5 billion public works bill to be funded by a proposed gasoline tax hike. Hoover, who had accused other legislators of "playing politics with human misery," reacted angrily to the Speaker's liberal relief measure. "This is not unemployment relief," the president declared. "It is the most gigantic pork barrel ever proposed to the American Congress. It is an unparalleled raid on the public treasury. Our nation was not founded on the pork barrel, and it has not become great by political log-rolling!"

Garner fired back: "It would be just as logical to refer to the Reconstruction Finance Corporation Act as a 'pork barrel' for the banks, insurance companies, railroads, and financial institutions of the country. The Democrats did not expect to receive real cooperation from the President in any manner benefiting the masses."

When Hoover lobbied against this bill, Garner denounced him as a failed president whose tenure was ending. "I have no personal feeling in regard to the President's criticism of the measures I have offered," the Speaker said. But Garner accused Hoover of attempting to blame Congress for his lack of success in fighting the Depression. "His necessity [to blame Congress] is the more apparent," the Speaker asserted, "as he is a candidate for re-election this year."

Garner viewed Hoover as well intentioned but politically inept. "I had to fight him because I thought he was wrong—and I still think he was wrong," he said two decades later, "and I think the results of his administration and immediately thereafter show he was wrong."[14]

While sparring with Hoover, Garner also had to contend with a powerful House Democratic rival. Appropriations Committee chairman Joseph Wellington Byrns, a leader of the Democratic opposition to Garner on the sales tax, now challenged Garner on his liberal relief program. For the first time since 1913, Democratic House members were called into caucus to settle a policy dispute. Byrns, who opposed liberal relief programs, rallied fifty votes against Garner's measure, but the Speaker mustered seventy-two votes. After this showdown, the caucus voted by an overwhelming margin to bind Democratic members in full support of Garner's aid program. "If they didn't stay bound," he later recalled, "I'd put 'em down in my book and they'd never get through paying for it."

With the support of all but three Democrats, Garner passed his bill in the House, and a Senate version sponsored by Robert F. Wagner of New York was also approved. On the eve of the Democratic convention, Hoover threatened to veto both measures unless they were amended to eliminate what he disparaged as "pork barrel" provisions. "We loan the shipping interests many millions of dollars at a very low rate of interest and it's all right," Garner replied. "When we try to do something for all the people, it's 'pork barrel.' To serve special interests is statesmanship; to serve the people is pork."

Unmoved by Garner's plea, Hoover vetoed the bills. When Garner and Wagner passed an alternative measure that provided about the same level of emergency relief and public works, Hoover reluctantly signed this legislation into law.[15]

During his first six months as Speaker, he made it a policy to avoid commenting on issues that were not pending before Congress. "Thus far we have been successful in preserving harmony, and I have no intention of making any declaration or otherwise doing anything that will disrupt this condition and thereby create a hazard to legislation vital to economic rehabilitation," he explained. "I am not particularly interested as to how my determination in this respect will affect my political future."

As delegates headed for Chicago, Garner ended his silence. Since Congress was still in session, he would not be attending the convention. But with the outcome in doubt, the Texas Democrat moved toward a more active candidacy by issuing a policy statement. "Many of my friends, not only those residing in my own district and state, but throughout the country, have asked me repeatedly to express myself on various public questions," he said. Garner advocated the removal of tariff barriers to open up foreign markets for American products; a one-third reduction of governmental expenditures; and relief measures "to keep the people from starving."

But it was his attack on Prohibition that made national headlines and had immediate impact on the delegates. "When the prohibition amendment was proposed, I, as a member of Congress, voted against it," he declared. "I have never believed it sound or workable, and it should be repealed."

Roosevelt's camp regarded the Speaker's declaration for repeal as an attempt to make himself more acceptable to the urban machine Democrats of the North and East and also to open the possibility that Garner could be the second choice of the Smith and Ritchie forces. In concluding his remarks, Garner signaled that he was no longer a reluctant candidate. "I appreciate the support of my friends," he said, "and I am willing to serve my country and my party to the limit of my capacity."[16]

If Garner forged an alliance with Smith, they would have enough votes to determine or veto the party's choice. One of them might even emerge as the nominee. "Roosevelt is both strong and weak," the Speaker confided to Timmons. "He seems to have practically no second-choice delegates. He has got just about a third of the New York delegates. Smith has the others, and nearly all from New England, New Jersey, and half those from Pennsylvania. . . . The stop-Roosevelt men could, with a little help, deadlock the convention."

Garner, who had been appalled by the 103-ballot convention at Madison Square Garden, did not want a similar fiasco in Chicago. As campaign manager Rayburn was about to embark for Chicago, he stopped by the Speaker's office for his instructions.

"There is one thing we've got to make sure that we don't do, Sam," Garner began. "We are going to win the election this fall unless we make damn fools of ourselves as we did in 1924. If we deadlock that convention and pick a compromise candidate, we will lose that election, and I want to live long enough to see a Democrat in the White House again. So we must make certain that we don't have a deadlock in Chicago. Sam, you and I both know that I am not going to be nominated for President. But a lot of these people who have been pushing me are loyal friends, and they think they are doing me a big favor so I couldn't very well say no to them."

On the eve of the convention, Garner told another friend that Roosevelt was in trouble. "He will have a majority, but not two-thirds," the Speaker observed. "Al Smith will have around 200 delegates and they will hold out until the last against Roosevelt. Ritchie will have some and they will be against Roosevelt all the way. Senator Lewis will not be a candidate and Cermak will hide out his anti-Roosevelt votes behind Melvin Traylor."

Garner did not know what to expect. "An ugly situation," he said, "can develop at Chicago."[17]

8

THE VIRGINIAN

O N HIS WAY to Chicago aboard the Capitol Limited, Harry Flood Byrd was jolted from his sleep. Just before midnight, as the ten-car Baltimore & Ohio train moved out of Pittsburgh, the boiler of the steam locomotive exploded instantly, killing engineer O. P. Smith and fireman H. E. Scott. Most of the train's fifty passengers, including the former Virginia governor, had been sleeping in the berths of their Pullman cars. Even though many passengers were in shock, none died and most escaped serious injury.

Byrd was not hurt and reacted calmly. When asked about the train wreck, he called it "purely accidental." An investigation would later find that a clogged valve, which prevented water from reaching the boiler, had caused the blast. "When I heard the first explosion," a witness recalled, "I thought it was a dynamite cap on the tracks and paid no attention to it. About four seconds later the second and larger explosion occurred. I looked out my bedroom window and saw the locomotive trucks coasting up the tracks, the whole front of the train obscured by clouds of steam."[1]

The first of the Democratic presidential hopefuls to arrive in Chicago, a week before the convention's opening gavel, Byrd had the potential to be more than a favorite son. His home state of Virginia had produced four of the nation's first five presidents and he had been the youngest governor of the oldest American commonwealth since Thomas Jefferson. As Byrd rose to prominence, H. L. Mencken wryly noted that Virginia, the mother of presidents, had not been pregnant in a hundred years. "The Virginians believe he is a man of destiny," Robert W. Woolley reported to an FDR ally, "and will hold the delegation for him for a long, long time before releasing it to Roosevelt or anyone else."[2]

A short man with an outgoing and engaging personality, the forty-five-year-old Byrd was a link between Virginia's past glory and its future promise. "Harry Flood Byrd comes as close to being of noble birth as is possible for an American," Gerald W. Johnson observed in *Life* magazine. The former governor was a direct descendant of William Byrd, who immigrated to the New World from England in 1670 and became one of the colony's most influential figures. His son William II founded the city of Richmond, served as president of the Virginia Council of State, and built Westover, one of Colonial America's great mansions, on the James River. The unhappy William III, who squandered the family's wealth, took his own life in 1777.

Harry Flood Byrd inherited political influence if not wealth. His father, Richard Evelyn Byrd, who was known as Mr. Dick, founded the *Winchester Star* in the apple-growing region of the Shenandoah Valley. The elder Byrd, a University of Virginia law graduate, served two decades as Commonwealth Attorney for Frederick County, and became one of the state's leading Democrats as Speaker of the Virginia House of Delegates. He had known Woodrow Wilson since they were law students in Charlottesville and in 1912 coordinated Wilson's presidential campaign in his native Virginia. On winning the presidency, Wilson nominated the elder Byrd as U.S. Attorney for Western Virginia. The future governor was the namesake of his uncle, Congressman Harry Flood, chairman of the House Committee on Foreign Affairs during the Wilson years and author of the resolution declaring war against Imperial Germany in 1917.[3]

At the age of fifteen, Harry dropped out of the Shenandoah Valley Academy to take over the management of his father's newspaper, which was then on the verge of bankruptcy. He paid off the newspaper's debts by establishing an advertising policy of pay-as-you-go that would become the guiding philosophy of his public career. In Winchester he bought out and closed a competing newspaper. Byrd did so well that he later acquired two other newspapers in the region.

While still in his teens, he became an apple grower on the side by leasing a group of small orchards. By 1911 he bought the first of what would eventually become in partnership with his brother Thomas the world's largest privately owned orchards. They owned more than two hundred thousand trees that produced about 1 percent of all the apples in North America. Among the sixteen varieties of apples that he raised were Red and Golden Delicious, Albermarle Pippins, Grime's Goldens, Yorkshires, and Winesaps. The brothers also built the nation's largest cold storage warehouse, which could hold 1.5 million bushels of apples. The Byrds, who sold their apples throughout the Middle Atlantic region and also exported to England, were the first apple growers to ship their fruit in crates instead of barrels.

Before he was eligible to vote, Harry won his first elective office, as a member of the Winchester City Council. He also served as president of the Valley Turnpike Company, which managed Virginia's first paved highway. At twenty-eight Harry started a decade of service in the Virginia Senate, where he voted as a fiscal conservative and moderate on social issues. He backed legislation for workmen's compensation, protection for child laborers, and increased aid to public schools.[4]

It was in the development of the state's highway system that Byrd made his mark. He sponsored legislation establishing the state highway commission and wrote the law that turned the Valley Turnpike into a freeway. But he opposed a 1920 ballot measure to amend the state constitution to allow the issuance of general obligation highway bonds. Despite Byrd's efforts, this amendment was approved by a majority of the state's voters. Byrd favored the construction of new roads but thought that the best way to pay for them would be through an increase in the gasoline tax and automobile license fees. In 1923, he successfully led the opposition to a statewide $50 million highway bond referendum.

This victory established Byrd as the rising star of Virginia politics. In 1924, as a delegate to the Democratic National Convention in New York, he shared a taxi with the Methodist bishop James Cannon, a major influence in Virginia's Democratic Party. The bishop advised the state senator that he should not run for governor in 1925 because his allies had already chosen another candidate, Byrd's Senate colleague G. Walter Mapp of Accomack. As Cannon soon learned, the apple grower was not easily intimidated. Before this encounter, Byrd was uncertain about his political future. Once the bishop attempted to deny him this opportunity, Byrd called his bluff.

In the 1925 Democratic gubernatorial primary, building on the popular backing that he won in the referendum fight, Byrd captured 61.4 percent of the vote. When Governor Byrd took office in 1926 at the age of thirty-eight, he was the state's youngest chief executive since the thirty-six-year-old Jefferson in 1779 during the American Revolution.[5]

Although Byrd was limited to a single four-year term under the Virginia constitution, he got more done during his tenure than any governor in the state's history and established a national reputation for innovation and progressive reform. He made government more efficient and accountable by merging one hundred agencies into fourteen departments under the governor's control. By changing the state constitution, he reduced the number of statewide elected officials from eight to three and gave the governor the authority to appoint the other five.

Byrd gained legislative approval for a gasoline tax and automobile license fees that produced the equivalent of $250 million in today's revenues for the construction of new roads. Before the young governor's administration, the Automobile Club of America had advised motorists to avoid the Old Dominion. After Byrd opened up modern highways and made his state accessible to the rest of the country, Virginia became a popular tourist destination. During the Byrd years, John D. Rockefeller Jr. began his restoration of Colonial Williamsburg to its eighteenth-century splendor. And, near Charlottesville, the newly organized Thomas Jefferson Foundation bought Monticello to preserve it as a national shrine. Byrd, who loved the Blue Ridge Mountains, was the prime mover in the creation of the Shenandoah National Park and the majestic Skyline Drive.

Byrd, always a keen student of public finance, established tax incentives to attract new industry and eliminated the state tax on land to help farmers. He abolished eight hundred tax officials by consolidating the state tax department in Richmond and ended the duplication of taxes. By implementing his pay-as-you-go policy in state expenditures, he transformed a $1.25 million deficit into a $2.6 million surplus by the end of his term. To prevent his state from going into long-term debt, Byrd passed a constitutional amendment that prohibited the state from issuing general obligation bonds.

He confronted oil companies and telephone companies to obtain lower rates for consumers. Byrd also promoted rural electrification and conservation.

In the most admirable of his reforms, Byrd obtained legislative approval of the nation's first antilynching law, making all members of a lynch mob subject to murder charges. Byrd declared that this most vicious of hate crimes was "intolerable." After he signed this measure into law there would not be another lynching in Virginia during his lifetime. His relationship with the few African Americans that he knew well, mostly servants or employees, was described as "kindly and paternalistic."

Byrd showed less courage when the legislature passed a measure requiring racial segregation in public places. Most of the state, like the rest of the South, followed this practice. But Hampton Institute, which had a rich cultural heritage, had a tradition of mixed audiences at public performances. John Powell, a concert pianist, led the campaign to make Jim Crow laws apply to the entire state. When this ugly legislation reached the governor's desk, Byrd would not sign the bill but allowed it to become law.

During the 1928 election, Bishop Cannon fanned the flames of religious bigotry against Alfred E. Smith, the first Roman Catholic nominated for the presidency. Cannon, urging Democrats to abandon Smith, denounced the Catholic Church as the "mother of ignorance, superstition, intolerance, and sin." Byrd, who was offended by these tactics, campaigned hard for Smith but failed to carry the state for his party's national ticket. It was among Byrd's finest moments when he rebuked Cannon for his hateful rhetoric. Just as he rejected unfair attacks on Roman Catholicism, Byrd would later use his political influence to end discrimination against Jews at a Norfolk resort.[6]

By the fall of 1928, Byrd had risen to such prominence that he was featured on the cover of *Time* magazine in the same issue that Roosevelt's gubernatorial nomination got secondary treatment. "Above all," the magazine noted of its cover subject, "he has the aid of that cohesive spirit of aristocracy-in-democracy, which despite his flair for mixing with chambers of commerce and booming the shipping facilities of Hampton Roads, he has helped to revive in Virginia politics."[7]

For all his accomplishments, the Virginia governor was the second-most famous Byrd of his generation. His younger brother Richard, a naval commander, achieved world renown as the first American to explore the North and South Poles. "His daring and courage have thrilled each one of us," President Herbert Hoover said, "because he has proved anew the worth and power and glory of qualities which we believe are latent in our people." Promoted to rear admiral after his mission to the South Pole, Byrd was awarded the Navy Cross for extraordinary heroism. In the first year of his brother's governorship, he received the Congressional Medal of Honor for his flight over the North Pole. Roosevelt, who had been close to Byrd since the Wilson administration, collected mementos from his friend's explorations. "By the way, as you had already given me the envelope which you carried over the North Pole and the little silk flag which you took over the ocean, I wish much that you could send me a scrap of something which you took over the South Pole flight," FDR wrote, "—even if it is a piece of your sock—as I much want to have all three framed together to hang in my office."

Roosevelt, who threw a gala reception for Admiral Byrd in Albany, was presented with an American flag that the explorer had flown over the Antarctic. FDR jovially suggested that the explorer would make a good candidate for high public office. But his old navy friend took great pride in his brother Harry's political accomplishments and had no interest in competing with him.[8]

If Harry F. Byrd could have run for a second term in 1929, he would have been overwhelmingly reelected. Dr. John Garland Pollard, dean of the School of Government and Citizenship at the College of William and Mary, a former attorney general, was tapped by Byrd to run for governor. In a mandate for the Byrd agenda, Pollard won the Democratic gubernatorial primary with more than three-fourths of the vote.

After leaving the governor's office, Byrd and his wife, the former Anne Douglas Beverly, moved into Rosemont, a stately and columned mansion that stood on a hilltop near Berryville in the midst of his orchards. From the small balcony of his upstairs study, the former governor enjoyed a spectacular view of the Blue Ridge Mountains, his orchards, and more than sixty acres of the estate's lawns and formal gardens. When he took up residence on the great estate, Byrd put up a sign in front of the stone gateposts that said, "Visitors Welcome."[9]

Among those who made the pilgrimage to Rosemont was Franklin D. Roosevelt, whose first year as governor overlapped with Byrd's final year. Beginning in 1930, there had been speculation about a possible FDR-Byrd ticket. As Democratic national committeeman from Virginia and vice chairman of the National Committee, Byrd led southern opposition to John Raskob's attempt to commit the party to policy positions more than a year in advance of the presidential election. "I am appealing to you to prevent an action which I understand is contemplated by the National Democratic Committee, and which in my judgment will create a division in the Democratic Party which it may be impossible to heal," the former governor wrote FDR. "Above everything else now we want a united party. . . .

"The Democratic Committee has no right to make a platform for the party," Byrd added. "It has never done so before. It is proposed to take this action, I understand, by the use of proxies, and this will still further increase the resentment. It is not a courageous action because it is taking a short cut as it is traditional that the Democratic party makes its policies by the action of the individual Democrats speaking through precinct meetings, thence to the state convention, and thence to the national convention.

"I would not trouble you with the matter but for its seriousness," Byrd concluded. "I know you have the interests of the party at heart just as much as I have, and I feel that you understand our Southern conditions better than many other leaders. Prompt action on your part will be necessary."

Roosevelt was quick to join forces with Byrd. "You are absolutely right that the Democratic National Committee has no authority, in any shape, manner or form, to pass on or recommend national issues or policies," FDR replied. On his instructions the New York Democratic Party passed a resolution opposing Raskob's power play.[10]

At the March 1931 meeting of the Democratic National Committee, Roosevelt dispatched Farley to help Byrd and Cordell Hull prevent Raskob from getting his way. In the face of growing opposition, Raskob withdrew his proposal. This marked the start of a close collaboration between Roosevelt and Byrd. "During these early days of the fight, Governor Byrd of Virginia participated in most of the strategy meetings called by the Roosevelt side," Farley recalled, "and he was looked upon as an inner member of the council."

While in Roosevelt's camp, Byrd warned about the risks of overexposure and peaking too soon. "Byrd believes [the] Governor should refrain from too many public utterances and allow the organization work to go ahead silently," a journalist close to the Virginian wrote a Roosevelt strategist. "He thinks favorite son candidates are the greatest danger in that they play directly into Mr. Raskob's hands. He thinks early understandings with them should be reached."

As Smith launched his comeback and Garner moved into possible contention, Byrd began to sense that he might have a chance for the nomination in the event of a deadlock. Henry Skillman Breckinridge, scion of the Kentucky political dynasty and assistant secretary of war in the Wilson administration, led the movement to draft the former Virginia governor. Colonel Billy Mitchell, one of the great combat commanders of World War I and advocate of an independent air force, also touted Byrd for the presidency. The financier John W. Hanes, heir to a North Carolina tobacco fortune and a future undersecretary of the Treasury, was among Byrd's earliest supporters for the 1932 Democratic presidential nomination. Robert Maynard Hutchins, the thirty-three-year-old president of the University of Chicago, did not make a public endorsement but privately favored Byrd for the Democratic nomination. Colonel Edward M. House, FDR's liaison with southern Democrats, thought Byrd's candidacy was folly. "He has no earthly chance for the nomination, either first or second place," House wrote a mutual friend, "and he should strengthen his hand by letting you steer his political course for the time being."[11]

In January 1932 the Virginia Senate and House of Delegates unanimously endorsed Byrd for the Democratic presidential nomination. "If nominated and elected President of the United States," the resolution stated, "he will bring to that office the qualities of clear common sense, assured grasp of perplexing problems, decisiveness in difficult questions, capacity for cooperation with the Congress and other branches, and a spirit of leadership sympathetic with the masses of people, that is just to all men."

Byrd, who neither drank nor smoked, had always supported dry legislation and advocated temperance. At the Jefferson Day Dinner in Washington, he proposed a national referendum on Prohibition. "We must recognize that no law is stronger than the public sentiment to sustain it," the former governor declared. "No problem has ever touched the lives and morals of our citizens more closely than prohibition. It should be removed from party politics and submitted directly to the people themselves for decision." After his proposal was endorsed by leaders of the Democratic Party's wet and dry factions, Byrd made the referendum a centerpiece of his campaign.[12]

IN THE CONVENTION issue of *Collier's* magazine, Byrd called for bold government measures to fight the Depression, including farm relief, providing food to the hungry, lowering tariffs to restore international trade, expanding the tax base, and increasing taxes on unearned incomes and inheritances. "As a Democrat I exercise my right to demand that my party nominate an able man who . . . has the physical and moral courage to place his political welfare second to the country's and to the welfare of the great unorganized majority," Byrd wrote. "A man who would rather serve one term well than two weakly and indifferently."

Of the leading contenders, he favored Baker with whom he shared a Jeffersonian philosophy of representative democracy, fiscal integrity, and individual rights. That was not all they had in common, for Baker and Byrd shared the birthplace of Martinsburg, West Virginia. If Baker went on to win the presidential nomination, he intended to offer Byrd the vice-presidential nomination. "Baker told my father that he wanted him as his running-mate," recalled Harry F. Byrd Jr. "And my father was interested."

"My party is as much a part of me as my religion," the elder Byrd said on the eve of the convention. "But my party must survive or perish in this election. If we perish as an organization it will be our fault. If we fail, let us do it courageously."

Byrd was also on Roosevelt's short list of potential running mates. "I had a long talk with Franklin and Louis Howe," Admiral Byrd wrote his brother. "As long as you have any chances Franklin, of course, wants you to stand firm for yourself, but he would like you to feel that, at any time, should you feel there is no chance for you, you will turn over your influence and votes to him. . . . I believe they would be in favor of you for the vice presidency." On the former governor's instructions, the resolution adopted by the Virginia delegation gave them the option to support another candidate. If Byrd decided not to have his name placed in nomination and released his delegates to Roosevelt, the vice presidency was his for the taking. Howe, partly because of FDR's friendship with the Byrds, calculated that Virginia would be the key to breaking a convention deadlock. Farley, who had worked more closely with Byrd, did not share Howe's optimism.[13]

9

EAST SIDE WEST SIDE

A LFRED E. SMITH, who had more presence than anyone in American politics, was a born performer. In his youth, he watched Broadway plays from the balcony and dreamed of a professional acting career. On the Lower East Side, Smith learned the actor's craft in the lyceum society of St. James Parish Church. He was a quick study and had a keen sense of timing, a strong voice, and a light comedic touch. Smith also excelled in dramatic roles and could sing and dance. Years later he confided that his favorite role was that of Bardwell Slote, the scheming congressman in *The Mighty Dollar*. "The reason the part was my favorite was because he had 450 speeches," Smith recalled. "He was on stage all the time; he dominated the piece. He was the whole show. That's why I liked it."[1]

From the moment he stepped off the Twentieth Century at Chicago's La Salle Street Station five days before the convention, Smith held center stage. "Politics is easier than acting," he wryly observed. "Our next president!" someone shouted as the former governor waved his straw hat at the cheering throng. Thousands of the party faithful had turned out for his arrival. It would take more than fifteen minutes for Smith to march up the station platform and make his way through the lobby to the car that awaited him. Along the way he signed autographs and allowed a schoolgirl to pin a button on his lapel with the picture of a donkey and the slogan: "Kick out the Depression with a Democratic vote."

Soon afterward, Smith was in top form as he met more than three hundred reporters in a ballroom at the Congress Hotel. In making his entrance, the former governor carried a walking stick, smoked a thick cigar, and looked dapper in a dark blue suit with a red necktie. Then something extraordinary happened. The news media burst into warm and sustained applause. "If it were left to the newspapermen Al would be nominated on the first ballot—not unanimously—but nearly so," Frank R. Kent reported. "They were never known to applaud anyone else on such occasions. . . . The Happy Warrior looked happy and at home."

Holding up his hand, Smith acknowledged the ovation and then put down his cane, sat down in a chair behind a long flat desk, and read a brief statement calling for the repeal of Prohibition. "The Eighteenth Amendment should never have been put into the Constitution. It is unworkable. I attacked it from the time it was first proposed and stated that it would be proved to be the greatest curse ever put over on an unsuspecting people. I fought it when it was unpopular to take that side of the issue in many parts of my own state and when every weapon of narrow-minded intolerance was turned against me. I carried the banner when the army was small, the stragglers numerous and the opposition bitter." Smith also called for a revision of the Volstead Act to allow "the sale of beverages of reasonable alcoholic content."

This press conference marked the first reunion between Smith and many of the reporters who had followed the 1928 presidential campaign.

George Morris of the *New York World Telegram* smiled mischievously as he opened the news conference with a question that parodied the trivial questions of local reporters on Smith's national campaign swing.

"What did you have for breakfast?"

"Ham and eggs," Smith jovially replied.

Asked for his prediction about the Democratic presidential contest, the former governor smiled and bit down on his cigar. "The convention will decide," he said.

Did he have a preference for the Democratic nomination?

"The honorable Alfred E. Smith of New York."

What about a running mate?

"I have not thought that out yet."

SMITH DISMISSED FARLEY'S claim that Roosevelt would be nominated on the first ballot. "I can only repeat what I said to reporters at Grand Central Station yesterday—it is ballyhoo," the former governor said.

As for his own support, the 1928 Democratic nominee played it coy. "My strength in the nation is a matter of record," he asserted. Smith denied that his candidacy was a front for the "Stop Roosevelt" movement. "Nothing to it," he asserted. "I am here to combat a 'Stop Smith' movement which commenced a year and a half ago. I am here to get myself nominated."

Smith refused to name a second choice. "There is no second choice," he declared. "I'm for myself alone."

The former governor then offered his scenario for a Democratic victory: "Write an honest, concise, clear platform and nominate me."

Smith created a sensation when asked whether he would pledge to support the party's eventual nominee. Even though he had been a

Democratic stalwart since his youth, it was unknown whether his dislike of Roosevelt outweighed party loyalty.

"I don't want to answer that question now," the former governor
answered. By hinting that he might bolt the party, Smith signaled that
he would go the distance to stop Roosevelt's nomination.[2]

IN PRIVATE CONVERSATIONS, Smith denigrated Roosevelt as an un-
principled opportunist. "Al Smith had very bitter personal feelings for
Frank Roosevelt," Thomas L. Stokes recalled. "I was impressed with
this when I talked to him in his office high up in the Empire State Building on my way to Chicago. It appeared to be a deep, personal grudge."

The unraveling of the Roosevelt-Smith friendship changed the 1932
Democratic presidential race. If FDR had the support of his gubernatorial predecessor, his first-ballot nomination could not have been
stopped. "Governor, you hold in the palm of your hand the assurance
of an overwhelming Democratic victory next year, or you are in a position where you could jeopardize the present prospect of sure success,"
Atlanta Constitution publisher Clark Howell told Smith in late 1931.
"With your support of him all opposition to him will vanish and his
nomination will be a mere formality. The country expects you to support
him, and it will not believe that you can do otherwise."

"The hell I can't," Smith shot back. "But I do not mean that I will
not support him. I am for the party first, above any man, and I will support the man who seems best for the party."[3]

Smith did not think that man was FDR. Even when Roosevelt had
been among his more visible public allies, the former governor regarded him as a dilettante. "Franklin just isn't the kind of man you
can take into the pissroom and talk intimately with," he once confided
to a friend.

FDR, who had longed for membership in the older man's inner cir-
cle, felt patronized and unappreciated. "Smith and his friends never
took me into their counsel," he would later recall. "I could work hard
for him at the New York convention—but I always was on the outside,
never on the inside with him." It was not for lack of trying. On several
occasions during Smith's administration, Roosevelt telephoned Robert
Moses, the governor's confidant, and asked if they might go together to
Smith's suite at the Biltmore Hotel. Although Moses let FDR tag along,
Roosevelt was never accepted as part of this group.[4]

Yet Smith, as the dominant figure in New York Democratic politics,
would do more than anyone to put Roosevelt within striking distance
of the presidency. There were many Democratic leaders who coveted
the opportunity to deliver Smith's presidential nominating speeches at
the 1924 and 1928 national conventions. In twice choosing FDR, Smith
gave him invaluable national exposure. It was to boost his 1928 presidential campaign that Smith drafted his younger friend for the Democratic nomination for governor. FDR at first declined to make the race
because he might not physically be up to it. But Smith appealed to his
party loyalty. "I need you, Frank," he said in a telephone call to Roosevelt in Warm Springs. "This is why. The progress which the Democratic party has made in this state must go on. We've got to carry on our
program. You've got a great name. We believe you are the man to carry
the state for the ticket. We need a big vote to swing to New York. It all
depends on you."

Roosevelt waged a vigorous campaign against the popular Republican attorney general Albert Ottinger. "He ran primarily to support
Smith," Frances Perkins remembered years later. "It never crossed his
mind that he could be elected if Smith did not carry the state. When the
news came to headquarters that Smith had lost the state, Roosevelt
went home convinced that it was all over. He was disappointed, as we

all were that Smith was not elected. That he himself would win was out of the question."

As the late returns were counted, Roosevelt squeaked through. While Smith was losing the state by 103,481 votes, FDR prevailed by 25,564 votes or 0.6 percent. "I certainly do not expect ever to run for public office again. I have had all I can stand of it," Smith declared after his 1928 defeat. "I will never lose my interest in public affairs, that's a sure thing; but as far as running for public office is concerned—that's finished."[5]

Smith, who had been the longest-serving chief executive in the history of New York State, had assumed that the new regime in Albany would be an encore for his own administration. But when he recommended the appointment of his senior adviser Belle Moskowitz as Roosevelt's chief aide and the retention of Moses as secretary of state, FDR politely declined both suggestions. "It was clear from what Smith told Roosevelt before his acceptance of the nomination that Smith felt he would be invaluable to the new governor in dealing with affairs of state. It was equally clear to me that, after Smith's defeat for the presidency, he felt that he could retain a more or less active interest in affairs at Albany by giving advice to the new governor," recalled Bronx Democratic leader Edward J. Flynn, who replaced Moses as secretary of state. ". . . Smith did not reckon with the independent and stubborn nature of the man with whom he was dealing. Having been elected governor of New York on his own merits, Roosevelt was determined to go it on his own. He felt that he would be better off completely divorced from Smith's influence."[6]

The Roosevelt-Smith friendship would never be the same. "I have always thought that if Al had been elected and gone to Washington to be President of the United States," Perkins observed, "he would have been completely absorbed in planning his national work. But, as it was, he could not take his mind off the comparison between his own experience and wisdom and Roosevelt's new and perhaps amateurish approaches to New York state political and administrative problems."

In his 1929 autobiography *Up to Now*, Smith did not express his real feelings about his gubernatorial successor. "The speech putting me in nomination [for the presidency] in 1924 was made by Governor Franklin D. Roosevelt, who was probably the most impressive figure in that convention," Smith wrote. At the 1930 New York Democratic convention, Smith returned the favor and delivered the speech nominating FDR for a second two-year term. "No man has accomplished more in the office he occupied than Franklin D. Roosevelt," declared Smith. "He has a clear brain and a big heart. For his humanity, the love and devotion he has shown the poor, the sick, and the afflicted, Almighty God has showered down on his head the choicest graces and his choicest blessings."[7]

By 1931, Roosevelt openly challenged Smith's leadership of the Democratic National Committee. On learning that national chairman John J. Raskob, Smith's closest ally, intended to have their party take an official position for the repeal of Prohibition, FDR forged an alliance with southern Democrats and thwarted this effort. "No doubt was left in my mind that a complete separation between the Smith and Roosevelt forces had thereby occurred," said Senator Cordell Hull of Tennessee. "After Roosevelt's withdrawal from the Smith organization and his assertion of an independent political course, all or most of those opposed to the Smith movement were gradually and ultimately to turn to Roosevelt as the most effective way of killing off Smith."

Smith struck back later in the year by leading the opposition to a Roosevelt-backed referendum that would amend the state constitution and provide up to $20 million for the purchase and reforestation of farmland adjacent to the Adirondack and Catskill forest preserves. The former governor accused Roosevelt of allowing the plunder of these public lands by special interests. "While I am able to talk and while I have got the power of speech and while I have got the determination to protect the Adriondack reserve," Smith declared, "no lumber dealer or lumber thieves or paper men will ever get in there and take the trees out. They belong to us."

The problem with Smith's argument was that Roosevelt's amendment specifically protected the forest reserves as "wild forest lands" and stated that this timber could not be sold or leased by private interests. Smith also alleged that the proposed bond was an excessive expenditure at a time when the state faced a deficit. FDR had the support of both major political parties, the State Federation of Labor, New York State Grange, and conservationist groups. In the November 3 election, the forestry referendum passed by more than two hundred thousand votes.

"What a queer thing that was for Al to fight so bitterly," Roosevelt wrote a friend. "I cannot help but remembering the fact that while he was Governor I agreed with almost all the policies he recommended but I was against one or two during those eight years. However, for the sake of party solidarity, I kept my mouth shut. I could readily have taken a public position in opposition to the Governor but, frankly, I did not think the issue was of vital enough importance to cause a party dispute."[8]

Annoyed by Smith's persistent criticism, Roosevelt became scornful of the man he had twice nominated for the presidency. "Smith was a poor governor," FDR told the former Democratic presidential nominee James Cox. "He left things in a mess at Albany, and I have had great difficulty in trying to straighten them out." Among the reasons for this harsh and unfair assessment was that Roosevelt now regarded Smith as not just a critic but a future rival. FDR had long suspected that Smith would come out of retirement and make another run for the presidency.

Smith, though, insisted that he had no such plans when Flynn dropped by the former governor's office at the Empire State Building in late 1931 and told him that Roosevelt had decided to run for president. "As a personal friend of Smith's who respected his position in the party, I wanted to get his opinion," Flynn wrote in his 1947 memoir. "Smith gave it to me in a very forceful way. He told me that he was completely through with politics and that no one could induce him to enter the political arena again." The former governor opened a drawer of his desk and showed him a stack of papers. "Ed, these are all debts that I must clear up," Smith said. "Financially, I am in an extremely bad position." Several members of his family had suffered major losses in the stock market. "He assured me that it would probably take the rest of his life to clear up these financial burdens," Flynn said.[9]

In addition to these economic factors, Smith worried that another political setback might make him seem like a perennial candidate. As the first Democratic governor of New York in forty years to win reelection, he had defeated two sitting Republican governors, a future secretary of the Treasury, and the son and namesake of Theodore Roosevelt. From 1902 through 1928 he won nineteen out of twenty-one elections and even in his loss to Hoover gained more votes than any presidential nominee in the history of the Democratic Party. When his daughter Emily asked him about a possible comeback, Smith outlined his reasons for not making the race. It had been twenty-four years since the Democratic Party had given another chance to an unsuccessful presidential candidate, the three-time nominee William Jennings Bryan. Smith did not expect to be renominated. "In order to build up any great amount of support for me, somebody would have to go all over the country. It would take a lot of money—more than I could put up," he said. "And I don't want to ask my friends to do it. I just don't want to do that anymore. In 1920 my name was offered to the convention, though it was just a gesture. In 1924 I made a fight for the nomination. In 1928 I was actually nominated. So I don't want to go looking for it again in 1932. I don't want to be the Bryan of the party."[10]

Finally, the religious issue made it doubtful that Smith could win a rematch over Hoover despite his unpopularity. As the first Irish Catholic nominated for the nation's highest office, he had to put up with more prejudice and bigotry than anyone who had ever sought the White House. Denounced from the pulpits of many Protestant churches as a threat to America's Anglo-Saxon heritage, Smith was depicted as a tool of the pope. "If you vote for Al Smith," thundered one preacher, "you're voting against Christ and you'll all be damned!" Smith's nomination revived, if only temporarily, the Ku Klux Klan, which distributed hate literature against him in twenty states, taunted him in the Bible Belt, and in several instances provided burning crosses as the backdrop for Smith rallies. Even the liberal *New Republic* contributed to this backlash. "The Catholic Church will remain an alien guest in the American body politic," the progressive journal asserted, "as long as it tries to form the minds of American Catholics by educational methods different from those which are used to form the minds of other Americans." The *Atlantic Monthly* printed an open letter that questioned Smith's fitness for the presidency because he might follow the teachings of his church instead of the U.S. Constitution.

"I recognize no power in the institutions of my church to interfere with the operations of the Constitution of the United States or the enforcement of the law of the land," Smith replied. "I believe in absolute freedom of conscience for all men and in equality of all churches, all sects, and all beliefs before the law as a matter of right and not as a matter of favor. I believe in the absolute separation of church and state."

Smith's religion did not cost him the presidency in 1928. Hoover could not have been defeated in this era of Republican prosperity. But bigotry undermined Smith's chances throughout the country and contributed to his loss of two hundred counties in the traditionally Democratic South. The prospect of Smith heading another national ticket alarmed party leaders in the South and West. "While I think Governor Smith would make a great President," Senator Pat Harrison of Mississippi observed, "I do not believe he could be elected. I believe Governor Roosevelt can be elected." Senator Alben Barkley of Kentucky was even more blunt: "Kentucky is anti-Catholic. Smith could not carry it under any circumstances." Former Oregon governor Walter M. Pierce, who had accepted the Klan's support in previous campaigns, wrote after Smith's 1928 loss: "We must never again nominate a Catholic or a wet. . . . Because I did not denounce Smith all the Protestant churches were against me."[11]

Alva Johnston, weighing Smith's comeback chances in *The Forum,* noted that the former governor had a record of more solid accomplishment than any living Democrat but predicted that the religious issue would not go away. "If Al were a Methodist, a Mennonite, a Muggletonian, a Holy Roller or Hook-and-eye Amishman," wrote Johnston, "his nomination and election in 1932 would be foregone conclusions."

Smith felt the same way. When Arthur Mullen, Nebraska's Democratic national committeeman, sounded him out about a 1932 comeback, the former governor was emphatic. "There's no chance for a Catholic to be President. Not in my lifetime or in yours, Arthur," Smith replied.

"I know it. I knew it in '24. I knew it in '28," said Mullen. "I knew we couldn't carry Nebraska for you, and I knew then, just as in '24 that you couldn't win; but you almost read me out of the Catholic Church in '24 because I knew it."

"Well, you were right," Smith noted. "I can't win against the bigots."[12]

But as the prosperity issue turned against the Republicans, Smith became more optimistic about his prospects and decided that his religion would cost him fewer votes than in 1928. He noted that a shift of

10 percent would have given him the edge in the 1928 popular vote and that a change of fewer than five hundred thousand votes could have produced a different outcome in the Electoral College. If the Democrats would give him another chance, Smith believed that he could beat Hoover.

Stopping Roosevelt would be more difficult. Yet this gave Smith a reason to run. Belle Moskowitz, Smith's longtime adviser, urged him to make the race. "It was his right to run again," she told Frances Perkins. Moskowitz wrote Felix Frankfurter that Smith had to run in 1932: "Prior to his [announcement] we were faced with an absolute foreclosure of the convention. This seemed to him unwholesome for the party.

"Many of us feel that the party needs a well-equipped candidate, able to lead, courageous and willing to take responsibility. We do not think that the record of the candidate who at that time was leading the field gave that kind of promise.

"Governor Smith made a real sacrifice in his own feelings and his own desires in the matter by injecting himself into the situation just far enough to hold the convention open," Moskowitz wrote.

Smith talked with bitterness about how the religious issue was used against him in 1928 and said that he wanted vindication in 1932. "He felt so terribly hurt, so outraged by that, and the point that he was making was that having been defeated on that issue in a year in which he was bound to be defeated, everybody, including FDR, should have stepped aside to let him have the nomination in a year in which he could have been elected," Perkins recalled. "He was very much wrought up about it, he pounded his fists and his voice got loud. He shouted at times in that conversation."[13]

Shortly before the convention, Mayor Frank Hague of Jersey City and former New York Supreme Court Justice Joseph M. Proskauer cosigned a confidential letter, with Smith's approval, to a selected list of the former governor's supporters asking them to generate one hundred thousand telegrams urging Smith's nomination. Hague and Proskauer had made arrangements with Western Union to have these messages delivered to the permanent chairman of the Democratic convention. By authorizing this activity, Smith demonstrated that he was playing to win and not just to stop Roosevelt.

Smith announced Hague would be his floor leader at the Chicago convention and that Governor Joseph B. Ely of Massachusetts would deliver the nominating speech. At a press conference, Ely was asked if he would borrow FDR's words in referring to Smith as the Happy Warrior. Ely shot back, "We've graduated from that high-school stuff, I hope."[14]

10

DOLLAR BILL

A S HE ARRIVED in Chicago aboard his private plane, *The Blue Streak,* former secretary of the Treasury William Gibbs McAdoo beamed with confidence. It had been eight years since his epic battle with Alfred E. Smith left their party in ruins. In the wake of that fiasco, Woodrow Wilson's son-in-law withdrew from public life and returned to his law practice. But the two-time presidential contender had staged an extraordinary comeback and would play a leading role at the convention. He was favored to become the first Democratic U.S. senator from California in a dozen years. His active involvement in the Golden State's presidential primary was a major factor in John Nance Garner's upset victory over Roosevelt. By barnstorming up and down the coast in his Lockheed-Vega cabin aircraft, he attracted crowds for Garner and showed how the new technology would change the future of presidential politics. With his election as chairman of the California delegation and as the Golden State's new Democratic national committeeman, McAdoo would have major influence in

Chicago. "The situation looks more confused than ever, and there is no telling what the outcome of the convention is to be," he wrote his old friend Bernard M. Baruch, who was among the leaders of the "Stop Roosevelt" movement.[1]

The tall and angular McAdoo parted his hair in the middle, wore a high starched collar and double-breasted blue suit, and looked a generation younger than his sixty-eight years. On meeting reporters at Chicago's Hotel Sherman, he expressed the hope that the approaching convention would not be another three-week stalemate such as the battle for Madison Square Garden that would make "victims" of the leading contenders as he had been a "victim" in 1924. Since McAdoo had deftly undermined Roosevelt's prospects for a first-ballot nomination, few believed that he would be greatly troubled by a deadlocked convention.

In his next breath, he suggested in his southern accent that FDR might well be the next victim of the two-thirds rule. "This talk of Roosevelt with 691 votes reminds me very much of Champ Clark at the Baltimore convention in 1912," he said. It had been twenty years since McAdoo showed his toughness and political skills in pulling the strings that changed the course of that convention. He talked Woodrow Wilson out of withdrawing when he trailed in the delegate count by a wide margin and had already dictated a telegram conceding to Clark. And it was McAdoo who forged the alliance with the three-time presidential nominee William Jennings Bryan that revived Wilson's candidacy and resulted in his nomination.

As for himself, McAdoo vowed to support Garner "all the way." A reporter then asked if he had a fallback choice. "Yes," the chairman of the California delegation replied. "Garner first, second, third, and all the time."

"Of all the men mentioned," McAdoo had written privately of Garner, "I think best of him. He is not a scholar nor a statesman like

Woodrow Wilson, but he has the cardinal virtues, is a loyal and dependable man, and I believe would make a better President than any of those who are prominently being mentioned for the office."[2]

He downplayed speculation about a possible meeting with his old rival Smith. "I'm here to meet and talk to people," McAdoo asserted. "I hope to meet everybody. Smith, Ritchie, Garner, Roosevelt, and all the others." Even though he would have conversations with all of the contenders or their strategists, it was regarded as most significant that McAdoo publicly indicated that he would indeed be conferring with his old rival Smith. Several weeks earlier, Herbert Bayard Swope, former editor of the *New York World*, had reached out to McAdoo by telephone from Smith's office in the Empire State Building and offered him a full partnership in the alliance to stop Roosevelt. McAdoo indicated that they might very well have mutual interests and agreed to confer with Smith in Chicago.

Roosevelt's camp also courted McAdoo. Daniel C. Roper, FDR's chief southern ally, had served under McAdoo in the Wilson administration and managed his 1924 presidential campaign. "He gave no indication of what his attitude would be toward the Roosevelt candidacy," Roper later wrote. "I hope much that Roper and House and you," FDR wrote Homer Cummings, "can pour oil on the somewhat troubled waters of his mind. Mac is a fine fellow, but I don't think that he has any perspective about the present situation and that it is only his real friends who can persuade him that a last-minute insurgence will get him nowhere and will do harm to the progressive ideals with which all of us were associated in the old days."

Following McAdoo's arrival in Chicago, Roper was among his first visitors. "He did not feel that he could shift the California delegates, but I persisted in my efforts," Roper recalled. Breckinridge Long, former assistant secretary of state in the Wilson administration and a senior strategist in both of McAdoo's presidential campaigns, was among Roosevelt's convention floor managers. "As soon as I arrived—three days before the convention met—I got in touch with McAdoo," he recalled. "He was obdurate. I had two long conversations with him. He introduced me to [Sam] Rayburn in his apartments. But from McAdoo I got the distinct impression he was playing his own game and could not be counted on to help at all—or unless Baker became a real threat."[3]

Farley, who kept in close touch with most western states for Roosevelt, detested McAdoo and assigned Roper and Long to that task. "I have always thought that he is one of the most arrogant men I have ever met. He always thinks he is right. He is rather a difficult fellow to get along with. I have always felt the only way to deal with him is to be outspoken," Farley wrote in his diary. "I have always thought he was selfish and thinks of McAdoo."

The erstwhile presidential contender, who had the longest memory in American politics, never forgot a slight or what he perceived as an injustice. He had old scores to settle with at least three of the rivals for the 1932 Democratic presidential nomination. For a grudge holder like McAdoo, the Chicago convention was an opportunity to get even. He viewed Roosevelt as an ingrate who had used him to gain favor in the Wilson years. McAdoo had offered FDR a job in the Treasury Department and sponsored his appointment as assistant secretary of the navy. When Roosevelt ran for the U.S. Senate as an independent Democrat in 1914, McAdoo was among his more prominent supporters. As a delegate to the 1920 Democratic National Convention in San Francisco, Roosevelt broke with Tammany Hall and was among the minority of New York delegates voting for McAdoo. But he could not forget that FDR helped to block his nomination at the 1924 New York convention. Since Roosevelt's election as governor of New York, McAdoo regarded him as a sellout for making peace with Tammany

Hall. "Don't you know," he asked Roper, "that he'll Tammanyize the United States?" Roper told McAdoo that he was mistaken.[4]

For months prior to the convention, McAdoo had been harsh and blunt in his comments about the Democratic front-runner. He dismissed FDR as a lightweight. "I can't think of Roosevelt as being equal in ability to the demands the White House must make on its occupants in the next four years," he wrote Chattanooga editor George Fort Milton, a longtime ally and friend. "I don't believe that there is any chance now for the nomination of Roosevelt, particularly in view of Smith's entry into the field," he told Baruch. McAdoo hinted at his enmity toward FDR when a Kentucky delegate asked about the possibility of California switching from Garner to Roosevelt. "It would be as impossible for the delegation to vote for Roosevelt," he replied, "as it would for me to walk on the waters of Lake Michigan."[5]

The renomination of Smith in 1932, McAdoo wrote a friend from the Wilson years, "would be a colossal blunder." He had never forgiven Smith for destroying his best chance at the presidency and for allowing his cohorts to unfairly portray McAdoo as the front man for the Ku Klux Klan. McAdoo had nothing to do with Smith's 1928 presidential campaign and gloated about his loss to Hoover. "It is amazing to me that men learn no lessons, apparently from disaster," McAdoo wrote when Smith made Prohibition repeal the central issue of the 1932 campaign. "I think there are infinitely more important questions than liquor and I know perfectly well that if the Democratic party in 1932 is asinine enough to risk its whole future on a fight to restore the liquor traffic, to the exclusion of the really grave economic and social problems that face us, it will be plunged into a deeper abyss of defeat than it suffered in 1928."

Another reason that McAdoo opposed Smith and Roosevelt was their New York residency. "As it looks to me at long range," he wrote Colonel Edward M. House, "a New York candidate is about the weakest that the Democratic party can put forward. . . . You can't imagine the distrust the country at large has of a New York candidate identified with and acceptable to Tammany. In fact, there is a wide distrust of New York anyway. This may be unjust but it is a fact which must be considered." In fact, Smith's relationship with Tammany Hall had been strained since he left the governorship in 1929, and Roosevelt had angered Tammany chieftains by authorizing a probe of New York City corruption. Nevertheless, McAdoo asserted that the selection of Roosevelt or Smith "would be tragic for the Party."[6]

So, when William Randolph Hearst "approached McAdoo to head a delegation against both Smith and Roosevelt, it was easy enough to get McAdoo's sympathy," recalled the California editor and McAdoo confidant Thomas M. Storke. "They saw eye-to-eye on the whole deal."

McAdoo also had issues with Baker. "A talk with Mac developed that he disliked Baker because of differences while in Wilson's cabinet," their mutual friend George Creel recalled. "No two men were ever more dissimilar, for the Secretary of War was scholarly, philosophical, and contemplative, while the Secretary of the Treasury shot ahead with the speed and directness of a bullet. . . . Mac raged against Baker's cautious approach to problems, and the two were in continual dispute." McAdoo brooded that despite his family connection to Wilson, Baker stood higher in the president's esteem than McAdoo and was now viewed as the more legitimate heir to the Wilson legacy. He launched a behind-the-scenes campaign to undercut Baker. "I don't know why it is," McAdoo wrote Colonel House, "but Baker seems to have no large popular following. He has never appealed to the rank and file of his party, nor to the masses of the people. In fact, all of our so-called leaders are lacking in this very essential element of vote-getting success."

If McAdoo had given up his presidential hopes, he might have been more generous in his assessment of the Democratic field. But he was relentless in his ambition and still dreamed of becoming only the third Democratic president since the Civil War. "Who, of all the men on our side now being mentioned," he wrote House, "has any popular hold upon the imagination or interest of the American people? Without meaning to be vain, but speaking merely of the fact, I think I had a very strong hold upon the masses. I don't know how strong it is now. Certainly it is far less strong than it used to be, but it might be vitalized if I were willing to make the effort. I have no such designs, however, although I am constantly receiving letters, some from very strong people, urging me to get back into politics. Both the Democratic and Republican parties are so badly split that a very extraordinary realignment in the voting might take place in 1932 if the Democrats could put forward some militant and progressive man who has some hold on the popular imagination, who is free from boss and machine taint or control, and who is, at the same time, sound on prohibition (I mean against repeal of the Eighteenth Amendment) and who has some really definite and constructive ideas about the economic and sociological problems of the day." In his judgment only he could meet this standard.[7]

McAdoo would not allow his name to be entered in presidential primaries. But in his private correspondence he made it known that he still coveted the prize. "I can see no reason, and I say this confidentially, why you shouldn't arouse interest among our old University of Tennessee boys and elsewhere in the suggestions you make about my availability," he wrote a former classmate, "although I am in no sense a candidate and will not seek the presidency. I have always felt that it was the duty to respond favorably to a call to public service if it came unsolicited. You must not quote me to this effect because it would be misunderstood; it would be construed as an implied candidacy."

In the winter of 1932, with many Americans turned off by both major political parties, McAdoo briefly pondered making an independent bid

for the White House. "So far as the presidency is concerned," he wrote
son-in-law Brice Claggett, "I have no illusions about a Democratic nomination so long as the wet and machine elements dominate the party machinery and are backed by unlimited money. I am still convinced that if
the necessary finances could be had an independent movement could be
led with more than an even chance of success this year. I would rather
lead such a movement than do anything else in the political line, but one
might as well fight a nest of machine guns with his hands as to undertake
a campaign of that sort. . . . It is a reflection upon our system of government that we are relegated in our choice of a President to one of two
men, handed out to us by the machine-controlled national conventions,
each dominated in the background by the same sinister influences."

So McAdoo kept working within the more traditional structure of
the Democratic Party. Colonel House advised McAdoo that he might
have another opportunity to win the presidential nomination in the
event Roosevelt fell short of the two-thirds majority. "That would be
the chance for your friends to spring your name upon the convention,"
House told the former Treasury secretary.[8]

To keep his name before the American people and showcase his ré-
sumé, McAdoo wrote his memoirs, *Crowded Years*, which were published
in 1931 by the Houghton Mifflin Company. McAdoo sent autographed
copies to party leaders across the country.

By any measure, he had led a life of considerable accomplishment.
A native of Georgia who grew up in Tennessee and moved to New York
as a young lawyer, he first gained national prominence at the turn of
the century as the builder of the tunnel underneath the Hudson River
that linked New Jersey to Lower Manhattan. This project had first been
attempted in 1874, and, following the deaths of twenty workers, engi-
neering experts said that it could not be done. But McAdoo would make
a career out of defying such challenges.

Few men in American history have exerted more power than McAdoo during the Wilson years. "I like movement and change; I like to make things better, to reshape old forces and worn-out ideals into new and dynamic forms," he wrote in his memoirs. "Nothing else gives me so much joy as the solution of a difficult problem." As secretary of the Treasury, he wrested control of the nation's finances from Wall Street and created the Federal Reserve System. McAdoo split the country into a dozen districts and selected the headquarters for each central bank, depositing billions in southern and western banks. To help preserve the family farm, he used his office to press for lower interest rates and created the federal farm loan system. He was involved in the creation of the first federal income tax.[9]

His influence extended beyond his department. Within the Wilson cabinet, he was among the most forceful advocates for intervention in the Great War. He raised the billions to support the American war effort and billions more in loans to Great Britain, France, Belgium, Italy, and Russia. When the war broke out, he took the lead in the creation of the merchant marine. At the time, American ships carried only 8 percent of the nation's foreign commerce. By the end of the Wilson years, the United States had the largest merchant fleet in the world. When Wilson placed the nation's railroads under government control, he named his son-in-law as director-general and had him transform a nineteenth-century rail network into a modern transportation system. The poet Arthur Guiterman captured McAdoo's wide-ranging influence in a popular verse:

> *The Who, preeminently Who,*
> *Is William Gibbs, the McAdoo.*
> *(Whom I should like to hail but daren't,*
> *As Royal Prince and Heir Apparent.)*
> *A man of high intrinsic Worth,*

The Greatest Son-in-Law on Earth—
With all the burdens thence accruing,
He's always up and McAdooing.
From Sun to Star and Star to Sun,
His work is never McAdone.

As early as 1914, when it was unclear whether Wilson would run for reelection, McAdoo had confided to the president that he would one day like to have his job. But Wilson would do nothing to help him achieve this goal and privately questioned whether he was presidential timber. "Now nobody can do things better than Mac," Wilson observed, "but if Mac ever reflects, I never caught him in the act."[10]

After the massive stroke in October 1919 that left him paralyzed on the left side and permanently affected his speech and judgment, Wilson would not change his attitude. Wilson resented it when his son-in-law advised him to compromise with Republican senators to gain approval of the Versailles Treaty and American participation in the League of Nations. When Wilson held out unrealistic hope that he could win renomination to a third term at the 1920 Democratic National Convention, McAdoo declined to campaign for the nomination. Even so, he led for more than twenty ballots at the San Francisco convention. "I am happy in my escape," McAdoo wrote a friend. "We are all young yet . . . and the world is before us."[11]

Not long after moving to Los Angeles in 1922, where he opened a law practice, McAdoo began his quest for the presidency. He was widely viewed as the inevitable 1924 Democratic nominee until his name was dragged into the Senate investigation of the Teapot Dome oil scandal. Edward L. Doheny, president of the Pan-American Oil Company, had paid $100,000 to Interior secretary Albert Fall who then awarded leases that allowed private development of naval oil reserves at Elk Hills,

California. Fall had also opened up the naval reserves at Teapot Dome, Wyoming, in a similar arrangement with another oil baron. During the Senate hearing, Doheny testified that McAdoo had been on retainer as a counsel for his oil company. Three other members of the Wilson cabinet had also been on Doheny's payroll, and Franklin D. Roosevelt as vice president of the Fidelity & Deposit Company had once approached McAdoo about obtaining bond business from Doheny. In contrast with Fall, none of these people were in public office when they were paid by Doheny. The former Treasury secretary demanded a hearing, rushed to Washington, and told senators that he had not been involved in the leasing of the oil reserves. "McAdoo as a man and as a lawyer cleared himself beyond any doubt," Mark Sullivan reported in the *New York Tribune*. But he never fully recovered from this controversy, which slowed his political momentum and probably cost him the nomination.[12]

Over the course of two national conventions, McAdoo had led in the presidential balloting for more than a hundred roll calls. At Madison Square Garden, he had support from delegates in thirty-four of the forty-eight states. Four years later, with his political fortunes diminished, he withdrew as a candidate, leaving Smith uncontested for the 1928 nomination. McAdoo took no part in the campaign and did not pledge his support to the ticket until the eve of the election. "I doubt very much if the Tammany outfit would have done as much for me," he wrote his former campaign manager, "if the conditions had been reversed."

But in the spring of 1932, the old rivals who had not spoken in eight years would join forces in opposition to Roosevelt. On the weekend before the convention, their mutual friend Bernard Baruch telephoned Smith and invited him to have lunch with McAdoo in Baruch's suite at the Blackstone Hotel. "Bernie," Smith replied, "I don't like him. I don't trust him and I won't be comfortable while I'm with him, but in this fight I would sleep with a Chinaman to win, and I'll come."

When Smith arrived, McAdoo greeted him warmly and extended his hand. "How're you?" he asked. "Out of sight," Smith responded.

"Well, we both got licked," McAdoo said.

"Yes," Smith shot back, "but it was better for me to beat you and you to beat me than for either of us to take a fall from Coolidge."

As they sat down to start lunch, McAdoo brought up the business at hand. "What are you going to do out here?"

"Well, I'm going to be on the level with you," Smith responded. "We're both against Roosevelt or you wouldn't be here. Is that right?"

McAdoo nodded in agreement.

"All right," said Smith, "if we work together we can beat this feller."

McAdoo, who had been predicting Roosevelt's defeat, now questioned whether he could be stopped. Smith then listed delegations in each part of the country that were wavering in their support of Roosevelt and could break if the convention deadlocked. "What then?" McAdoo asked.

"If we go to the fifth ballot," Smith said, "we've got him licked. Then my candidacy is out the window. I can't be nominated. But we can then sit down around a table and get together on a candidate."

"When you sit around the table will I be there?" asked McAdoo.

"If you're not there," Smith replied, "I won't be either."[13]

11

RITCHIE OF MARYLAND

ALBERT CABELL RITCHIE, the four-term governor of Maryland and longest-serving chief executive of any state in sixty years, was philosophical about his chances for the 1932 Democratic presidential nomination. "If it comes, it will be wonderful," the white-haired governor said with a wry smile. "If it doesn't, well, I have gone a good deal farther than I ever expected to." Among the favorite sons to be placed in nomination at Chicago Stadium, he alone had a realistic chance of becoming a contender. It was often noted that Ritchie had more friends and fewer enemies in Chicago than any of the candidates. If the convention deadlocked, he hoped to emerge as the compromise choice. "Even his most hopeful admirers do not expect a great deal on the first ballot," Mark S. Watson reported in *The Forum*. "They are much more interested in the last ballot, and certainly they have ample precedent." In the event of a deadlock, Ritchie's strategists liked their prospects. "Have talked to scores of Democrats from numerous southern states and was surprised at the number ready to jump to Ritchie if

Roosevelt is stopped," floor manager Robert B. Ennis wired his candidate from Chicago, "and it looks as though he will be stopped." The *New York Times* reported from Chicago that the Maryland governor "is looked upon as the candidate to whom the anti-Roosevelt forces may rally if they can delay Governor Roosevelt's nomination."[1]

On his arrival at Chicago's Grand Central Station, Ritchie got a hero's welcome. In the crowd that mobbed him, he lost a shoe when someone stepped on his heel. The governor recovered the shoe, leaned down to put it back on, and worked his way through the cheering throng. Escorted by police bodyguards to an open car, he stepped on the back seat, took off his hat, and waved it to the Democratic faithful.

As his motorcade moved slowly out of the station and north to Jackson Boulevard, Ritchie was overwhelmed by the rousing reception. Roosevelt's camp viewed the parade as a clear indication that Ritchie was Mayor Cermak's preference. Peter Carey, chairman of the Chicago Board of Trade, organized this remarkable tribute. A thousand marchers, including three bands playing martial music, followed the governor's car. In the absence of Roosevelt, Garner, and Baker, Ritchie drew the week's biggest crowd. More than a hundred thousand people cheered Ritchie's triumphant procession. "Win with Ritchie" signs and red-white-and-blue bunting adorned the parade route. As he moved past the Chicago Board of Trade, the Maryland governor was showered with ticker tape, confetti, and pieces of torn-up telephone books. When the parade approached the Federal Building on Dearborn Street, government workers crowded windows to catch a glimpse of Ritchie. From down below, a man in a megaphone shouted to them: "Take a good look at your next boss."[2]

On Michigan Avenue, the crowd roared as the governor approached the Congress Hotel. It took him more than ten minutes and considerable help from his bodyguards to struggle through the crowd and make his way to the elaborate rosewood-paneled Florentine room. As he made his entrance through the huge French doors, the band struck up "Maryland! My Maryland!" Attractive young women from Maryland pinned campaign buttons on visitors to Ritchie's elaborate headquarters. "One of our young men achieved eighteen Ritchie buttons in one day," Thomas L. Stokes of Scripps-Howard recalled. "The girls were pretty."

Later in the afternoon, when Ritchie tried to hold a press conference in the Florentine room, sixty political correspondents were outflanked by about eight hundred of the governor's more ardent supporters. "They swarmed around, pushed the reporters off their chairs, barred those who were late from pushing to the front," observed W. A. S. Douglas of the *Baltimore Sun*, "and otherwise interfered with the business of the moment."

Even after Ritchie asked them to clear the room and allow him to meet the press, the partisans would have none of it. They were determined to hold their ground and did not understand why the Fourth Estate should get preferential treatment. A frustrated candidate left through a side door and invited reporters to meet him in his eighth-floor suite.

"Ritchie looked somehow like a wax figure in a show window. His dress was elegant, as always," Stokes remembered. "He was pleasantly reserved, seeming to hold himself in for fear that he might disturb that bland equanimity which was his public self. His face was constantly alight with a beneficent smile that never became openly joyous. His chuckle often was strained and artificial. He just wouldn't let himself go."[3]

His background contributed to this restraint. He had led a life of privilege and had the demeanor of a southern aristocrat. The governor was the son of Judge Albert Ritchie of the Supreme Bench of Baltimore and Elizabeth Cabell, whose family had been prominent in Virginia since before the American Revolution. Her grandfather William

Cabell, seventh governor of Virginia, was among Thomas Jefferson's friends; and her great-uncle Joseph C. Cabell served four decades as rector of the University of Virginia and was Jefferson's right-hand man in creating the school. Governor Ritchie's cousins included the novelist James Branch Cabell and the Pulitzer Prize–winning historian and former U.S. senator William Cabell Bruce, whose son David K. E. Bruce became one of the nation's more accomplished diplomats, serving in six major ambassadorial positions under six administrations.

Ritchie, who was described by the *Chicago Tribune* as "the handsomest man in American public life," was the only bachelor among the 1932 contenders. A Baltimore newspaper once gave a best-looking-man contest and an embarrassed Ritchie was the winner. "He is the cutest boy in America," declared the operatic soprano Mary Garden, a longtime friend. "I have yet to see him give anybody a thrill," Robert W. Woolley wrote privately in 1931, "other than a few passionate ladies who were looking for a handsome man." In an era when the news media gave less scrutiny to the personal lives of politicians, there was no mention in the public prints of Ritchie's marital history. In 1907, at the age of thirty-one, he married Elizabeth Catherine Baker. They did not have children and were divorced nine years later. Ritchie would never remarry.[4]

His marriage was the first casualty of his political career. In 1915 he won his first election as attorney general of Maryland and soon made known his ambitions of running for governor. Ritchie said that he did not seek public office out of a sense of noblesse oblige or because he heard "voices from somewhere" calling him "to save the commonwealth." Ritchie was straightforward in saying that he wanted to make a name for himself and build a record of distinction.

Ritchie took a leave of absence as attorney general in 1918 to serve in the Wilson administration as legal counsel to the War Industries Board. Bernard M. Baruch, the board's chairman and an influential figure in national Democratic politics, adopted Ritchie as his protégé and did much to promote the younger man's political fortunes.

As the first Maryland governor to serve more than one term, he compiled an impressive record. He transformed the state's school and public health standards from low to high among the forty-eight states. Ritchie made state government more efficient and accountable by consolidating eighty agencies and departments into nineteen, introducing merit hiring and promotion, and reducing taxes by 25 percent.

"What most people outside of politics think of Ritchie in Maryland," Frank R. Kent wrote in *Scribner's*, "is that he has made the best governor the state has ever had, that he knows more about the state's business than any other man, that he is attractive, companionable, clean, capable, a governor of whom the state can be proud."[5]

Ritchie, a pro-business Democrat who was among the first members of his party to address an annual meeting of the U.S. Chamber of Commerce, called for a rollback of federal regulations on industry and advocated a bill of rights for American business. "I believe that as long as business recognizes and fulfills its political and economic obligations," he declared, "it is entitled to its own measure of self government instead of bureaucratic control superimposed upon it."

Intellectually consistent in his views, Ritchie turned down President Harding's request that governors of coal-mining states send in troops to settle a coal strike. "I felt, and said respectfully," he recalled, "that the strike should be settled by mutual agreement and not by the bayonet. That was the way it ultimately was settled." Organized labor, which did not agree with the governor's economic conservatism, never forgot his stance on the coal strike.

As the Depression worsened and he sought national support, Ritchie softened his stance against federal intervention to help the unemployed. "I think the government should get as much needed public work done as can be done," he said in Chicago, "but not just for the sake of doing it." He opposed more direct relief by the federal government because it would mean "a bureaucracy so great that it would outbureaucrat all our bureaucracies put together."

In the tradition of his ancestors, he believed in the political philosophy of the sage of Monticello. "I am content to be called a conservative in that I think we ought to go back to certain fundamentals—notably the fundamental of governmental noninterference, on Thomas Jefferson's theory that the country is best governed which is least governed," Ritchie said.[6]

Ritchie also viewed another Democrat, the conservative Grover Cleveland, as a model of presidential leadership. Richard F. Cleveland, a Baltimore lawyer and son of the late president, was among Ritchie's supporters and would second his nomination at the Chicago convention.

The most forthright of the Democratic hopefuls about his presidential ambitions, Ritchie was equally candid in discussing his chances. In a 1931 straw poll of national Democratic leaders, he trailed FDR and Smith but led Baker, Garner, and Murray. Months before Chicago, he confided to a friend that Roosevelt would probably be the nominee and expressed doubt that the New York governor could be stopped. At the same time, Ritchie thought that he had enough of a chance to justify making the race.[7]

When he arrived in Chicago, Ritchie had just picked up the endorsement of the *New York Daily News* as the Democrat who would have the best chance of defeating President Hoover. The *New York Times* reported that Tammany Hall and its allies might throw their support to Ritchie if Roosevelt failed to clinch a first-ballot nomination. The Chicago Board of Trade listed the Maryland governor as a three-to-one favorite to win the nomination. As his fellow governor was getting all this attention, Alfalfa Bill Murray commented that the Maryland Democrat "would make a good president if he wasn't so damn lazy." An amused Ritchie replied, "That means I'll have to start working twenty-four hour days instead of only twenty, as I've been doing heretofore, just to please the Governor of Oklahoma."[8]

Despite the big parade in the Loop and the perception that he was gaining momentum, his candidacy had already peaked. Ritchie had been encouraged by Smith to seek the presidency and assumed that he would pick up Smith's delegates in the event of a deadlock. Four years previously, he had withdrawn from the Democratic presidential race and seconded Smith's nomination. It came as a jolt in Chicago when Smith told him that he was going all out to win the nomination. "He told me that he never realized that Smith was a candidate until he reached Chicago because Smith had led him to believe his only interest was to stop Roosevelt," James A. Farley wrote in his diary. "I got the impression from Ritchie that he felt he had been double-crossed."

His name figured prominently in speculation about the vice presidency. At the Madison Square Garden convention, he had been open to that possibility. "As I feel now, if I can get the presidency I'd like it, and I'd take it," he told a friend who had urged him to reject the second spot. "And if I can't, but can get the vice presidency—as I feel now—then I'd like that, and I'd take it. Let's not be too proud and haughty."

But Ritchie, who had pledges of delegate support in several southern and midwestern states on later ballots, was determined to play out his candidacy.[9]

12

DEEP RIVER

E ARL B. DICKERSON, an African American lawyer from the South
Side of Chicago, appearing in behalf of the National Association
for the Advancement of Colored People, made a compelling argument
before the all-white Resolutions Committee of the Democratic National
Convention. If they adopted a civil rights plank, Dickerson predicted
that two million black voters in northern states would abandon the party
of Abraham Lincoln and "go Democratic." He asked his party to take a
firm stand "against discrimination by reason of race, creed or color, as
being outdated, barbarous, unscientific and un-American."

Dickerson, a native of Mississippi and graduate of the University of
Chicago Law School, was, at forty-one, a senior executive with the
Supreme Life Insurance Company of America, the nation's largest black
enterprise, and would soon be appointed as the first African American
assistant attorney general of Illinois. He was among the record number
of six African American alternate delegates to the 1932 Democratic
National Convention. In the history of the party, there had never been

a black delegate to its national convention and only a single alternate, in 1924, at Madison Square Garden.[1]

He had been part of the great migration from the Deep South to the black metropolis of Chicago's South Side. Most of the residents near Dickerson's office on South Parkway were from Alabama, Arkansas, Georgia, Louisiana, Mississippi, and Tennessee. Republican Oscar De Priest, the nation's only black congressman and the South Side's dominant political figure, was born in Alabama and had lived briefly in Kansas before moving to Chicago in his teens. He described himself as "congressman at large" for the nation's twelve million blacks. Social reformer Ida B. Wells, whose bold reporting from the South in the 1890s exposed racial violence, lived on the South Side for nearly forty years and had died in 1931. Other notable residents of Black Chicago included Jack Johnson, the first African American heavyweight boxing champion; Archibald Motley, the nation's most renowned black painter; jazz legends Earl Hines, who was in his fourth year at the Grand Terrace nightclub, and Louis Armstrong, who was dubbed "Satchmo" in 1932 by a British critic during Armstrong's first visit to England; Claude A. Barnett, founder of the Associated Negro Press, which provided news to 150 black newspapers; Robert S. Abbott, founder and publisher of the *Chicago Defender*, the nation's most influential and largest-circulation black newspaper; and the poet Gwendolyn Brooks, who would become the first African American winner of a Pulitzer Prize.

For blacks leaving the Deep South, Chicago symbolized the promise of a better life. But Jim Crow was alive and well in the big city. Most of Chicago's hospitals were closed to blacks, and the public schools were segregated. In the downtown hotels, African Americans were unwelcome as overnight guests and could not dine with whites in restaurants. Shortly before the convention, two black lawyers won a three-year legal battle against a Loop restaurant after its manager turned them away with the comment: "It is the policy of this restaurant not to serve colored people."[2]

In his presentation, Dickerson focused on the cotton kingdom of the old South. Two-thirds of the nation's blacks still lived in what had once been the Confederate States of America. Less than 5 percent of the 4.2 million blacks of voting age were registered to vote in these eleven states. In three constitutional amendments, sponsored by Republicans and ratified between 1865 and 1869, blacks were guaranteed freedom, equal protection under the law, and the right to vote. African Americans voted in large numbers and won state, local, and national political offices in the Reconstruction Era. But when federal troops withdrew from the South in 1877, the Democratic Party asserted itself as the Party of White Supremacy. Through intimidation and violence blacks were chased out of southern politics. In a series of cases, the Supreme Court effectively nullified the Fourteenth and Fifteenth Amendments when it held that civil rights were a matter of state law and placed strict limits on federal authority to enforce voting rights. Across the South, blacks were denied the right to vote in Democratic primaries. The Louisiana rule allowed only "electors of the white race" to vote in Democratic primaries. In Arkansas, "legally qualified white electors, both male and female" were eligible for party membership. The rules of the Virginia Democratic Party stipulated that "all white persons who are qualified to vote at the next ensuing general election" were declared to be members of the party. A month before Democrats met in Chicago, the Supreme Court struck down a Texas law under which the Democratic state executive committee prohibited blacks from voting in primaries. Justice Benjamin Cardozo, writing for the majority, ruled that this law violated constitutional rights because the executive committee was a state-created political unit. Soon after this ruling, Texas Democrats convened in Houston and adopted new bylaws stating that their primaries were open to "all white citizens of the State of Texas who are qualified to vote."[3]

As Dickerson testified, he faced some of the very politicians who had written the rules that had disenfranchised black voters. Senator Carter Glass of Virginia, a member of the committee, had rewritten his state's constitution three decades earlier and denounced black voting rights as "a crime to begin with and a wretched failure to the end." There was no chance that the all-white panel would vote to invalidate the white primary. Yet Dickerson pressed the issue. "To Negro citizens," he said, "the party pledges its opposition to the 'White Primary' movement and offers full and untrammeled participation in party councils, conventions, primary elections and all phases of party activity without discrimination of race or color."[4]

Dickerson also urged the committee to repudiate the hate crime of lynching. The Tuskegee Institute in Alabama reported that 4,643 persons were executed by lynch mobs between 1882 and 1934. Three-fourths of these victims were African Americans. More than half of this white violence took place in the states of Mississippi, Georgia, Alabama, Louisiana, and Texas. Before they were put to death, the victims were often savagely beaten, dragged through the streets, and tortured. These sadistic rituals often attracted thousands of spectators. An antilynching bill sponsored by a Missouri Republican, Leonidas C. Dyer, passed the House of Representatives in 1921 but was blocked in the Senate by southern Democrats.

The eloquent Dickerson urged the committee "to bring about an end to the barbarous crime of lynching whereby law is dethroned and the mob is made judge and executioner, and to enact a federal law for this purpose." But the Resolutions Committee would not vote to make lynching a federal crime. Southern racial conservatives asserted that lynching was a matter for state and local authorities. All too often, sheriffs were more than willing to release prisoners into the custody of angry mobs.[5]

Dickerson also called on the party to oppose discrimination against blacks in federal employment, on projects funded with public revenues, and in the administration of unemployment relief. Unless the committee responded to at least some of these issues, Dickerson said that the Democrats should not expect African Americans to change their political allegiance.

After outlining the NAACP's civil rights agenda, Dickerson raised the issue of pensions for the elderly, guaranteed health care, and unemployment insurance for all American citizens "regardless of race." Dickerson also advocated "drastic taxes of large incomes for the express purposes of producing more equal distribution of wealth."

"I received an ovation at the end of my talk," Dickerson reported to NAACP executive director Walter White. "This does not matter much, but at least the leaders of the Party are in a frame of mind to deal with colored people on a more friendly basis."[6]

White, a black man with light skin who often passed as white, had been among the founders of the NAACP in 1914 and after many years as a senior official in the civil rights organization began his long run as executive secretary in 1931. He had been striving for months to build a new political coalition that would build popular support for the struggle for racial equality. During the 1928 presidential campaign, Smith courted White's support. "I know Negroes distrust the Democratic Party, and I can't blame them," Smith told the civil rights leader. "But I want to show them that the old Democratic Party, ruled entirely by the South is out, and that we northern Democrats have a totally different approach to the Negro."

Belle Moskowitz, Smith's adviser, was openly sympathetic to the black cause and believed that the Democratic Party needed African

American votes in northern industrial states to have any chance of regaining the White House. White supported Smith but lost enthusiasm when the presidential nominee declined to issue a strong policy statement in support of civil rights. Smith's running mate, Senate Democratic leader Joseph T. Robinson of Arkansas, and Senator Pat Harrison of Mississippi persuaded Smith that the traditionally Democratic South would be lost if he endorsed White's views. Later, after Smith lost half of the South, he regretted this decision.[7]

Frederick Douglass, black America's greatest leader of the nineteenth century, had once described the Republican Party as "the ship and all else the sea." But among the reasons that some civil rights leaders were looking to the Democrats in 1932 is that the Republicans took the black vote for granted. The party of Lincoln and Frederick Douglass, which had written the constitutional amendments to help blacks achieve freedom, had been less than steadfast in upholding these principles.

President Hoover, who won three-fourths of the black vote in 1928, had a mixed record on race. When he purchased his home on S Street in the nation's capital, Hoover would not sign a restrictive covenant against blacks and Jews. As secretary of commerce in the Harding and Coolidge administrations, he ended segregation in his department. As president, he hosted a dinner for Dr. Robert Moton, president of the Tuskegee Institute. This marked the first time in three decades that an African American had dined at the White House. First Lady Lou Henry Hoover included Jessie De Priest, wife of the black congressman, at a congressional tea. The Republican president commuted the sentence of an African American man whose conviction of murdering a white woman was based on flimsy evidence.

Hoover abhorred lynching, and it is now known that he considered the use of federal troops to fight mob violence. When advised that he lacked the constitutional authority to take such a bold step, he held back.

If he had shown more resolve in the fight against lynching, blacks might have been more forgiving when he nominated U.S. Court of Appeals judge John J. Parker for the Supreme Court in 1930. A decade earlier, as a Republican candidate for governor of North Carolina, Parker had embraced white supremacy and suggested that blacks were unfit to participate in the democratic process. Led by White, the NAACP launched a major campaign against Parker and played a key role in forging the bipartisan coalition that defeated his nomination by a single vote.[8]

In his 1932 reelection campaign, Hoover approved what became known as a "lily-white" strategy to purge the black leadership of southern state Republican organizations. Hoover had carried seven southern and border states in 1928 and sought to expand his base among white voters in this region at the expense of the GOP's most faithful constituency. At the 1932 Republican convention, Hoover's men replaced black-led delegations from South Carolina, Georgia, and Louisiana with all-white groups and unsuccessfully sought to prevent the seating of the Mississippi delegation headed by Percy Howard, the state's veteran Republican national committeeman. Walter White began referring to Hoover as "the man in the lily-white house." There were only twenty-six black delegates to the 1932 Republican National Convention, which represented only 2.2 percent of all delegates and about half the number seated at the previous GOP convention. "No one in our day," observed the black intellectual W. E. B. DuBois, "has helped disenfranchisement and race hatred more than Herbert Hoover by his 'lily-white' policy."[9]

When the GOP convention ousted black delegates, the *Chicago Defender* editorialized: "The managers of the Democratic Party now have an unparalleled opportunity—if they will grasp it. It is their privilege to profit by the blunders of the Republicans." White wrote Dickerson that a Democratic Party endorsement of their resolution, "contrasted with the refusal of the Republican National Convention to go on record against lily-whitism, will have repercussions throughout the country."

The *Defender* offered its own plank demanding a black in the next presidential cabinet, full voting rights for all citizens, a federal antilynching law, fair representation of African Americans in police forces across the nation, and "the opening up of all trades and trade unions to blacks as well as whites."

On the politics of race, the 1932 Democratic presidential contenders were content with the status quo. Garner, Ritchie, and Byrd favored states' rights and opposed federal intervention in the Jim Crow South. Baker largely shared this view. As secretary of war during the Great War, he had done nothing to end the army's segregationist practices. His racial conservatism and heritage as the son of a Confederate officer made Baker the leading alternative to Roosevelt among southern delegates headed for Chicago. Murray was the crudest in his appeal for racist votes. During the Alabama primary, he publicly asserted that blacks were inferior to whites in culture and morals.[10]

Roosevelt, who did not yet have the two-thirds vote required for the nomination, had enough of a majority to dominate the Resolutions Committee. Without the New York governor's support, there would not be a civil rights plank in the Democratic platform. Roosevelt had overwhelming support among delegates from the racially segregated South. A month before the convention, as he traveled by train through the South, FDR greeted friendly crowds from the back platform. "Dixie is with you," a man cried out in Greenville, South Carolina. "That's right," the Democratic presidential candidate replied. "I'll have every state below the Mason and Dixon line except Texas and Virginia."

In dealing with African Americans, Roosevelt would do nothing to jeopardize his white southern support. Howe bluntly advised the New

York governor "to remember our southern brethren" and not "the anxious colored brethren." Senator Pat Harrison of Mississippi, one of FDR's more important allies, reflected the views of the southern political establishment. "The Negro is satisfied down there from a political standpoint," Harrison said. "In my state, the Negro has played no part in politics for 40 years and has no desire to do so. We are all content to leave the situation alone as it is."[11]

So was Roosevelt. As a member of the Hudson River aristocracy, he grew up with the prejudices of his social class. Into his early political career, he used the word *nigger* in private conversation and family correspondence. Roosevelt's biographer Geoffrey Ward disclosed that the text of a 1911 speech included FDR's handwritten reminder to add "story of nigger." As assistant secretary of the navy, he helped carry out the segregation of the department. Roosevelt, who did not initiate these policies, followed orders and never questioned the reduction in the number of black sailors. From the Civil War through the Spanish-American War, African Americans made up between 20 and 30 percent of the navy's sailors. By World War I, this number had diminished to 1.2 percent. In 1919, following race riots in the nation's capital, Roosevelt wrote a Harvard classmate in Little Rock: "With your experience in handling Africans in Arkansas, I think you had better come up here and take charge of the Police Force."

Roosevelt, who spoke so eloquently about the plight of the forgotten man, would make no public reference about the status of race relations during his preconvention campaign. Nor did he talk about this issue at the dinner table. Years later, his son James could not recall "a single discussion" with his parents about "voting rights in the South." When the NAACP sent FDR a questionnaire about civil rights, he declined to respond.[12]

He was not a hater. During World War I, he wrote a warm letter of recommendation to the surgeon general in behalf of an African American doctor who wanted to join the Army Medical Reserve. As governor of New York, he signed legislation expanding the judiciary that made possible the election of two black judges. "They are both Democrats and excellent judges," he said later. Roosevelt did not appoint blacks to senior positions in his administration and was silent about the struggle for racial equality.

Roy Wilkins, who had moved to New York in 1931 when White named him as assistant executive secretary of the NAACP, regarded FDR as indifferent and uncaring. "He was a New York patrician," Wilkins remembered. "Distant, aloof, with no natural feel for the sensibilities of black people, no compelling inner commitment to their cause."

Indeed, Roosevelt often referred to himself as an "honorary southerner." During his long struggle with polio in the 1920s, he sought therapy in the soothing mineral waters of Warm Springs, Georgia. In 1926 he bought the old resort, which he would convert into a center for the treatment of fellow polio victims. But its doors were closed to African Americans. Like other health facilities of this era, Warm Springs was a segregated institution. This discriminatory policy would remain in effect throughout the 1930s and into the next decade. Roosevelt, according to his biographer Frank Freidel, never "sufficiently challenged Southern traditions of white supremacy to create problems for himself."[13]

In Chicago, Roosevelt accepted existing racial laws and customs. Despite the friendly reception that Dickerson got at the Congress Hotel, none of his language would be incorporated into the platform. "No vote was taken on a specific racial plank," a member of the committee later explained, "as it was thought inadvisable to put the vote on record."

In the final version of the platform, the Democrats pledged "equal rights to all; special privilege to none." Senator Burton K. Wheeler of

Montana, a Roosevelt ally, said that blacks were unmentioned because the committee did not want to single out an individual group.

"We urged these planks with no hope of getting them adopted," a disappointed White wrote a friend, "but simply to have them put up as a yardstick by which the failures of the Republicans and Democrats would be made more evident."[14]

13

EYE OF THE TIGER

JOHN FRANCIS CURRY, the leader of Tammany Hall, who controlled the largest bloc of delegates at the 1932 Democratic National Convention, had yet to play his hand. As New York Democrats embarked for Chicago on a half dozen special trains, they awaited Curry's instructions on for whom to vote in the presidential balloting. "Whatever John F. Curry decides will meet their views perfectly," the *New York Herald Tribune* reported. While there were published reports linking him to at least five of the Democratic contenders, Curry had not instructed his delegation and indicated that he was in no hurry to announce his choice. "I do not believe in a party hitching itself to a star," the Tammany chieftain told the *New York Times*. "There is no star important enough for that. That is the reason that I do not believe in building a platform to fit a candidate. The candidate must be selected to fit the platform. The success and duties of a party are more important than the ambitions of any individual."[1]

*   *   *

CURRY WAS OF course referring to Roosevelt. It had been known for months that he did not regard the New York governor as his kind of Democrat. In a private meeting with Jim Farley at the Madison Square Garden Club, he rebuked Farley for using his position as state Democratic chairman to advance FDR's candidacy and accused him of sending the false message "around the country that New York State would be instructed for Roosevelt." Even though Farley insisted that he was doing no such thing, Curry's allegations were based on solid information. In promoting Roosevelt's cause, Farley had overstated his support in the New York delegation.

At this same meeting, New York mayor James J. Walker warned Farley that Roosevelt's candidacy was in trouble. Walker, Curry's longtime ally, noted that there was a good chance that the New York regular Democratic organization would not be for Roosevelt and predicted that the leaders of the Democratic Party's big-city machines would join forces in Chicago to stop FDR. "Presidents come and go," Walker told his friend Farley. "The organization goes on forever."[2]

TAMMANY HALL, founded shortly after the American Revolution as the Society of St. Tammany or Columbian Order, began as a patriotic fraternal organization. Most of its early members came from the ranks of enlisted men in the Continental Army, in contrast with the Society of the Cincinnati, which had been formed by officers and whose members belonged to aristocratic families. Tammany, according to the society's constitution drafted by John Pintard, is "a political institution founded on a strong republican basis whose democratic principles will serve in some measure to correct the aristocracy of our city." The organization selected Tammanend, a legendary chief of the Delaware tribe, as its patron, and adopted Native American rituals and traditions. Their headquarters became known as the Wigwam and its governing board was made up of thirteen sachems, one for each tribe or Tammany district, headed by the grand sachem, and the society's members were referred to as warriors and braves.

By the election of 1800 Tammany emerged as an influence in national politics with its support of Thomas Jefferson for the presidency and one of its own, Aaron Burr, as the third vice president of the United States. And it was with the society's backing that Martin Van Buren in 1836 became the first New Yorker to win the presidency.

The expansion of the right to vote was Tammany's first great cause. From the postrevolutionary era into the early nineteenth century, white male property owners were the only eligible voters in New York State. To break the dominance of the aristocratic elite, Tammany championed full voting rights for all classes. At the Constitutional Convention of 1821, over the protests of legal scholars and others who feared democratic government, an amendment was passed that gave every white male in New York the right to vote. In the wake of this victory, Tammany established its base among the working class and became the model for big-city political machines. By reaching out to immigrants and helping them to become citizens of the New Country, the regular Democratic organization showed strength in even greater numbers.[3]

William Marcy Tweed, the Scottish American who became grand sachem on the eve of the Civil War, transformed the society into a statewide force, rewrote the city charter, and built a new wigwam on such a large scale that it was the stage for the 1868 Democratic National Convention. As a young man, he had been foreman of Big Six, the city's best-known volunteer fire company, and Tweed made its insignia, a tiger's head, the official emblem of Tammany. If he had been less greedy,

Tweed might have left a legacy of accomplishment. But he was so blatant in his looting of the public domain that his name would live on as the very symbol of graft and corruption. He stole $20 million in public funds, got caught, and in 1878 died in his cell at the Ludlow Street jail.[4]

After Tweed's fall, the Irish took control of Tammany and were still dominant in 1932. Under the leadership of Charles Francis Murphy, who became chairman in 1902 and ruled for twenty-two years, Tammany achieved its greatest power and gained a new respectability. More than any of the Tammany sachems, he understood the importance of adapting to changing times. In the Progressive Era, Murphy neutralized his opposition by forging alliances with reformers and adopting some of their issues. He supported progressive labor laws, women's suffrage, and improving public education. During his long tenure Murphy was responsible for the elections of three mayors of New York City (George B. McClellan, William J. Gaynor, and John F. Hylan) and three governors of the Empire State (John A. Dix, William Sulzer, and Alfred E. Smith). When Sulzer turned on him, Murphy had him impeached and removed from office. Smith, future U.S. senator Robert F. Wagner, and Judge James A. Foley, who became a jurist of national stature and was also the Tammany leader's son-in-law, were among the new generation of political leadership whose careers were advanced by Murphy. When the party chairman died in 1924, Tammany wielded more power than at any time in the organization's long history.[5]

In 1932 Curry had the chance to take Tammany to an even higher level. Since the Civil War the regular Democratic organization of New York had been on the wrong side in the only national conventions that nominated winners (Grover Cleveland and Woodrow Wilson). As the convention neared, there was growing speculation that Curry would determine the nominee.

Curry, an Irish immigrant, was born on November 23, 1873, on a farm in County Fermanagh. Six months later his parents brought him to New York City. He grew up on the West Side of Manhattan, where his father had a dairy farm near Sixtieth Street and Tenth Avenue and Curry tended the cows. In his youth, he was a star athlete, a sprinter for the West Side Athletic Club and shortstop for the Palisades Baseball Club. "When I was very young," he recalled years later, "I was not sure whether I wanted to be a cowboy or a sailor." Curry, who dropped out of school to take a job with Western Union, became active in Democratic politics and in 1897 began his public career as financial clerk in the office of the city paymaster of New York. At the age of twenty-eight, he was elected to the State Assembly but quit after just one term.

In 1904, Curry became a member of Tammany's governing council when he successfully challenged longtime sachem Daniel "Two-Spot" McMahon for the district leadership of the San Juan Hill section of the middle West Side. On the same block where his father had once farmed, he established the John F. Curry Association, which became the most active social welfare agency in the area. "Take care of the poor," Curry said, "and the poor will take care of you." Curry and his precinct captains found affordable housing for his constituents, fed the hungry, and sought to find jobs for the unemployed. He made a good living in the insurance business and also served as the city's commissioner of records. For a quarter century, he was among the city's more effective district leaders.

As party chairman, in the tradition of "Silent Charlie" Murphy, Curry preferred to work behind the scenes, never made speeches, and seldom made himself available to the news media. "I will carry out the politics in which I grew up," he said. In his second-floor office at the new party headquarters on Union Square, he sat at Murphy's old oak rolltop desk. A three-foot carved wooden tiger stretched across Curry's desk, another of equal size but made of bronze rested on a window ledge, while another, made of inlaid tropical wood, hung on the wall. "No matter where a visitor sits," a reporter noted in June of 1932, "he is staring at one of the huge cats."[6]

Brooklyn's Democratic boss John H. McCooey, who had been Murphy's closest ally, was Curry's chief lieutenant in running the New York Democratic Party. At sixty-eight, McCooey had been Brooklyn's Democratic leader since 1909 and would soon be installed by Curry as New York's Democratic national committeeman. Edward J. Flynn, the Bronx Democratic leader, who had been chosen by Murphy, was frozen out by Curry. "I did not agree with Curry's policies," he recalled, "and as a result Tammany and the Bronx organization did not work in harmony."[7]

Curry and McCooey, though, had forged alliances with three of the Democratic Party's great urban machines: the Cermak organization in Chicago, the Hague machine in Jersey City, and the O'Connell organization in Albany. A week before the 1932 Democratic convention, Cermak went to New York and conferred with Curry and Hague about strategies to thwart Roosevelt's nomination. Their reasons for opposing Roosevelt were not complicated. The urban bosses, who stood to control their city's liquor licenses, were determined to have the party come out strongly for the repeal of Prohibition while FDR preferred to keep this controversial issue out of the campaign. A larger factor in their opposition was that these tough, hard-boiled men regarded FDR as a "goo-goo" reformer unfriendly to their interests. When Hague interviewed presidential contenders, his first question was whether they would "cooperate with, or disregard the party organization."[8]

From the beginning of his career, Roosevelt had an uneasy relationship with party regulars. As a young state senator, FDR showed an unmistakable anti-Irish bias when he scorned Murphy "and his kind" as "beasts of prey." At the time, FDR led an insurgent group that blocked the election in the New York legislature of Tammany stalwart William F. Sheehan to the U.S. Senate. "Those who called themselves the better people of New York have always had mixed reasons for opposing Tammany Hall," FDR's adviser Raymond Moley observed years later. "The reasons which they do not express are that Tammany suggests alien ancestry, religious affiliations antagonistic to those of most native Americans, and generally the 'lower' and poorer elements. The reasons expressed are the corruption, the misgovernment and the autocracy of the machine. These latter evils are not to be minimized. The former, however, are important and pervasive."⁹

In a 1911 interview with the *New York Times*, Roosevelt defended his independence. "There is nothing to gain by the Democratic party through an alliance between Tammany Hall and the up-State Democrats," he asserted, "until the character of leadership in the Tammany organization has changed." As he would soon learn, it was easier to criticize than seriously challenge the regular Democratic organization. In 1912, he attempted to launch a new party coalition, "Empire State Democracy," which never got off the ground. Two years later, as a member of the Wilson administration, he ran as an independent in the Democratic primary for the U.S. Senate and sought to make the election a referendum on ending the domination of party bosses. Tammany's candidate James Gerard, a wealthy lawyer and the U.S. ambassador to Germany, crushed the insurgent by four to one in New York City and more than two to one in the statewide primary vote. What these setbacks taught Roosevelt is that he could not go it alone. By extending an olive branch to the party leadership, he kept himself politically alive. In the summer of 1917, FDR delivered the main speech and shared the stage with Murphy at the 128th annual Independence Day celebration of the Society of Tammany. As a result of this reconciliation, Roosevelt suddenly found himself touted for the governorship. Though he did not pursue this opportunity, the accommodation with Tammany opened future possibilities. It was with Murphy's approval that Democratic presidential nominee James Cox selected FDR as their party's nominee for the vice presidency. Roosevelt had the support of the regular Democratic organization in both of his successful campaigns for governor and showed his gratitude in 1929 by speaking at the dedication ceremonies for Tammany's new wigwam on Union Square.[10]

The erstwhile independent defended his alliance with party regulars. "To accomplish almost anything worthwhile," FDR observed in 1932, "it is necessary to compromise between the ideal and the practical. . . . But these compromises must never condone dishonesty, extravagance, or inefficiency." This was the dilemma that Roosevelt confronted as he sought the Democratic presidential nomination.[11]

Judge Samuel Seabury, a noted reformer who was the namesake and great-great-grandson of the first Anglican bishop in the United States, in the summer of 1930 launched the most comprehensive investigation of municipal corruption in the nation's history. Roosevelt recommended the judge's initial appointment to investigate the New York judiciary and later gave him broader authority to look into the district attorney's office in Manhattan. Within a short time, Seabury exposed vast corruption in the criminal justice system and brought down crooked magistrates, clerks, and policemen. His investigation of New York district attorney Thomas C. T. Crain concluded that the aging Tammany politician and former judge was an incompetent but not a crook. In 1931 Republicans in Albany created the Joint Legislative Committee to Investigate the Affairs of the City of New York with Seabury as chief counsel.

In building his public corruption cases, Seabury pioneered the technique of using bank accounts and other financial records. By the end of that year, the judge disclosed that Thomas M. Farley, the sheriff of

New York County, had banked $396,000 over the previous seven years during which time his public salary had ranged from $6,500 to $15,000. During Seabury's interrogation, Farley testified that he had saved this money in "a tin box." Seabury presented his findings to Roosevelt and urged the governor to oust the sheriff. After Farley submitted to questioning at a public hearing convened by FDR, the governor invoked his power of removal from office. Roosevelt asserted that a public official had an obligation and public duty to explain when "his scale of living, or the total of his bank deposits far exceeds the public salary which he is known to receive. . . . The state is a just but jealous master."[12]

As he competed for presidential delegates, FDR did not like being put on the spot. "On the one side was an angry and outraged political machine which would control most of New York's votes in the national convention," recalled FDR's adviser Raymond Moley. "On the other side was the reformer Seabury, most of the New York press, and 'good' citizens, an army of them throughout the nation, whose support a presidential candidate would most assuredly need."

Under this pressure, Roosevelt vented his frustration. The Reverend John Haynes Holmes and Rabbi Stephen Wise urged him to use the Farley case as his precedent and remove Sheriff James A. McQuade of Brooklyn and John Theofel, chief clerk of the Queens County Surrogate's Court, who was also the borough's Democratic leader. Like Farley, McQuade and Theofel had mysteriously acquired hundreds of thousands of dollars. Instead of going after the corrupt officials, FDR accused the civic reformers of impertinence. "It would perhaps be easy for me to question the good faith in which these letters were written, or to assume that you care more for personal publicity than for good government," Roosevelt wrote the clergymen in a public letter.

"Let me tell you two gentlemen straight from the shoulder, that I am becoming convinced from your letters that corruption in public office and unfit servants in public office are both far less abhorrent to you than they are to me. A rushing into print early and often, with extravagant and ill-considered language, causes many of our decent citizens to doubt your own reliance on law, on order and on justice.

"The time which you two gentlemen now spend in bringing charges and asking your Governor to perform unconstitutional functions and to ignore the principles of representative government could be more profitably spent. If you would exert yourselves patiently and consistently in pointing out to the electorate of New York City that an active insistence on their part would result in better qualified and more honest and more efficient public servants, you would be rendering a service to your community which at the present time you are not performing."[13]

As the convention neared, Roosevelt faced another unpleasant choice. James J. Walker, the dapper and popular mayor of New York City, had long been the focal point of Judge Seabury's investigation. The judge produced evidence suggesting that Beau James had accepted more than a million dollars from city contractors. In late May, for two days, Walker took the stand and had no credible explanation for taking what he described as "beneficiences" from "many kind friends."

Less than three weeks before the convention, Seabury presented his charges to Roosevelt and concluded that Walker "has failed properly to execute the duties" of his office, that he was motivated "by improper and illegal considerations" and "guilty of gross improprieties."

A week before the convention, Roosevelt sent Walker a copy of the judge's report and asked for a response to the allegations. "I plan to go to the convention in a day or two," the mayor told reporters. "Upon my return I will immediately take up the matter of the Governor's communication."[14]

Walter Lippmann, who was using his column to undercut Roosevelt at every opportunity, used the Walker case to question his leadership.

"It is, of course, an unpleasant thing to have to consider the removal of Mayor Walker just before the convention meets," Lippmann wrote. "If he removes the Mayor, Mr. Roosevelt will be accused of playing politics. If he does not remove him, he will also be accused of playing politics. It is a perplexing problem. But the problem is entirely the consequence of Governor Roosevelt's indecision during the last year. . . .

"This squalid mess is due to nothing but Governor Roosevelt's own weakness and timidity. If months ago he had done what he should have done, if he had broken with Tammany and put himself unequivocally at the head of the forces struggling for good government, there would be no dilemma today. He elected, instead, to play an intricate game with Tammany, to act against corruption only when he was forced to do so, to feed Tammany patronage, to consort with the Tammany bosses, and to go along with Tammany in trying to discredit Mr. Seabury and the active forces fighting Tammany corruption."[15]

Roosevelt had reason to be suspicious of the judge. While fighting municipal corruption in New York, Seabury was also maneuvering to make himself available for the Democratic presidential nomination. He had once been the Democratic nominee for governor of New York and now viewed the nation's highest office as his destiny. The starchy judge, whose investigation had been widely acclaimed on the editorial pages of the nation's largest newspapers, believed that independents, progressives, and Bible Belt moralists would rally behind his presidential candidacy. Louis Howe reported to FDR that the judge had sent representatives to meet with Democratic senators in Washington to get their assessment of Seabury's chances at a deadlocked convention. Copies of a new book about the judge by a friendly New York journalist were being distributed to delegates and party leaders. "The Seabury plan," Moley later wrote, "was to strike down Walker, maim Tammany, if necessary embarrass Governor Roosevelt's presidential ambitions and perhaps present himself to the nation . . . as a suitable occupant for the White House." A week before the convention, the *New York Times* disclosed on its front page that Seabury had reserved a suite at Chicago's lakefront Drake Hotel and would be attending the convention.[16]

Earlier that month, FDR privately expressed his rage over the judge's timing. "This fellow Seabury is merely trying to perpetuate another political play to embarrass me," he wrote Colonel House. "His conduct has been a deep disappointment to people who honestly seek better government in New York City by stressing the fundamentals and eliminating political innuendoes."

Roosevelt was being urged by some allies to remove Walker or risk losing the nomination. One night in June of 1932, Marion Dickerman, a close friend of the Roosevelt family, sat in the study at Hyde Park as FDR listened to three nationally prominent Democrats make the case for Walker's ouster. According to Dickerman, Roosevelt "remained remarkably calm" during this discussion and gave no hint of his leanings. After the politicians left without a commitment, Dickerman spoke up. "They're right, Franklin!" she exclaimed. "You know they are! The convention will never nominate a Tammany-controlled candidate, and that's what your enemies will call you. You must remove the mayor."

"Never," an irritated FDR shot back, "never will I let it be said that I climbed to a position of power on the back of someone else!" Dickerman, who had known Roosevelt for years, had never seen him this angry.

In explaining his reluctance, FDR became more reflective about the Walker case. "I have at times acted on the advice and counsel of others when it was contrary to my own judgment, and on occasion the results have been good. The advice proved to be good. But one act leads to another," he told Dickerman, "and when the time comes to act again the same counselor may not be there. The first time, you acted out of

character; the second time, you are confused. The path you are following is not the one that you would have chosen by yourself, and because
it isn't you make mistakes. This is a vital matter. It's more important
than any immediate political advantage. You must let me be myself."[17]

Roosevelt, though, conferred with numerous advisers about the
Walker case, including Moley, who had worked with Seabury in earlier
corruption probes. At one point, FDR asked, "How would it be if I let
the little mayor off with a hell of a reprimand?" Then, answering his
own question, Roosevelt said firmly, "No. That would be weak."

CURRY, WHO OWED his election as party chairman to Walker, showed
his support for the embattled mayor by choosing him as New York's
member of the Resolutions Committee. "At the present minute an efficient government in New York is being attacked. This would never have
happened," Curry asserted on the eve of the convention, "if the city had
its proper representation in Albany."[18]

14

GRAND ILLUSION

A S THE CONVENTION got closer, with FDR short of the required two-thirds majority, the Stop Roosevelt movement intensified a whispering campaign that questioned his fitness to serve as president of the United States. A major political party had never nominated a presidential candidate with a massive disability. "He is crippled both mentally and physically," asserted Jersey City mayor Frank Hague, Smith's floor manager. Hague, who stood over six feet tall, with a slender athletic build and the cold eyes of an IRA shooter, was taking dead aim at FDR's handicap. "Supreme belief in himself appears in every expression and gesture. As he argued with delegates on the sidewalks and in the corridors," Alva Johnston of *The New Yorker* observed, "Hague's countenance had a deadly earnestness exceeding that of a poker-faced comedian; his blue eyes protruded fiercely from his lean, ruddy face; shifting his cane from the crook of one elbow to another, he enforced his points with cleaver strokes of the right and left hand. He has the accuracy of a knife-thrower in narrowly missing the listener's face with these fierce overhand chops."[1]

Other prominent Democrats joined in. "We don't want a dead man on the ticket," William Gibbs McAdoo, the chairman of the California delegation, told a Roosevelt ally. In this same conversation, McAdoo declared with certitude that FDR could not possibly withstand the rigors of a national campaign. Smith, who shared this opinion, wrote in the preconvention edition of the *Saturday Evening Post* that the presidential nominee was expected to wage a four-month national campaign. "It requires a man of great vigor and bodily strength to stand the physical strain of it," Smith said, "to make no mention whatever of the tax he has to put upon his mental qualities to permit him to conduct the campaign intelligently over so long a period." At a national conference of Democratic women, the group's president made a slurring reference to Roosevelt's health. "This candidate while mentally qualified for the presidency," Mrs. Jesse W. Nicholson averred, "is utterly unfit physically."[2]

Enraged but not surprised by these comments, FDR had long recognized that the health issue had the potential to undermine his chances for the nomination and thereupon adopted the strategy of attempting to conceal his disability from the American public. Roosevelt, who was essentially a paraplegic, had the cooperation of his security detail and the press in this elaborate deception. The news photographers and newsreel cameramen never took pictures of FDR in a wheelchair or on crutches and political reporters seldom made reference to his handicap in their stories. Only the upper part of Roosevelt's body was photographed. With his well-chiseled patrician features, that exuberant tilting of the head, and the cigarette holder extending from the strong jaw, FDR projected an image of optimism and confidence.

Roosevelt, who had no use of his legs, went to great lengths to hide the fact that he was paralyzed from the waist down. He could neither walk nor stand on his own but created the appearance of standing by wearing heavy leg braces jointed at the knees and supporting himself by leaning against a wall or holding the arm of another person, often his son James or a member of his security detail. Beginning in 1928, he could with difficulty and on rare occasions give the illusion of walking by swinging his hips forward and, with his braces locked to keep legs from buckling, take a few awkward steps supporting himself by two canes as if on stilts. For the rest of his life, he relied on a wheelchair as his means of getting around.[3]

But he did not want the public to know that he was confined to a wheelchair. As part of his elaborate deception, Roosevelt manipulated country editors by giving them misleading information about his condition. "I am not in any sense an invalid and have not been since an attack of infantile paralysis," he told a Kansas editor. "Literally, the only thing the matter with my health is that I have to walk with braces on my legs and a couple of canes. The legs are constantly improving." In a letter to a Montana editor, Roosevelt took issue with a friendly editorial that noted that he had not given up his wheelchair. "As a matter of fact," FDR claimed, "I don't use a wheelchair at all except a little kitchen chair on wheels to get about my room while dressing before I am dressed, and solely for the purpose of saving time. I don't think this can be properly considered 'use of a wheelchair' because in my work in the Capitol and elsewhere I do not use one at all."

The historian Alan Brinkley has written of Roosevelt's strategy: "His determination to hide his condition from those around him probably strengthened what was already his natural inclination to dissemble, to hide behind an aggressive public geniality, and to reveal as little about himself as possible."

Among polio survivors Roosevelt was hardly unique in his denial. As Dr. Lauro S. Halstead, a polio survivor, has written, "Virtually every polio survivor I have met has displayed an element of this self-deception." Long after his doctors told him he would never walk again, FDR expected to prove them wrong.[4]

After being stricken in the summer of 1921 with infantile paralysis, as polio was then known, Roosevelt fought back with extraordinary will. While lying in bed he would spend hours in a futile effort to move a single toe. As his leg muscles withered, FDR built up his upper body by working out on parallel bars, swimming in the pool of his neighbor Vincent Astor, and learning to pull himself across the floor of the family library by dragging his legs. "Each new thing he did took not only determination but great physical effort," Eleanor Roosevelt recalled.

FDR adapted to his paralysis by inventing devices that gave him greater freedom. He designed his own wheelchair, using a small wooden chair and a metal frame with wheels, a huge improvement over the large and bulky wicker wheelchairs that were then the standard. He had a small car rebuilt so that he could drive it without foot pedals and also developed a gadget for his Florida houseboat that enabled him to be lowered into the water for swimming.[5]

From 1924 through the rest of his life, Roosevelt drew strength from the invigorating mineral waters at Warm Springs, an old resort and spa in western Georgia. By swimming in the thermal pool fed by a subterranean spring, he developed his broad shoulders, barrel chest, and powerful arms. In the pools, supported by the warm water, FDR felt life in his toes for the first time since 1921, could stand without braces in water up to his shoulders, and even give the illusion of walking. In 1926, he spent two-thirds of his personal fortune, more than $200,000, to buy the resort, cottages, and pools, which he developed into a center for the treatment of polio. Next to this property, FDR also bought more than a thousand acres of mountain farmland.

The establishment of the Georgia Warm Springs Foundation in 1927 must be ranked among Roosevelt's great accomplishments. In this era, the few medical institutions for people with disabilities were gloomy asylums with names like the New York Society for the Relief of the Ruptured and Crippled and the Children's House of the Home for the Incurables. Many polio patients were packed into open wards of contagious hospitals. In contrast with these grim places, FDR provided an environment of sunshine and hope. There were 150 patients in the center's first two years, and Roosevelt worked and stayed in touch with many of them. He had cottages built that were more accessible for the disabled, opened a new therapy pool, and hired an orthopedic surgeon, nurses, and physiotherapists. As the rehabilitation psychologist Richard Thayer Goldberg has written, "FDR's concern was the patients. He envisioned Warm Springs as a transitional facility where patients could learn to function independently and develop personal and social relationships. He saw Warm Springs as a preparation for community living, not as a hospital with strict regulations and bureaucratic institutionalization."[6]

Roosevelt's disability brought out an inner strength, made him more focused and disciplined, and gave him a larger sense of purpose. "There are times," Louis McHenry Howe later observed, "when I think that Franklin might never have been President if he had not been stricken. You see, he had a thousand interests. You couldn't pin him down. . . . Then suddenly there he was flat on his back with nothing to do but think. He began to read, he began to think, he talked, he gathered people around him—his thoughts expanded, his horizon widened."

Frances Perkins, who had been a young social worker when she met Roosevelt, was impressed by his personal growth in the wake of the ordeal. "I noticed when he came back that the years of pain and suffering had purged the slightly arrogant attitude he had displayed on occasion before he was stricken," she later wrote. "The man emerged completely warmhearted, with humility of spirit and with a deeper philosophy. Having been to the depths of trouble, he understood the problems of people in trouble."

Roosevelt, who refused to give in to his disability, did not think of himself as a victim and among the reasons for his campaign of deception is that he wanted to be judged on his own terms. "Now, I don't want any sob stuff," he told a reporter who interviewed him about his work at Warm Springs. At home FDR took the same attitude. "Never to my knowledge," recalled James Roosevelt, "did he rant or rail against the blow fate had dealt him in making him a cripple."[7]

As Roosevelt prepared to run for the presidency, he understood that his health was a topic of political discussion and that the issue could not be easily dismissed. In the fall of 1930, while running for his second term as governor, FDR publicly announced that he had qualified for $500,000 in life-insurance policies from twenty-two companies with the Georgia Warm Springs Foundation as the beneficiary. Roosevelt, who was then forty-eight years old, qualified for the normal rate for a person of his age. "I would say that his examination disclosed conditions which were comparable to a man of thirty," said Dr. Edgar W. Beckwith, medical examiner of the Equitable Life Assurance Company. "His chest expansion is five and one-half inches, whereas the average individual has from three to three and a half inches." Beckwith added that Roosevelt's blood pressure of 128 "compares with that of a man forty-five and is better than gilt-edged for a man of forty-eight. He has no internal weaknesses."[8]

In spite of this glowing report, the health issue did not go away and not just because of doubts about Roosevelt. Warren G. Harding had died of a heart attack in 1923 and Woodrow Wilson suffered a massive stroke in 1919 that left him incapacitated for the remainder of his presidency. In 1893, Grover Cleveland underwent a secret operation for cancer of the jaw aboard a yacht in New York harbor. Cleveland lived another fifteen years, but the records of his surgery were not opened until a decade after his death. By 1932 there was a growing recognition among politicians and the voting public that presidential health was an issue of legitimate concern.

FDR, who was eager to dispel any doubts about his health, enlisted the help of trusted allies. "I find that there is a deliberate attempt to create the impression that my health is such as would make it impossible for me to fulfill the duties of President," he reported to a friend in May of 1931. "To those who know how strenuous have been the three years I have passed as Governor of this State, this is highly humorous, but it is taken with great seriousness in the southern states particularly. I shall appreciate whatever my friends may have to say to dispel this perfectly silly piece of propaganda."[9]

During his western tour, Farley was confronted about the health issue by Democratic officeholders at virtually every stop. Less than pleased with this news, Roosevelt had already been considering ways to neutralize the issue. It was with his cooperation that a Republican writer, Earle Looker, published a dramatic article in the July 25, 1931, edition of *Liberty* magazine entitled "Is Franklin D. Roosevelt Physically Fit to Be President?"

Looker, a resident of former President Calvin Coolidge's hometown of Northampton, Massachusetts, and longtime friend of the Oyster Bay Roosevelts, answered in the affirmative. "I had watched him working and resting. I had noted the alertness of his movements, the sparkle of his eyes, the vigor of his gestures. I had seen his strength under the strain of long working periods," he wrote. "In so far as I had observed him, I had come to the conclusion that he seemed able to take more punishment than many men ten years younger. Merely his legs were not much good to him."

After interviewing forty-three of Roosevelt's associates, Looker wrote that their consensus opinion was that he was in good health and his condition had improved since his election as governor. Looker also disclosed that Roosevelt had been examined by a panel of medical specialists chosen by the director of the New York Academy of Medicine, including a neurologist, orthopedist, and diagnostician. "We have today carefully examined Governor Roosevelt," the doctors reported to Looker. "We believe that his health and power of endurance are such as to allow him to meet any demand of public and private life."

The doctors reported that Roosevelt's organs and functions were "sound in all respects," that he did not suffer from anemia, had a strong chest, and normal spinal column. They were less than accurate in claiming that FDR "has neither ache nor pain at any time," that his legs were getting stronger, and that he "can maintain a standing position without fatigue."[10]

The *Liberty* article became the Roosevelt campaign's official response to the health issue. "It answers fully the questions that were put to me," Farley told FDR. Howe mailed out fifty thousand copies of Looker's piece, sending the article to state and local officeholders, every county chairman in the nation, individuals who had questioned whether Roosevelt was up to the demands of the office, and allies seeking to refute the latest whispering campaign.

Even though Roosevelt had seemingly turned the health issue to his advantage, his enemies were not letting up. "I had thought the article in *Liberty* would have stopped [the whispering campaign]," FDR told downstate Illinois supporter V. Y. Dallman, "but the story is still being circulated industriously in all parts of the country, and I suppose it will have to be handled all over again." Roosevelt had faith that the public would give him the benefit of the doubt "because I am quite as able to get around as the most sturdy citizen and cover an average of twenty to thirty thousand miles in my state each year."[11]

In the spring of 1932, when FDR planned a trip to Warm Springs, some advisers expressed concern about the timing of the visit. Robert W. Field, a New York lawyer and native Texan, who was helping Roosevelt in the South, urged him to cancel the trip. "The only two of our group whom I have seen," Robert W. Woolley confided to Colonel House, "agree with Mr. Fields' suggestion that the Governor go not again to Warm Springs until after next November. They fully appreciate the importance of doing everything possible to discount the effect of the whispering campaign as to the Governor's health, which seems to be well under way."

But FDR would not back down. "Roosevelt is determined to go to Warm Springs," House answered Woolley. "He has made many engagements there to meet people and he feels that he cannot disappoint them. The effect of his going will be minimized and the health feature of it will be eliminated." In late April, FDR embarked for southern Georgia and stayed for about three weeks.

On this trip, while delivering a speech in Georgia, Roosevelt was driving home a point when he moved away from the rostrum on which he had been leaning, lost his balance, and to the shock of the crowd, abruptly fell over. "Several friends on the platform rushed forward and helped him to his feet," Robert S. Allen recalled. "Without a loss of a word he resumed his address at the point where he had broken off when he fell. The audience was so stirred by this exhibition of willpower that it broke into cheers."[12]

Roosevelt demonstrated similar resolve that spring when President Hoover held a dinner at the White House for the nation's governors and their wives. Eleanor and Franklin arrived early and, as tradition dictated, stood with other guests in the East Room awaiting the president's arrival. When Hoover did not appear for thirty minutes, Roosevelt was in pain. "My husband was twice offered a chair," Eleanor later wrote, "but he thought that if he showed any weakness someone might make an adverse political story out of it, so he refused each time. It seemed as though he was being deliberately put through an endurance test, but he stood the whole evening very well, though the half hour before President and Mrs. Hoover appeared was an ordeal."

The Roosevelts, who had reason to be suspicious about Republican involvement in the whispering campaigns, would never forgive the president. But Hoover was not a mean-spirited man and it is doubtful that he was deliberately hurtful. "I greatly admired the courage with which he fought his way back to active life and with which he overcame the handicap which had come to him," Hoover wrote of Roosevelt in 1958. "I considered that it was a great mistake that his friends insisted upon trying to hide his infirmity, as manifestly it had not affected his physical or mental abilities."[13]

Some of FDR's Democratic rivals took a different view. Former Virginia governor Harry F. Byrd, who had been among Roosevelt's earliest allies before launching his own presidential bid, told friends that he doubted that FDR could stand the strain of the presidency. When Roosevelt visited the former governor at his Virginia mansion, it took three men to carry him up the broad front steps. Whatever his private doubts, Byrd would never publicly question Roosevelt's fitness for the presidency.

Oklahoma governor "Alfalfa Bill" Murray, who had never been accused of subtlety, took the Democratic presidential race into the gutter. Less than three weeks before the convention, Murray said of Roosevelt: "How much less can a man think who has locomotor ataxia, a nervous disease that affects the spinal column, and ultimately the brain. I know they say it is infantile paralysis, but locomotor ataxia never came from that source."

With these reckless innuendoes, Murray became the first public figure to embrace the anonymous hate campaign alleging Roosevelt's condition had been produced by syphilis and that his mental health would also be affected. Sympathetic letters poured into Albany and FDR ignored the desperate Murray.[14]

At the convention, Hague took the lead in seeking to discredit FDR. In private conversations with party leaders, he viciously mocked Roosevelt's disability. The Jersey City mayor, with Smith's encouragement, went public with his vitriolic comments.

"Governor Franklin D. Roosevelt, if nominated, has no chance of winning at the election in November," Hague said in an appeal to delegates. "I have felt out public sentiment not alone here, but in practically every state in the union, particularly those states east of the Mississippi, and I am brought to the conclusion that he cannot carry a single state east of the Mississippi and very few in the Far West."

While reiterating his support for Smith, Hague noted that the Democratic Party had "a wealth of material" and "outstanding statesmen," including Ritchie, Traylor, Garner, Baker, White, Murray, Reed, and Lewis. When Hague got around to Roosevelt, he made an unmistakable reference to his disability: "Why consider the one man who is weakest in the eyes of the rank and file."

After conferring by long-distance phone with FDR, Farley responded, "Governor Roosevelt's friends have not come to Chicago to cry down, criticize or defame any Democrat from any part of the Union."

Governor Richard B. Russell of Georgia, chairman of that state's delegation and at thirty-four the nation's youngest governor, took the lead in moving from delegation to delegation advising party leaders that he knew Roosevelt well, had spent time with him at Warm Springs, and could vouch for his health.

The good-humored Farley, who had been balding since youth, wryly noted that Roosevelt's condition was no more of a handicap than "a glass eye or premature baldness."[15]

15

HYDE PARK

HORTLY BEFORE THE opening of the Chicago convention,
FDR summoned Democratic leaders to Hyde Park for a strategy
meeting. As the visiting politicians stepped off the train at the Pough-
keepsie station, they were met by a fleet of cars including state troopers
for the six-mile drive north on Albany Post Road. The Roosevelts had
ties to the Hudson River Valley going back to the seventeenth century
and had lived along the eastern shore since 1818. The town of Hyde
Park, with its green rolling hills and Dutch colonial stone fences, was
incorporated in 1821 on land that had been granted by the British
crown more than a century earlier to several parties, including the personal secretary of the then royal governor of New York.

Springwood, FDR's birthplace and country estate, was on a bluff
overlooking the Hudson, and the "Big House" reflected the warm and
cheerful personality of the New York governor. In 1915 he and his
mother, Sara Delano Roosevelt, renovated the house, replacing the old
clapboard exterior with stucco, adding many windows and large two-

story wings at each end, replacing the old porch with a fieldstone terrace and sweeping balustrade, and raising the pitched roof to add a
third story. The mansion contained thirty-five rooms, nine baths, and
four chimneys. On top of the colonnaded portico, the American flag
and New York State flag were flying. Surrounded by thick forests and
terraced lawns, the estate included formal gardens, coach house and
stables, greenhouse, icehouse, pump house, and an arboretum with
hundreds of trees of many varieties cultivated by FDR. The stable built
by his father was adorned with ribbons won by several generations of
Roosevelts in horse competitions. Of Roosevelt's five children, only
Franklin Jr. and John, who were both students at Groton, still spent
their summers at home. Eleanor and Franklin lived with the governor's
mother, Sara, who owned the estate, and Howe, a member of the
household since FDR's crippling polio attack.[1]

The arriving guests included Senators Cordell Hull of Tennessee,
Thomas J. Walsh and Burton K. Wheeler of Montana, Clarence Dill of
Washington, and John S. Cohen of Georgia, James A. Farley, Edward J.
Flynn, and Robert H. Jackson, former Democratic national chairman
Homer S. Cummings, former Internal Revenue commissioner Daniel
C. Roper, former attorney general A. Mitchell Palmer, Democratic na-
tional committeeman J. Bruce Kremer of Montana, former Pennsylva-
nia Democratic chairman Joseph F. Guffey, and Kansas congressmen
Guy T. Helvering and William A. Ayers.[2]

WITH HIS NOMINATION in doubt, this would be the last time before
the opening of the convention that Roosevelt would be in the same
room with most of these party leaders and he wanted their advice on
strategy and tactics. As this group convened, there were swirling ten-
sions. Hull, Wheeler, and Dill were ambitious for the vice presidency

and that topic was not on the agenda. Of these three senators, only Hull was on Roosevelt's short list of possible running mates. The courtly and dignified Hull, who was addressed even by members of his family as Judge Hull, was among the more respected members of the Senate, and he was Roosevelt's most important southern ally. As a congressman in the Wilson era, he sponsored and passed into law the nation's first income tax and now was promoting free trade and the reduction of high tariffs imposed by Republicans. Hull, a former chairman of the Democratic National Committee and favorite son of his state at two national conventions, supported FDR as their party's best hope of recapturing the presidency. Hull was uncomfortable with the high-profile roles in the campaign of Wheeler, an outspoken western progressive, and Dill, whom he suspected of leaking information to political columnists about confidential strategy meetings like this one.[3]

Walsh and Wheeler, who had often battled the mighty Anaconda Copper Mining Company, had an intense dislike for Kremer, a lawyer and lobbyist with longtime ties to Anaconda. When Wheeler had been their party's nominee for governor, Kremer worked against him. He also supported Smith over Walsh in the 1928 Democratic presidential race and had talked about running against Walsh for senator. But the feuding Montanans had been among FDR's earliest supporters for the presidency and, at least for now, were working together.

Cummings and Roper, veterans of national politics going back to the Wilson era, were being touted by Colonel Edward M. House for the leadership of the campaign. The old Wilsonians blamed Farley and Howe for FDR's setbacks in the late primaries. Roosevelt thought well of Cummings and Roper but stood by his team. Farley resented published reports that suggested that Cummings was running the campaign. Even though Cummings apologized for this confusion, Farley viewed him as a self-promoter.[4]

On this first Sunday in June, with the primaries behind them, Roosevelt convened the strategy meeting in the huge living room, which occupied the entire lower floor of the south wing of the house. Designed by FDR, the paneled room measured one hundred by forty feet and had two fireplaces, built-in bookcases filled with leather-bound collections, portraits of Roosevelt ancestors, European and Oriental antiques, and naval paintings. The governor loved this room and particularly enjoyed the view from the southwest window that extended for miles down the Hudson River.

The first topic on the agenda, which was drafted by Howe and Jackson, secretary of the Democratic National Committee, was the Chicago compromise over the permanent chairmanship. Less than a week after Jouett Shouse gave up probable election as keynoter and temporary chairman in exchange for the subcommittee's endorsement for permanent chairman, he began hearing that Roosevelt's camp would fight his candidacy. But at the Hyde Park meeting, the party leaders were presented with the options of retaining Shouse or choosing another permanent chairman "if this is unwise."[5]

Wheeler, the first member of the Senate to endorse Roosevelt for the presidency, suggested in the clipped accent of his Massachusetts youth that it would be folly to honor the terms of the Chicago compromise. "If Shouse becomes chairman," he warned Roosevelt, "you will not become President!"

The four other senators also spoke out against Shouse. Before this meeting, Walsh confided to Farley that "the selection of Shouse should not be tolerated." In a letter made public at the Montana State Democratic convention, Walsh made an unmistakable reference to Raskob and Shouse as "a sinister combination" seeking to thwart the will of the people. "The unhappy result in 1920 and again in 1924 of the selection of a candidate by a deadlocked convention ought to dissuade any

Democrat from looking eagerly to the occurrence of such an issue," he asserted, "and little hope is entertained of the nomination of any one of the able and eminent gentlemen whose names have been mentioned in connection with the nomination, other than Governor Roosevelt, except through a deadlock."[6]

Roosevelt and Howe, who had been wary about the Chicago compromise, did not have to be converted. Since the April meeting in Chicago, there had been ample evidence of Shouse's anti-Roosevelt activity. He had urged Smith to run in Massachusetts, successfully encouraged favorite-son candidacies in Ohio, Illinois, Missouri, and Virginia, and publicly welcomed Garner into the race. If Roosevelt fell short of a two-thirds majority on the early ballots, Shouse could, as permanent chairman, start a rally toward another candidate.

Walsh, who had gained high marks for his steady performance as chairman of the 103-ballot 1924 Democratic National Convention, soon emerged as the group's consensus choice. He had been widely acclaimed and was a hero in the Democratic Party for exposing the theft of the nation's oil reserves in the Teapot Dome scandal of 1923–24. His investigation led to the indictment and conviction of Interior secretary Albert Fall for taking a $100,000 bribe. Walsh's probe also forced the resignation of secretary of the navy Edwin Denby for negligence and incompetence. "His steel eyes when he is in action seem to bore through a witness," the *New York Times* reported. "The questions come through with the speed of machine-gun fire." Because of the senator's tenacity, Fall became the first cabinet member in American history imprisoned for a felony committed while in office. The Supreme Court supported Walsh's interpretation of official misconduct. In June of 1932, Teapot Dome was still very much in the news as Fall completed his prison term and conspiracy charges were dropped against the major figures in the scandal. There was

A two-thirds majority was required to win the 1932 Democratic nomination. When the convention opened on June 27, a deadlock seemed likely as Roosevelt was about one hundred votes short. *Kaufmann & Fabry Studio*

Governor Franklin D. Roosevelt, observing the tradition that front-runners stayed home during the convention, had a direct line installed from Albany to the command center at Chicago's Congress Hotel. *Roosevelt Library*

Louis McHenry Howe, Roosevelt's alter ego and confidant, spent twenty years grooming him for the presidency. Throughout the convention, he never left Suite 1702.
Roosevelt Library

Campaign manager James A. Farley was more hopeful than confident in predicting a first-ballot Roosevelt nomination.
Wide World

In an attempt to sway uncommitted delegates, Farley put up a map at the Congress Hotel that showed FDR had more support than all his rivals combined. But it overstated Roosevelt's vote. *Chicago Sun-Times*

Former New York governor Alfred E. Smith, arriving in Chicago with his wife, Catherine, had the second-largest bloc of delegates and was the sentimental favorite among newspapermen covering the convention. *Chicago Sun-Times*

Former Virginia governor Harry F. Byrd (*left*), the Old Dominion's favorite son, got celebrity support from his brother, Admiral Richard E. Byrd, famed explorer of the South Pole. *Wide World*

Oklahoma governor "Alfalfa Bill" Murray threatened to lead a third-party movement if Roosevelt's forces overturned the two-thirds rule. *Chicago Sun-Times*

Mayors Frank Hague of Jersey City, Jimmy Walker of New York, and Anton J. Cermak of Chicago were leaders of the "Stop Roosevelt" alliance. *Wide World*

Cermak, taking a lunch break at the stadium, controlled the galleries and the convention hall. His companion is Michael Igoe, Illinois Democratic national committeeman. *Chicago Sun-Times*

Al·Smith (*left*) and
William G. McAdoo,
whose bitter rivalry
split the Democratic
Party in 1924, made up
in Chicago and plotted
how to stop Roosevelt.
Wide World

Clarence Darrow,
Chicago's renowned
lawyer, attended the
convention as a
Roosevelt supporter.
Chicago Daily News

Jane Addams, winner of the 1931 Nobel Peace Prize, lobbied for a peace plank in the Democratic platform. *Chicago Daily News*

In the most important credentials fight of the convention, Senator Huey Long of Louisiana made the case for the seating of his delegation. *Chicago Sun-Times*

Boston mayor James Michael Curley, whose Roosevelt slate was trounced in the Massachusetts primary, seconded FDR's nomination as a delegate from Puerto Rico. *Wide World*

Former senator Gilbert Hitchcock announcing that the Democratic platform advocated the repeal of Prohibition. Across the great hall, Democrats cheered the return of legalized liquor. *Chicago Sun-Times*

Listening to the convention on radio, FDR would not comment about his prospects. *Roosevelt Library*

During the Roosevelt demonstration, the candidate's sons James and Franklin Junior carried the New York standard. On the right, sporting an FDR button, is Roosevelt's son-in-law, Curtis Dall. *Chicago Daily News*

Garner and Byrd had modest demonstrations. Although Ritchie got more cheers in the hall than Roosevelt, the shouts were from the nonvoting galleries. *Wide World*

For sheer emotion, the Smith parade topped them all. *Chicago Sun-Times*

At the beginning of the Roosevelt demonstration, stadium organist Al Melgard played "Anchors Away," which had been the candidate's theme song, but switched to "Happy Days Are Here Again." *Kaufmann & Fabry Studio*

Tammany Hall boss John F. Curry (1) led a New York delegation that included Judge Daniel F. Cohalan (2); Smith (3); Max Steuer (4); Mayor James J. Walker (5); Dudley Field Malone (6); and Brooklyn leader John McCooey (7). *Chicago Daily News*

Mississippi senator Pat Harrison, who returned to his downtown hotel after the second ballot, thought that the convention had adjourned. When he learned otherwise, Harrison rushed back to the hall to hold his state in line for FDR.
Chicago Daily News

After the all-night session, crowds flocked out of the stadium. *Chicago Sun-Times*

Michael G. McAdoo, once the crown prince of American politics, became the kingmaker of the Chicago convention in announcing California's switch to Roosevelt on the fourth ballot. *Wide World*

Embarking on the first flight in the history of American presidential politics, FDR showed there was nothing to fear from air travel. *Roosevelt Library*

On Roosevelt's arrival in Chicago, efforts at crowd control turned into bedlam.
Chicago Daily News

At the airport, FDR greets the cheering throng and is met by daughter
Anna Dall, FDR Jr., James, and campaign manager Farley. *Roosevelt Library*

Accepting the nomination, FDR pledges "a New Deal for the American people." James Roosevelt and his wife, Betsey, are sitting next to Eleanor. *Chicago Sun-Times*

In a masterful performance, Roosevelt takes command of the Democratic Party and gives hope to a troubled nation. "This is more than a political campaign," he asserted, "this is a call to arms." *Roosevelt Library*

Returning to Chicago in the fall of 1932, FDR threw out the first ball of the World Series between the Cubs and the New York Yankees. He is flanked by son James and Mayor Cermak. *Chicago Sun-Times*

speculation in 1932 that President Hoover might nominate the Democratic senator for the Supreme Court.

Walsh, seventy-three years old and a twenty-year member of the Senate, told Farley before the Hyde Park meeting that Roosevelt "ought to have someone else in mind" for the chairmanship because Walsh had voted for tariffs to protect the lumber industry in his state. Senator Alben Barkley of Kentucky, following his selection as temporary chairman, was criticized by Roosevelt's camp when he broke party lines to support a tariff on coal. "The fuss raised about Barkley's voting for a duty on coal may be renewed with emphasis should I be made permanent chairman," Walsh wrote privately. "Be good enough to write me about the matter and be assured I have not the slightest ambition to fill the place if you and the others in charge of the campaign think it unwise, under the circumstances, for me to be the choice."

But Roosevelt forces needed a candidate of Walsh's stature to take on Shouse, who had a two-month head start in building support among delegates. There were few decisions more badly handled by the Roosevelt camp than those involving the leadership of the convention. Shouse, who had not been straight with FDR, was double-crossed in return. Walsh's integrity and credibility made it easier for Roosevelt to sell his candidacy for permanent chairman.[7]

Another obstacle to Roosevelt's nomination was the two-thirds rule. Even though he had locked up the support of more than 600 of the 1,154 delegates, a majority would not be enough. Under a century-old rule, the Democratic presidential candidate had to be nominated with at least two-thirds of the vote. If Smith, Garner, Ritchie, and the favorite sons held together, Roosevelt was vulnerable. Walsh feared that Democrats could be headed for an encore of the debacle at Madison Square Garden. "If we could nominate Governor Roosevelt without any serious contest, say before as many as five ballots have been taken, his [nomination and election] would be assured," he predicted. "If the thing drags out our chances wane with every succeeding ballot."[8]

As Roosevelt understood better than anyone, leading contenders ran into trouble. It would be difficult for Roosevelt to overturn the two-thirds rule because in the Deep South, his strongest region, most Democratic leaders were opposed to a rules change. But unless the two-thirds rule was abrogated, chances were slim that a deadlock could be avoided at Chicago Stadium. FDR, though, was reluctant to publicly challenge the supermajority rule. "By the way, about the two-thirds rule, my thought is that it is an anachronism anyway, and, as you know, particularly in conventions," he wrote privately. "Nevertheless I hesitate to say anything about it because it might sound like a confession of weakness at this particular moment."

Walsh had similar misgivings. "It would, it seems to me, be a confession of weakness on the part of supporters of the leading candidate to urge the adoption of a majority rule effective at once," he commented.[9]

Several methods of ending the two-thirds rule were suggested at the Hyde Park meeting. FDR reiterated his view that the rule should be abolished and that was the consensus view of those gathered in the living room. But Roosevelt deferred action on this issue until the weekend before the convention and asked Farley to be his "direct representative" and "handle the entire situation."

Roosevelt would not be attending the convention but asked the group whether he should break tradition by making an appearance at Chicago Stadium if he won the nomination. Since before the Civil War it had been the custom in both political parties for candidates to be formally notified of their nomination in ceremonies held weeks after the convention in their hometown. "General discussion as to whether or not it is advisable for him to appear at the convention," Farley wrote in his diary, "and it was agreed he would show up and make a short speech from seven to ten minutes."

Hull, who had been working on the platform since the previous fall, was the group's unanimous choice as chairman of the Resolutions Committee. On Farley's recommendation, Arthur Mullen of Nebraska was chosen as Roosevelt's floor leader for the convention. Kremer was selected as chairman of the convention Rules Committee, but the committees on permanent organization and credentials were left open as bargaining chips for uncommitted delegates. It was decided that Farley would open headquarters at the Congress Hotel in Chicago at least two weeks in advance of the convention. "Decided . . . that we would try to get our people on the job as early as possible," Farley noted, "and get our program definitely formulated before the opening so it would be thoroughly understood what we have in mind."[10]

Roosevelt wanted his nominating speech to be delivered by a fellow New Yorker. Senator Robert F. Wagner, sponsor of the 1932 Emergency Relief and Construction Act, had quietly declined an invitation because he was up for reelection and reluctant to alienate Tammany Hall. Another reason Wagner took a pass is that he had longtime ties to Smith. "He is a smart fellow but has no courage; is always afraid of being put on the spot," Farley observed. "He is always fearful of having to take sides."[11]

The journalist and historian Claude G. Bowers, who had written readable and insightful books about Andrew Jackson and Thomas Jefferson, was Roosevelt's second choice to give the nominating speech. A native of Indiana where he won the state oratorical contest in 1898, Bowers became prominent in Democratic politics as the chief editorial writer for the old *Indianapolis Sentinel*. In making hundreds of speeches for the Democratic Party, he became known as the "Gatling Gun Orator of the Wabash" for his dramatic, quick-fire delivery. Bowers moved to New York in 1923 as an editorial writer for Joseph Pulitzer's *New York World* and became friendly with Roosevelt who admired his studies of Jackson and Jefferson. "I am thrilled at the prospect of another book from your pen," FDR wrote in the late 1920s. After publication of *The Tragic Era,* a book about Reconstruction, Roosevelt wrote Bowers: "The book has had, more than any other in recent years, a very definite influence on public thought. In addition, the book has done much to bring back a great many erring members of our party." At the 1928 Democratic National Convention in Houston, where Roosevelt nominated Smith, Bowers delivered a rousing keynote address in which he alleged that "privilege and pillage" were the legacy of the Harding-Coolidge years.[12]

"It was the consensus of opinion that Bowers is the best one to do the job," Farley noted. After the meeting, Senator Wheeler telephoned Bowers and told him that it "had been the unanimous decision that I should be asked to render a certain service, which all hoped I would give."

When Bowers was summoned to the Executive Mansion in Albany, he assumed that he would be invited to give the nominating speech. "Nothing could have been more embarrassing, because of several complications," Bowers recalled. "I was writing a political column for all the Hearst papers and it would appear daily during the convention in Chicago. At that time, Hearst was supporting the candidacy of Speaker Jack Garner. While my contract left me free in such matters, I could see that the delivery of the speech might be embarrassing to the paper in Chicago." Another problem was that Bowers had already agreed to be a member of Tammany Hall's delegation to the Chicago convention. "I had no idea what the position of the organization would be in the convention," he later wrote.

Roosevelt was in a jovial mood when Bowers arrived at the mansion. The governor had a servant bring them two bottles of beer. Then FDR got down to business and asked his friend to give the nominating speech. He had often talked with the historian about Jefferson but on this occasion cited Andrew Jackson as his model for presidential leadership. Roosevelt declared that he wanted a "fighting Jackson speech." Bowers "had no doubt of his complete adherence to the Jeffersonian principles of democracy, but he clearly had a preference for Jackson's methods."

Though honored by this invitation, Bowers explained that he might have a professional conflict. "I felt I could not agree without getting the consent of Hearst," he later wrote.

"Is there anything I can do?" Roosevelt asked. "Can I get Hearst on the telephone?" As FDR reached for the phone, Bowers cautioned "that this would be the surest way to get a negative answer, and that it would be better for me to submit the matter to him through the office."[13]

Given the trouble Hearst had caused Roosevelt, it would have been generous if the publisher had allowed Bowers to deliver the nominating speech for FDR. The Jefferson biographer was not the only big-name writer who would be covering the Chicago convention for the Hearst newspapers. Front-page columnist Arthur Brisbane, Damon Runyon, Will Rogers, Senator Pat Harrison, war correspondent Floyd Gibbons, novelist Mary Synon, former heavyweight boxing champion Gene Tunney, and humorist Bugs Baer were already being promoted as "one of the greatest galaxies of writers and political authorities ever gathered together."

Hearst responded promptly when asked whether Bowers could give the speech. "While I would not think of interfering in any way with Mr. Bowers' personal or political views and preferences, I think it would be less embarrassing to the papers," he wired from San Simeon, "if he did not too intimately identify himself with any one candidacy."

A disappointed Bowers sent the telegram with a note to FDR.

"Please do not take it too much to heart that things did not work out as we hoped," Roosevelt answered. "You must of course do what seems wise and for the best interest of all concerned. Certainly I would be the last to ask you to go against your own better judgment."

This would not be the last time that Bowers disappointed Roosevelt. As a Tammany Hall delegate from Manhattan, Bowers would follow the instructions of John F. Curry at the convention and vote down the line against FDR.[14]

16

MAGIC NUMBER

THE LAKEFRONT Congress Hotel overlooking Grant Park and Buckingham Fountain on South Michigan Avenue had long been known as "the home of the presidents" and was back in the limelight as the command post for the 1932 Democratic National Convention. Originally built as the Annex to Louis Sullivan's remarkable Auditorium, the hotel had opened for the 1893 Chicago World's Fair and would be renamed the Congress in 1911. From Grover Cleveland through Calvin Coolidge, seven of the nation's chief executives had stayed in the hotel's Presidential Suite.

The second floor of the hotel, along a red-carpeted hallway about five feet wide and a hundred yards long, housed the campaign offices for seven of the men vying for the Democratic nomination. The John Nance Garner banner hailed him as "a vital American," while Al Smith touted himself as "the man with a program," and Harry F. Byrd was "the farmer, the governor, the American." To show more flair, Farley portrayed his candidate as unstoppable, by placing a large map of the

United States with FDR territory colored in red. More than three-fourths of the country's geographical area was in crimson. "The map was one of those details that did not seem especially important at the time," Farley remembered. "But after the convention many delegates told me that it impressed them in graphic fashion with the fact that the Governor was actually the majority choice."[1]

The map showed that Roosevelt had a decisive lead over the field and a clear majority of the delegates, but that still wasn't enough. Heading into the convention, FDR was about 100 votes short of the 770 needed to win the nomination. If the opposition did not yield, this magic number could not be achieved. At three of the five previous Democratic conventions, this rule had slowed and ultimately stopped the front-runner. Since the Civil War there had never been a leader on the first ballot to gain the nomination if the convention went more than four ballots. "Never in my experience," former *New York World* editor Herbert Bayard Swope wrote his brother from Chicago, "was a convention so ripe for the picking."[2]

FDR's dilemma had confounded front-runners for generations and dated back to the party's first convention. President Andrew Jackson summoned Democrats to Baltimore in 1832 for the purpose of nominating Martin Van Buren as his vice-presidential candidate. The Jacksonians approved the rule "that two-thirds of the whole number of the votes in the convention shall be necessary to constitute a choice." William R. King, a member of the committee that drafted this rule, argued that "a nomination made by two-thirds of the whole body would show a more general concurrence of sentiment in favor of a particular individual, would carry with it a greater moral weight and be more favorably received than one made by a smaller number."

From the start, this rule sparked controversy. During the 1832 convention, the *Baltimore Republican* reported that a Virginia delegate "objected to the proposition for two-thirds as inconsistent with the fundamental principle upon which our government is founded, which provide that the rule of the majority shall prevail and because it might possibly be found to be impracticable to unite the voices of so large a proportion in favor of any one individual."[3]

Under the two-thirds rule, conventions mattered. To attain the nomination, presidential contenders had to fight until the last roll call. As a result of the two-thirds rule, the delegates were empowered and conventions were deliberative. Van Buren, for whom the rule was enacted, was its first casualty. After winning the presidency in 1836 and losing reelection four years later, he attempted a comeback in 1844. Van Buren's camp tried to eliminate the two-thirds rule, but this effort failed when 20 percent of his delegates voted against this change. On the first ballot, the former president got nearly two-thirds of the vote and led his nearest opponent by more than three to one. But his lead slipped on the second ballot and the erosion could not be contained. In the first great convention upset, the long shot James Knox Polk won a ninth ballot nomination.

It was not unusual for delegates to take their time. In three of the five conventions before 1932, the Democratic presidential balloting went for at least forty-four roll calls. House Speaker Champ Clark of Missouri, who led for twenty-nine ballots and commanded a majority for eight, could not overcome the two-thirds barrier at the 1912 convention in Baltimore. "That rule was a device of the pro-slavery propagandists to enable them to nominate Democratic candidates for the presidency in whom they could trust and in whose hand they felt that their interests would be safe," Champ wrote in his memoirs. "The pro-slavery men could not muster a majority of a convention, but they controlled more than one-third. Hence the two-thirds rule." At more than half of the Democratic Party's conventions since 1832, the early leader failed to attain the nomination.[4]

If William Gibbs McAdoo had changed the rules at the 1924 Democratic National Convention, he would have been the nominee. Before the Madison Square Garden convention, his strategists considered whether to abolish the two-thirds rule. Roosevelt, then serving as Smith's convention floor manager, defended the rule: "Leaving out the question of Smith, McAdoo, or any other candidate, I doubt if any rules of the convention should be changed after the delegates are elected."[5]

Now that Roosevelt found himself in a position similar to that of McAdoo eight years previously, he felt differently. Unless a simple majority ruled, there was a good chance that the Chicago convention would be long and drawn out. Yet FDR was reluctant publicly to challenge the supermajority rule.

On the night of Thursday, June 23, Farley presided over a meeting in the eleventh-floor Presidential Suite of the Congress Hotel attended by sixty-five leaders representing Roosevelt's delegations. His opening remarks made no reference to the two-thirds rule. Farley intended to discuss this matter with a smaller group later that night. "Almost before what we realized was taking place," he later recalled, "the meeting was stampeded into taking hasty and ill-advised action."[6]

Senator Huey Pierce Long of Louisiana, a spellbinding orator and important Roosevelt ally, took charge of the meeting. Denouncing the financial interests opposing FDR, he then introduced a resolution: "That it be the sense of this gathering of the friends of Franklin D. Roosevelt that we pledge ourselves to do all within our power to bring about the abolition of the two-thirds rule and the adoption of the majority rule in this Democratic convention."

Long was preaching to the converted. The Roosevelt forces, smoldering over Hague's vicious attack, were eager to crush the opposition through any means necessary. Senator Burton K. Wheeler of Montana, earliest ally among the western progressives, made a compelling argument for the rules change. Josephus Daniels of North Carolina, FDR's old boss at the Navy Department, said that the Roosevelt forces should refuse "to be hog-tied by a small element bent upon killing off the candidate shown to be the choice of the people." Senator Cordell Hull of Tennessee, a former Democratic national chairman, called for abolishing the rule, noting that "forces of destruction were trying to ruin the Democratic party." A dazed Farley allowed Long to second his own motion. After the resolution passed without a dissenting vote, Rules Committee chairman Bruce Kremer vowed to present the rules change to the full convention.

"The incident hit me like a blow on the nose," Farley later wrote. "My confidence was badly shaken for the first time. Besides that, there was no disguising the fact that the blame was mine for letting the meeting get out of hand, even though there wasn't any way to prevent it. I was annoyed and uncertain about what to do." Another Roosevelt strategist, Molly Dewson, remembered that Farley "looked bewildered, confused and pathetic."[7]

Farley could not reach FDR because a thunderstorm in upstate New York had downed some telephone wires. After a lengthy delay, he finally made a connection. Roosevelt took the news calmly and suggested a poll of their delegates to determine whether they could win a floor vote. A simple majority could abrogate the rule. Above all, the governor told Farley to control the resolution so that he could make a graceful retreat if necessary.

Years later, Farley said the runaway meeting was part of a calculated strategy. Before the meeting at the Congress, he had obtained FDR's approval to get rid of the two-thirds rule, which meant the nomination could be had by a simple majority of 578 votes. As a ploy, Roosevelt's camp decided to make it look as if Farley had lost control of the meeting.

Edward J. Flynn said that this was to "make it appear" that the governor had not taken the initiative.

Roosevelt played it to the hilt. Another participant in the meeting, who was unaware that this controversial decision had been cleared in advance, called FDR to get his reaction. "Why ask me what I think about it?" he answered. "You have done it. Why ask me what I think about it now?"[8]

If Roosevelt declined public comment, he could not avoid the crossfire. As James A. Hagerty reported in the *New York Times*, the effort to abolish the two-thirds rule was "the most sensational development in a national convention since 1912." More than any other event of the Democratic presidential race, the fight over the two-thirds rule united Roosevelt's opposition. "The spirit of American fair play will not tolerate any eleventh-hour, unsportsmanlike attempt to change the rules after the game has been started," Smith declared. "This radical change sounds like a cry for a life preserver."[9]

"They're hanging a millstone around his [Roosevelt's] neck," said John W. Davis, the 1924 Democratic presidential nominee, an at-large member of the New York delegation in Chicago.

Governor Richard B. Russell of Georgia, a Roosevelt stalwart, was untroubled by this argument, asserted that the two-thirds rule was unfair, and vowed to fight for its elimination. "The thing must be done, should have been done before, and will be done now," said Farley, whose initial count showed 697 delegates in favor of the change, 119 more than Roosevelt needed.

Texas congressman Sam Rayburn, Garner's campaign manager, asserted, "Mr. Farley should not, however desperate he may become, undertake to change the rules of the national Democratic convention for the single hope of nominating one man." From Cleveland, Newton Baker broke his silence. "Every member of the Democratic party who knows its traditions and is proud of its history has a duty to protest against the proposed abandonment of the two-thirds rule," he said. "Our representatives at Chicago have no right to change that rule after we have instructed our delegates. . . . Sensitive men would find it difficult to defend a candidate who started out with a moral flaw in his title."

Albert Ritchie, announcing that Maryland would vote for retention of the two-thirds rule, expressed regret that the divisive issue was being raised. McAdoo defended the century-old tradition and found fault with Roosevelt for attempting to rewrite the rules. Joseph T. Tumulty, who had been Wilson's chief aide, said that the late president believed in the sanctity of the rule and accused FDR of putting himself above the party.

"What was good enough for Andrew Jackson," thundered former senator James A. Reed of Missouri, "should be good enough for the rest of us." Murray threatened to organize a third party if Roosevelt succeeded in changing the rule. A strategist for the Stop Roosevelt forces came up with the idea of asking delegates to sign a pledge withholding their support from any candidate who won the nomination by changing the rules.

Former Ohio governor James M. Cox, the party's 1920 presidential nominee, whose choice of Roosevelt for the vice presidency made him a national figure, came out against his former running mate's proposal as "unworthy of our traditions." Ely Culbertson, the nation's leading authority on contract bridge, wired the Democratic National Committee: "In a straight game you cannot change the rules after the cards are dealt."

The Roosevelt ranks were beginning to break. Former senator Gilbert Hitchcock of Nebraska, FDR's selection as chairman of the Platform Committee, described the action of the Thursday night caucus as a "tactical mistake." In his view, Roosevelt still had a good chance to win under the existing rule and "the proposition to abolish the two-thirds rule would stir up unwarranted opposition."

Senator Pat Harrison of Mississippi, who was holding his state for Roosevelt by a single vote under the unit rule, said that the proposed rules change was "foolhardy and asinine." He would not object to changing the rule at the next convention but not "while the game is in progress." Senator Tom Connally of Texas, who had been chosen by Garner to deliver his nominating speech, said: "The Roosevelt people in threatening to abrogate the two-thirds rule are making a blunder and endangering party success. The party is bigger than any individual."[10]

Farley, taking his instructions from Roosevelt, responded that this criticism was misguided: "It is a grossly inaccurate statement to say that the friends of Governor Roosevelt have decided to 'abrogate' the two-thirds rule. There is no two-thirds rule at present binding on the convention, which will meet Monday. Nor will that convention be bound by any rule whatever except such rules as the delegates deliberately vote for after the convention is organized."

The two-thirds rule could "only be imposed upon a convention by a deliberative affirmative vote of the convention itself," Farley asserted. "Our contention is that this affirmative action should not be taken— that it has been outgrown and has been productive of disruption even to the extent of undoubtedly ruining all chance of Democratic success in 1924. That we should again deliberately lay ourselves open to the disaster of a minority control by again adopting the indefensible two-thirds rule merely because of its age is as absurd to insist that we should ride in post-coaches because they were the custom of our forefathers."

As a possible compromise, some party figures suggested amending the rule for future conventions. FDR in 1924 had made a similar recommendation. "It is foolish to talk about this convention abrogating the two-thirds rule for the next convention," Farley said. "This cannot be done. Each convention is a rule unto itself and makes its own rules."[11]

Judge Samuel Seabury, on arriving in town for the convention, handed down his opinion. "There are good reasons for adhering to the two-thirds rule. Like the principles upon which our government is established, it is designed to protect not only the rights of the majority, but of the minority as well," the judge asserted. "The maintenance of this tradition and the other reasons which support the rule are too important to be sacrificed to a rule or ruin policy in the personal interests of one candidate."

In making this argument, the judge aligned himself with the political machine he was trying to put out of business. "We will fight the abrogation of the two-thirds rule to the last ditch," vowed Tammany leader John F. Curry. At a caucus of the New York delegation, sixty-five voted with Curry, while only twenty-seven backed a rules change. Farley had been counting on a minimum of thirty-nine votes from his home state.

As the debate became heated, fistfights broke out in the Missouri caucus and some delegates walked out. The Iowa delegation, which favored Roosevelt, broke with him on the rules change. Farley had hoped for an even split among the fifty-eight Illinois delegates. But Mayor Anton Cermak announced that he supported retention of the old rule and locked up forty-eight votes for his side.

Roosevelt now faced trouble in his strongest region. Angered by the proposed change, Senator Josiah W. Bailey of North Carolina warned Farley and Flynn that FDR had put his southern support at risk. "He told us that we would not only lose the votes of North Carolina," recalled Flynn, "but that we would alienate every other southern state if we persisted in raising the question." Mayor W. A. Gunter of Montgomery, in an open letter, implored delegates to uphold "the birthright of the South" and reject "the emotions of temporary expediency."[12]

In the Deep South, John Sharp Williams of Mississippi embodied the old traditions and was the region's most beloved political figure. The son and grandson of Confederate officers who died in battle, he was later described by W. J. Cash in *The Mind of the South* as "one of the most notable men the South has produced since the Civil War." Although he supported segregation, the aristocratic Williams deplored racial politics and a quarter century earlier had ridiculed Governor James Kimble Vardaman's proposal to repeal the Fifteenth Amendment that gave blacks voting rights. His narrow triumph over Vardaman in their bitter 1907 senatorial primary was hailed nationally as a victory for moderation. During his long and distinguished public career, he lectured about Thomas Jefferson at Columbia University, served as House minority leader, temporary chairman of the 1904 Democratic National Convention, and as a member of the Senate, where he was President Wilson's ally and confidant. For a generation, he was among the Democratic Party's more respected voices. Since retiring in 1923 to the shades of his 3,000-acre Cedar Grove plantation, he guarded his privacy and stayed out of politics. But when former Senate colleague James Reed alerted him from Chicago of the Roosevelt proposal, Williams felt compelled to speak out for the first time in a decade.

"The two-thirds rule has been for a century the South's defense," Williams answered in a telegram to Reed. "It would be idiotic on her part to surrender it."[13]

This was the most punishing blow to the Roosevelt cause. Mississippi promptly voted against the proposed change. From Albany, Roosevelt appealed by loudspeaker telephone to the North Carolina caucus but got nowhere. The Tar Heel delegates overwhelmingly voted for retention of the rule. As the Alabama delegation joined the opposition, Roosevelt's strategists learned of growing dissension in the Tennessee, Kentucky, and South Carolina delegations. Senator James F. Byrnes of

South Carolina, who privately disagreed with the move against the rule, held his state in line out of loyalty to FDR. Elsewhere in the South, support faded.

Overall, there had been more than a hundred defections. On June 27, the opening day of the convention, the *New York Times* reported that support for FDR on this issue had fallen to 584 votes, with 565 for the opposition. He needed 578 votes to abolish the rule but the momentum was shifting against him, and Roosevelt called off the fight. "This is no time for petty strife and momentary advantage," he wired Farley from Albany. "That truth becomes more apparent when an honest difference of judgment is exaggerated by the opposition press into grave internal dissension. . . . I believe, and always have believed that the two-thirds rule should no longer be adopted. It is undemocratic."

Then, FDR told Farley that "the issue was not raised until after the delegates to the convention had been selected and I decline to permit either myself or my friends to be open to the accusation of poor sportsmanship or to the use of methods which could be called, even falsely, those of a steam roller. I am accordingly asking my friends in Chicago to cease their activities to secure the adoption of the majority nominating rule. . . . I trust, however, that the committee on rules may recommend some rule to insure against the catastrophe of a deadlock or prolonged balloting."[14]

On learning of Roosevelt's new proposal, Frank Hague replied with another personal attack. "It confirms my previous charge that he is lacking in loyalty to his friends," declared the Jersey City boss. "He encouraged them in the fight on the two-thirds rule. Then when it became apparent that he could not win he abandoned them all."

Under the circumstances, the FDR camp had no choice. "We found we did not have enough to carry it," Farley wrote in his diary, "or if we did the margin would be so slender that we would lose prestige."

Howe, who arrived in town as the controversy was breaking, told Farley and Flynn that they had been foolish "to go out on such a limb." Adviser Samuel I. Rosenman, who was staying that week with the Roosevelts at the Executive Mansion in Albany, wrote later that the move against the rule was "the major mistake" of the convention. "It was unfair to try to change the rules, for our own benefit, in the middle of the game," he recalled. "The attempt created great resentment in Chicago; it was responsible for much hard feeling which, had it persisted, might have cost Roosevelt the nomination."[15]

In his retreat, FDR was also looking beyond the convention. "If he gets the nomination, he wants it to be worth something," a friend said after talking with the governor. "He will need all the support he can get."

After this setback for Roosevelt, the *New York Times* reported that pressure was building for the nomination of Baker or Ritchie. "Any man who cannot secure the vote of two-thirds of the delegates," Smith defiantly asserted, "should not be the nominee of the convention."[16]

17

RAINBOW

J AMES HAMILTON LEWIS, the only sitting U.S. senator to seek the presidency in 1932, rolled up a larger vote in the primaries than Al Smith or John Nance Garner and headed into the convention fourth in the delegate count with fifty-eight pledged votes from his home state of Illinois. If Lewis endorsed Roosevelt and released these delegates, Farley believed that FDR had a good chance to win on the first ballot. Lewis had no chance of winning the nomination and he was more openly sympathetic to Roosevelt than any of the favorite sons.[1]

"J. Ham," as he was known, had long been the most elegant dresser in American politics, wearing perfectly tailored London suits with wing collar, billowing cravat, silk handkerchief, and gloves. When he was named by the Democratic caucus in 1913 as the first party whip in the history of the Senate, Lewis dressed for the occasion in top hat, formal black cutaway coat, and white vest. He often carried a walking stick, wore beribboned glasses, and introduced spats to North America. As a young lawyer in Seattle, he grew the Vandyke beard and dressed in bright colors to attract business. The starchy Thomas B. Reed of Maine, who was House Speaker when Lewis was a young congressman from the state of Washington, dismissed him as "that garrulous rainbow." A later House Speaker, Champ Clark, asserted that Lewis was "the greatest dude in America." Others nicknamed him "The Aurora Borealis of Illinois," "Jim the Whisk," and "Pink Whiskers." By 1932, his beard and mustache made him look like a throwback to the days of McKinley. But they also set him apart. Later in the decade, when the new *Life* magazine needed a distinctive face for the cover story about the Senate, its editors chose Margaret Bourke-White's unforgettable portrait of the old dandy.

"He's a strange combination of shrewdness, political, oratorical and legal ability, foppishness, and affectation. In the few months of his present term," Rodney Dutcher reported from Washington, "he has been more remarked for his habit of using and mixing the rainbow's colors than for any special legislative activity."

A shameless flirt, he once stopped an attractive young woman in front of the Senate Office Building, raised his hat, and asked: "My dear, can you direct me to the Senate Office Building?"

"Yes, I can," she replied. "And I can tell you that the number of your suite is 111, Senator."[2]

Lewis had a background even more colorful than his wardrobe. A native of Virginia, he was born in 1863 just after his father, a major in the Confederate Army, fell wounded in the Civil War. By the time he was a senator, Lewis was deceptive about his age. Lewis spent most of his youth in Augusta, Georgia, then studied briefly at the University of Virginia. On leaving Charlottesville, he headed for Savannah to read for the law and was admitted to the bar in 1882. Seeking to make his fortune on the Pacific Coast, he landed in San Francisco and took a job as a newspaper reporter before moving to Seattle and working as a longshoreman. He soon established a law practice, began teaching rhetoric at the University of Washington, and went into Democratic politics.

In 1887, Lewis, at twenty-four, was elected to Washington's last territorial legislature. Two years later, Washington would be admitted to the union as the forty-second state and only state named after a president of the United States. Soon afterward, he presided over the state's first Democratic convention. Elected to the state's only congressional seat by a plurality of 396 votes in 1896, Lewis sponsored legislation that preserved the majestic snow-capped Mount Rainier as a national park. Edged out for reelection in 1898, he served as an inspector general with the rank of colonel during the Spanish-American War in Cuba, Puerto Rico, and the Philippines.

After the turn of the century, he relocated in Chicago where he resumed the practice of law and was active in Edward F. Dunne's successful 1905 race for mayor. Appointed by Dunne as corporation counsel, Lewis helped pass laws that made it possible for the city to lower utility rates. Dunne was elected governor in 1912 and soon persuaded the legislature to choose his friend as U.S. senator. Just two months into his term, Lewis became the second-ranking Democrat in the Senate.

Lewis rounded up the votes that helped pass Woodrow Wilson's New Freedom legislative agenda including the graduated income tax, creation of the Federal Reserve, stronger antitrust laws, and the eight-hour workday for railroad workers. One of the Democratic Party's most effective orators, he was enlisted by Wilson in 1916 as his chief surrogate in the Far West. Lewis delivered a series of hard-hitting speeches that contributed to a near-sweep of states that were crucial to Wilson's narrow margin over Charles Evans Hughes.

A staunch supporter of Wilson's foreign policy, including American intervention in the Great War, Lewis went to the Western Front as Wilson's representative. At the shell-torn battlefield of Château-Thierry, he was grazed in the cheek by a sniper's fire as the army's Second and Third Divisions helped thwart the German offensive. On his return voyage, a German torpedo struck the *Mount Vernon,* but Lewis was uninjured. He was later awarded the U.S. Military Order of the World War and was also decorated by the governments of France, Belgium, and Great Britain. His internationalism may have cost him a second term in 1918 as he was narrowly defeated by the wealthy isolationist Medill McCormick.

After this setback, Lewis declined Wilson's offer to nominate him as ambassador to Belgium. Few senators had more foreign policy experience. Beginning in 1889, when President Benjamin Harrison sent him to London as a member of the panel that negotiated a dispute between the United States and Canada over the Alaskan boundary, he carried out a multitude of diplomatic assignments for presidents of both parties. Lewis was involved in the annexation of Hawaii as a territory, helped draft the treaty under which Spain surrendered Puerto Rico, and served on a commission that regulated customs laws with Canada. Wilson sent him to London as part of a team that negotiated international laws for the sea. Another reason that his foreign policy views could not be easily ignored was that Lewis chaired the Senate committee that had oversight over the State Department's budget. In the boom decade of the twenties, Lewis became one of the country's leading international lawyers, representing American oil companies in the Middle East and the government of Mexico for whom he negotiated a $28 million loan. "Senator Lewis, as one of the elder statesmen, has had an almost unparalleled continuity of experience with our foreign relations," the young Loop lawyer Adlai E. Stevenson said in introducing Lewis to the Chicago Council on Foreign Relations.

When Stevenson wrote Lewis for background to make this introduction, the senator responded, "As the folks at home know me enough to dislike me quite cordially or feel kindly generosity, it would be quite sufficient to call attention that 'this is Lewis.' "[3]

The former senator made a comeback in 1930 when Cermak engineered the party's endorsement for his old seat. He had lost none of his skills. "Colorful, brilliant J. Ham, with his classical torrents of eloquence, rapier repartee and ability to paint pictures vividly," recalled Chicago political writer William H. Stuart, "was the master of audiences of all classes, from all walks of life, never at a loss for witty, incisive replies." Walter Trohan, who covered the Lewis comeback for the *Chicago Tribune*, added, "He had an absolute genius for leaving out the commitment clause on any controversial issue, so that listeners on both sides of any question could feel that he was with them heart and soul."[4]

His opponent, Congresswoman-At-Large Ruth Hanna McCormick, daughter of political boss Mark Hanna and widow of the man who had ousted Lewis, had won her party's nomination by defeating the aging Republican incumbent. Setting an Illinois vote record that has stood for more than seventy years, Lewis recaptured his old seat with 64 percent of the vote. When Roosevelt won his second term as governor, he got a larger overall vote in New York, but Lewis won by eight more percentage points and a bigger plurality.[5]

By any measure, it was an extraordinary comeback. If Lewis had been twenty years younger and more understated in his sartorial choices, he might have been a genuine contender in 1932. "Qualities which aid a man among the home people may hurt him nationally. The rise of James Hamilton Lewis, for instance, was expedited in Illinois by the eccentric elegance of his dress and whiskers. Lewis is a man of ability," Alva Johnston observed in the convention-week edition of *The Forum*. "The tale of his climb from longshoreman to senator is more stirring than the life story of any of his rivals. But the country would never allow in the White House a man whose whiskers have been a national jest for more than forty years."[6]

Mayor Cermak had no illusions about making Lewis president. Through Lewis the mayor controlled federal patronage. "He'll make the appointments," said Cermak, "but I'll give him the names." In June 1931, more than a year before the convention, he summoned party leaders to City Hall and informed them that Lewis would be the state's favorite son. "Not only did Cermak desire freedom of action with respect to the various aspirants for the nomination," the mayor's biographer Alex Gottfried later wrote, "he wanted to allay rumors connecting him with a Smith-Tammany stop-Roosevelt movement."[7]

Some months later, Lewis began having second thoughts about being used for brokerage purposes. "Lewis called in person on the Governor and assured him that he was for him and only wanted a complimentary vote," Howe advised Daniel C. Roper. Former governor Dunne, a longtime Lewis ally, had been named by Cermak to the Illinois delegation and was openly for Roosevelt. "We knew that Senator Lewis did not for a moment regard himself as a serious contender and that he was extremely friendly to the candidacy of the New York governor," Farley later wrote. "After receiving a complimentary vote, we felt that he was willing to have the Illinois delegation switch perhaps before the result of the ballot was announced."

Trohan confided to Farley that Lewis was ready to break with Cermak. If Roosevelt's manager approached Lewis, Trohan said, "he would find him itching to lead a revolt that would chip a few votes from the Cermak bloc."[8]

As the convention approached, Farley made another run at the Chicago mayor. "Did not get anywhere," Farley wrote in his diary. "He indicated to me that he did not know what they would do because Lewis, of course, was insisting on a complimentary vote." At a meeting of the delegation, Cermak crushed a move to endorse Roosevelt as the alternative choice. "We in Chicago have no second choice," he declared. "We are with Senator Lewis so long as he stays in the field."[9]

On the eve of the convention, Lewis took himself out of the game. "Please say to the Illinois delegation," he wired Cermak, "that I release each and all from any obligation. . . . I will not assume to direct or even suggest any individual or joint action for the delegation." Lewis also sent a telegram to Vincent Y. Dallman, editor of the *Springfield State-Register*.

"Ham Lewis parted his red whiskers," quipped Will Rogers, "and fifty-eight delegates jumped out. He said to 'em, 'Boys, I can't feed you any longer. Go out and get the best offer you can.' "

Rogers told Alfalfa Bill Murray: "Bill, we can buy these Illinois delegates cheap. They are just home talent and belong around here and won't cost much."

Murray answered: "Buy 'em, hell, let's sell 'em ours."

"This is the beginning of the end," Farley proclaimed. "Roosevelt will be nominated on the first ballot." The Roosevelt camp predicted that FDR would pick up most of the fifty-eight Illinois delegates. "In the opinion of many this new element of strength clinches the nomination," Arthur Krock reported in the *New York Times*, "by repairing any damage caused by the sudden decision" to make the fight over the two-thirds rule.[10]

Cermak, it turned out, had a contingency plan. On learning that Lewis had quit the race, the mayor announced that Illinois would be placing another favorite son's name in nomination: Loop banker Melvin A. Traylor. "It is very seldom that a state is fortunate enough to have two favorite sons qualified for the presidency," Farley later wrote, "but the Illinois leaders were equal to the occasion. A few of the delegates came over to our side, although not at all the number we anticipated. The outcome was disappointing."[11]

18

TODDLIN' TOWN

ROM ALL DIRECTIONS, the Democrats arrived by train. Chicago
was the hub of the nation's transportation system with its seven
terminals serviced by twenty-two lines. The "James A. Reed for President" special train carrying three hundred Missouri Democrats aboard
the Rock Island Line pulled into the La Salle Street Station at about the
same time as the Chicago and Alton Railroad's "Garner Special" rolled
into Union Station. Meanwhile, Democratic senators and congressmen
took the Baltimore & Ohio's Capitol Limited into Grand Central Station. Envelope manufacturer George D. Gaw, the city's official greeter,
welcomed them all with the gusto of an old-style ring announcer. "I
represent his honor Mayor Cermak, who wanted to come himself but
was detained," Gaw told one and all. "It is a pleasure and a distinction
to welcome you to this wonderful city, sir."

Chicago, as the architect Daniel Burnham noted, had been made by
the railroads. From the days of the iron horse, it was America's convention center, and 1932 marked the fifteenth time that a major party

had come to town. Of the fifteen presidents between the Civil War and the Great Depression, ten had been selected in Chicago.

The rumble and roar of the elevated trains, speeding traffic of the outer drive, and bright lights of State Street gave visiting Democrats a sense of movement and excitement. So did Lake Michigan, the second-largest body of fresh water in North America, and the nation's busiest waterway. "There is something like the spirit of a carnival throughout Chicago," said radio commentator Lowell Thomas, attending his first political convention.[1]

From Twelfth Place to Thirty-ninth Street along the lakefront, the Democrats flocked to get a sneak preview of the 1933 Chicago World's Fair. Taking them back in time was a log replica of Fort Dearborn, an 1803 frontier outpost, and a reconstruction of the Wigwam, the rambling frame building where Abraham Lincoln was nominated for the presidency in 1860. And in contrast, delegates learned about new inventions and technological advances at the futuristic Hall of Science, a great U-shaped building covering nine acres, and the Electrical Complex, which featured air-conditioning and television. Workmen were just completing the Golden Pavilion of Jehol, a gleaming sixty-foot-high, red lacquer and gold reproduction of a Buddhist temple built in 1767 at the summer home of the Manchu dynasty.

During convention week, there were nightly fireworks along the lakefront and planes flying in formation above the George Washington Bicentennial military pageant at Soldier Field. Amelia Earhart, who had just made the fastest transatlantic flight in history, received a tumultuous welcome as she flew in for the opening ceremonies.

"A seven-cent streetcar fare took us to the Loop," recalled Saul Bellow, who graduated from high school that month. "On Randolph Street, we found free entertainment at Bensinger's billiard salon and at

Trafton's gymnasium, where boxers sparred. The street was filled with jazz musicians and City Hall types."[2]

Jane Addams, founder of Hull House and recipient of the 1931 Nobel Peace Prize, tried to influence the Democratic platform. Addams, in the city greeter's official car, led a peace parade of more than a hundred cars through the Loop. Appearing before the Democratic Platform Committee, she called for lower tariffs, reduction of war debts, and recognition of the Soviet Union. Addams, who had been denounced as a traitor for her pacifism, said that she was not endorsing Joseph Stalin's regime. "We venture to remind you," she told party leaders, "that when Thomas Jefferson recognized Russia, he did not commit himself to the government of the Czar."

The lawyer Clarence Darrow, who had gained prominence defending Socialist Eugene Debs and the radical labor leader Big Bill Haywood, had recently come back into the Democratic fold. When asked about his presidential choice, he declared himself for Roosevelt unless Newton Baker moved into contention. "I'm for everything possible to get rid of Hoover," he said. Darrow urged radical measures to fight the Depression. "If everybody had a minimum wage of fifty dollars a day," he declared, "there would be no crime."

Robert Maynard Hutchins, the University of Chicago's thirty-three-year-old president, was touted by Jim Farley and Josephus Daniels as a potential vice-presidential nominee even though he was two years younger that the constitutional requirement. "I believe the Democratic Party has the greatest opportunity of its career to enlist under its banner the younger generation of this nation," Hutchins told the Resolutions Committee, "but it must state in unequivocal terms its position on some of the fundamental problems of today."

Most important, Hutchins said, "The Democratic party must reaffirm its devotion to the interests of the common man and declare itself ready to bring to the aid of the underprivileged and distressed the full resources of the federal government."[3]

Adlai E. Stevenson, a thirty-two-year-old associate in a Loop law firm and grandson of Grover Cleveland's vice president, attended a Lake Shore Drive dinner party with Hutchins, Richmond publisher John Stewart Bryan, Resolutions Committee chairman Gilbert Hitchcock, and Richard Cleveland, the son of the late president.

Of the five local newspapers, the afternoon *Chicago Daily News* was the most nationally prestigious. Its convention team included political writers Paul R. Leach and Edwin A. Lahey, columnist Robert J. Casey, and the young editorial cartoonist Herbert L. Block, who had already compressed his signature into Herblock. "There never was and never will be again such a collection of real newspapermen who could really write as (editor) Henry Justin Smith put together and held together on the *Daily News*," New York journalist Gene Fowler later observed.[4]

After months of inactivity because of the Depression, the hotels were suddenly crowded. The elegant Drake Hotel on the Gold Coast hosted John F. Curry and more than six hundred New York Democrats. James J. Hines, a Tammany district leader, shared a lakefront suite with the underworld kingpin Frank Costello. On the same floor, former sheriff Thomas Farley, who had been removed from office by FDR, was rooming with the gangster Dutch Goldberg. Edith Bolling Wilson, the wife of the late president, and Alice Roosevelt Longworth, daughter of President Theodore Roosevelt, stayed at the Blackstone Hotel. William Jennings Bryan Jr., the son and namesake of the three-time Democratic presidential nominee, checked into the Congress. A half dozen delegations made their headquarters in the Palmer House, whose gilded lobby resembled an Italian Renaissance palace. Walter Gregory, the hotel's manager, prayed for a deadlock. The Stevens, which had more than three thousand rooms, hosted the delegations of a dozen states and six territories. Arthur Mullen, Roosevelt's floor leader, recalled: "The hotel corridors looked like the main street in a Texas oil town just before they're going to bring in a gusher. Big shots, little shots, candidates, delegates, national committeemen, reporters, photographers, lobbyists, gangsters, beer-runners, local politicians, curiosity seekers, all milled around with bands blaring and banners waving while, in locked rooms, shirt-sleeved Warwicks labored with and on each other."[5]

The California and Texas delegations, both committed to Garner, were on adjacent floors at the Sherman House. McAdoo, as chairman of the California delegation, kept a ceremonial suite in this hotel while spending most of the week at his penthouse in the more luxurious Stevens. "I expect to use these rooms as my personal headquarters," he advised the manager of the Stevens, "and I shall be glad if you will not make the fact public because members of my family will be with me, and we want to be able to get away from the business end of the convention."

Another prominent Democrat, New York mayor Jimmy Walker, like McAdoo chose not to stay with his delegation. Walker would spend the week as the guest of Vincent Bendix, chairman of the Bendix Aviation Corporation, in the old Potter Palmer castle on Lake Shore Drive. Beau James, who hosted parties throughout the week at the mansion, also made the rounds of the city's nightclubs and spent an afternoon at the racetrack.[6]

It was a city of endless distractions. The Chicago Cubs, led by outfielder Riggs Stephenson and their new second baseman Billy Herman, had four .300 hitters in the lineup and four pitchers who would each win at least fifteen games. During convention week the Cubs were knocked out of first place but would soon recover and go on to win the National League pennant. A turning point in the season was Cub president William L. Veeck's decision later that summer to replace manager Rogers

Hornsby with popular first baseman Charlie Grimm. Across town, Luke Appling, in his second season as the starting shortstop for the White Sox, was a quality player on a mediocre team. That fall, Bronko Nagurski and Red Grange would lead the Bears to their first National Football League title in a decade. In the championship game, fullback Nagurski threw a pass to halfback Grange for the game's only touchdown.[7]

On the day before the convention officially began, legions of delegates attended the opening of the Arlington Park horse-racing track and cheered Gold Step, a seventeen-to-one long shot, to a photo finish upset over western champion Polydorus. The heavily favored Jamestown faded in the stretch. For the visiting Democrats who did not want to make the long trek to Arlington, "Hinky Dink" Kenna's cigar store, at 311 South Clark Street, was the most centrally located of the city's five hundred handbooks that accepted bets on horses.

The young Henry Cabot Lodge Jr., covering the convention for the *New York Herald Tribune*, joined his friend H. L. Mencken for a tour of the Loop's speakeasies. "A taxi took us to a bar which was located in a long, narrow room," he recalled. "Near the front door and to the left was the bar itself. Standing before the bar was a young lady who could best be described as gorgeous. At the end of the room was a piano and a species of male singer, in vogue at the time, known as a crooner. Mencken and I ordered drinks and, as we stood drinking, the crooner's voice became more and more objectionable. Finally, Mencken said to the young lady behind the bar, 'I'd like to shoot that son of a bitch.' The young lady did not bat an eye or change her supercilious expression. She reached under the counter, pulled out a Thompson submachine gun, laid it on the counter, and with a condescending fluttering of her eyelids said, indifferently, 'Go ahead.'"

In the Loop, there were six hundred of these illegal establishments. Supplies for convention drinkers were reduced when whiskey barrels shipped from New Jersey sprang a leak in a Northwestern Railroad freight car. Amos W. W. Woodcock, chief of the nation's Prohibition enforcement, had 187 agents in Chicago to enforce dry laws during the convention. "Our work will be directed at the commercialized distribution of liquor, not against the individual who buys," Woodcock declared. His agents would not be permitted to make raids on the hotel rooms of visiting Democrats. Bootleggers anticipated a 400 percent increase in their business during convention week. The prices of cases of scotch and bourbon increased from $70 to $100. For delegates ordering room service, Loop hotels charged twelve dollars for a quart of scotch, ten dollars for bourbon, and two dollars for gin. "Out of every 5,000 bottles drunk the first two days," an underworld figure estimated, "3,000 will be from stock the visitors have brought along. After a couple of days, the stock people have brought along will be used up and they'll buy outside."

Grand Hotel, in which MGM showcased its stars Greta Garbo, John Barrymore, Joan Crawford, Wallace Beery, and Lionel Barrymore, was playing at the Woods Theatre, Randolph and Dearborn Streets. "If you want to see what screen glamour used to be, and what, originally, 'stars' were," Pauline Kael later wrote, "this is perhaps the best example of all time."

During convention week, the musical *Clowns in Clover* opened at the Apollo, Randolph and Clark Streets. *Do Your Stuff*, an African American musical revue, extended its run at the Adelphi. Duke Ellington, billed as "Harlem's Aristocrat of Jazz," performed at the Lincoln Tavern in suburban Morton Grove. Joe E. Lewis, whose theme song, "Chicago," celebrated his "toddlin' town," and Julia Gerity, "queen of the blues," were the headliners at the North Side's Vanity Fair. The Mills Brothers, the first African Americans to have their own show on network radio, had returned to the Palace on Randolph Street. And

Chicago was the home of the blues and of such jazz legends as the trumpeter Louis Armstrong, pianist Nat King Cole, and clarinetist Benny Goodman.

Through the *WLS National Barn Dance*, Chicago is where country and western music became nationally popular. By 1932, this program could be heard coast-to-coast and was receiving more than a million letters a year. Gene Autry, the barn dance's singing cowboy, had just become the recording industry's first recipient of a gold record for his hit, "That Silver Haired Daddy of Mine."

In the age of radio, Chicago was the center of the industry. The soap opera and the dramatic play written for radio were both invented in Chicago. *Amos 'n' Andy*, created by and starring Freeman Gosden and Charles Correll, aired six nights a week from the Merchandise Mart's NBC Studio and had an audience of forty million Americans. The *Lum and Abner* show, which was in its second year, would have a twenty-four-year run. Virginia Payne, twenty-two years old in 1932, was about to begin the first of twenty-seven seasons as "Ma Perkins." Another show, *Jack Armstrong, the All-American Boy*, would soon be launched in Chicago with Jim Ameche in the title role.[8]

The Great Depression had brought unemployment and chaos to Chicago. Just south of Union Station, where many of the delegates arrived by train, thousands of unemployed persons were living in shacks made of cardboard, scrap lumber, and tarpaper. "I think what makes the slums of Chicago more dreadful than any others," the novelist Mary Borden wrote in *Harper's*, "is that they are so flimsy, so shallow, so open, and so bleak. . . . There are thousands upon thousands of new, shabby, square wooden boxes, perched on the hard ground."[9]

In Grant Park, across from the convention's hotel headquarters, thousands of the jobless slept on the grass. At Washington Park, on the South Side, the Chicago Urban League reported that for ten blocks "every available dry spot of ground and every bench is covered by sleepers." John Dos Passos, covering the convention for *The New Republic*, observed the homeless on the lower level of Michigan Avenue. "Down here the air, drenched with the exhaust from the grinding motors of trucks, is full of dust and the roar of the heavy traffic that hauls the city's freight," Dos Passos reported. "They lie in rows along the edges above the roadway, huddled in grimed newspapers, men who have nothing left but their stiff hungry grimy bodies, men who have lost the power to want."

"Chicago is in desperate need," Mauritz A. Hallgren lamented in *The Nation*. "It cannot pay its debts; it cannot feed its hungry." A "Hooverville," where the unemployed lived in shacks and tents, was built next to the garbage dump at Thirty-first Street and Cicero Avenue. Large numbers of the destitute picked through the garbage for old slices of melon, discarded vegetables, and scraps of meat, which they would boil and sprinkle with soda. As a garbage truck unloaded, fifty men got into a fight over the pile of refuse. A week before the convention, more than two thousand street cleaners and garbage collectors quit their jobs in protest against two months of working without pay. Dr. Herman N. Bundesen, president of the Health Commission, urged local residents to reduce the risk of disease by burning all garbage. Throughout the city, piles of trash quickly accumulated and police guarded municipal dumps.[10]

As the convention neared, 759 Chicago teachers had lost their homes because the city had not paid them in five months. More than three hundred thousand parcels of Cook County real estate were about to be auctioned because of delinquent tax payments. Over a six-month period, municipal court bailiffs evicted fourteen hundred families. A few bailiffs even paid the rent to keep from throwing families into the street.

The Depression also brought down the mighty Samuel Insull. For three decades he had been the most powerful man in Chicago. Insull, a pioneer in the development of electric power, built massive generators that revolutionized the industry, and the first grid system, which made it possible to distribute power throughout the nation. He specialized in merging small power companies into larger units and eventually presided over a $3 billion empire that generated power in thirty-two states. When electrical consumption dropped sharply in 1931 and revenues fell, Insull borrowed more than $150 million from Chicago banks. Owen Young, chairman of General Electric, and a group of New York financiers, began buying shares of Insull's companies and forced several into bankruptcy. Insull lost his personal fortune of $170 million, and three hundred thousand people suffered financial losses. Shortly before the convention, he resigned the leadership of the Commonwealth Edison Company, the Public Service Company of Northern Illinois, the People's Gas and Light Company, Middle West Utilities, and the Chicago Metropolitan Traction Companies. It was also announced that Chicago's Civic Opera House, which he had built, would be closed for the fall and winter seasons. Just before the convention, Insull walked unrecognized through the lobby of the Blackstone Hotel. His eyes filled with tears when a longtime critic approached him to express condolences. That night he flew to New York and then, under an assumed name, sailed for France. He would later be indicted on charges of fraud, embezzlement, and violation of bankruptcy laws. When he was extradited from Greece to face the charges, Insull was acquitted on all counts. Although federal prosecutors had tried to make Insull a scapegoat for the Depression, juries were persuaded that powerful enemies, including New York's House of Morgan, had destroyed his empire.[11]

After his fall, thirty-nine Chicago banks closed that June. Most of these were small neighborhood banks. But as delegates arrived in Chicago, the panic reached the Loop. The Chicago Bank of Commerce was the first of the downtown banks to close. Between the Tuesday night and Friday before the convention, Melvin A. Traylor, chief executive officer of the First National Bank of Chicago and the First Union Trust, felt the crunch as depositors withdrew more than $50 million from his bank.

On Saturday morning, tens of thousands of people lined up to get into the First National, which opened at 9:00 a.m. Within two hours, millions of dollars had been paid out. Then Traylor stepped up to the challenge. Standing on the pedestal of a marble pillar in the savings department, he spoke in the soft mountain drawl of his native Kentucky. "I am delighted to see so many of our customers here, but I am really sorry that they are afraid of me," he said. "I don't blame you. There has been so much happening in the banking business in Cook County within the last two or three years that I suspect that if I were not really familiar with the situation I would also be frightened. But may I say this to you. We have been in business over seventy years. We have been criticized many times, but this is a place where you all have kept your money and a place to which you have looked for accommodations. We have been conservative and for that reason we are in a position to pay our depositors their money. . . . I don't blame people for being worried, but if you will talk to the Federal Reserve Bank, and if you will talk to the Governor of the Federal Reserve Board, at Washington, and if you will talk to people who know what our condition is, they will tell you we are sound.

"The bank will be open during the usual business hours," he went on, "and will be open on Monday morning. We will be willing and able to pay off any depositor who wishes to withdraw his funds."

At the end of his remarks, the crowd applauded. Traylor had saved his bank. But other Loop financial institutions were still threatened.[12]

Former vice president Charles G. Dawes, who had resigned that month as chief of the Reconstruction Finance Corporation, decided on Saturday night that he would have to close the Central Republic Bank and Trust Company. Over the past year the bank's assets of $240 million had diminished to half that amount. A brigadier general in World War I, the first director of the federal budget, ambassador to Great Britain, and the 1925 recipient of the Nobel Peace Prize, Dawes was regarded as Chicago's leading citizen. The failure of his bank, which had more than a hundred thousand depositors, including 755 other financial institutions, would have national repercussions.

On Sunday morning, Dawes informed Traylor and George M. Reynolds, chairman of the Continental Illinois Bank, of his decision. Unless his bank was kept open, they replied, the other four major banks in the Loop were also doomed. When the two executives offered several million dollars in loans, Dawes said that he would stay in business only if he could obtain a $100 million loan that would allow him to pay off every depositor. Traylor then telephoned President Hoover, at his Camp Rapidan retreat, advising him of the situation and asking for a federal bailout. "If we do not get such support by Monday," Traylor told Hoover, "every Chicago bank—ours among them, of course— will have to close its doors."[13]

Traylor then sought out his friend Jesse H. Jones, the Reconstruction Finance Corporation board member, who was in town as a member of the Texas delegation to the Democratic convention. "Mr. Traylor came to my hotel room and asked me to go with him to a meeting of bankers," Jones recalled. "He did not tell me the purpose of the meeting or where it was to be held, but his demeanor manifested that it was serious and urgent."

The meeting, in the boardroom of the Central Republic Bank, was presided over by Traylor. Jones was informed that the Loop banks had paid out more than $100 million in deposits since Tuesday night and had lost additional millions through clearinghouse withdrawals to banks in other cities. "It was clear to me that the bank should not be allowed to close," Jones later wrote. "I called President Hoover. As best I could by telephone, I explained the situation to him. I told him I thought it much too dangerous for the country to allow the bank to close. . . . I also felt certain that, if the bank closed, all Chicago banks would have to close, and that would soon mean a closing of all banks in the country."

Hoover did not want that to happen. "The situation demanded broad vision and comprehensive understanding of the problem, instant decision, bold and courageous action," he remembered years later. Secretary of the Treasury Ogden Mills and Jones became the administration's point men in the negotiations. "When the President called me back," Jones recalled, "he told me to make as good a trade with the other banks as possible, that is to take as much participation as they could, but to save the Dawes bank."

Under a tentative settlement, a group of New York bankers offered a $10 million loan, while Chicago banks pledged $5 million, and the Reconstruction Finance Corporation offered to provide $80 million. But this plan fell through when Dawes demanded a written commitment from the New York group. Mortimer N. Buckner, who represented the Wall Street bankers, could not reach several members of his group before the Monday morning deadline. Finally, after sixteen hours of negotiations, Jones raised the RFC loan to $90 million. The Dawes bank opened on Monday morning and, though the bailout was criticized when made public later in the week, banking in the Chicago area was stabilized.[14]

A week before the convention, Mayor Cermak was also looking for federal aid. He spoke in behalf of an amendment that would allow the Reconstruction Finance Corporation to make loans to cities. Cermak testified that Chicago had expenditures of $3 million a month for the jobless. He told of raising $10 million from private citizens and another $12 million through the sale of bonds. "These funds ran out June 1," he told the House Banking Committee. "Then more than $5 million of additional bonds were sold. This is sufficient to last until August 1." Unless federal relief could be obtained, the mayor warned, "I am unable to say what will happen in Chicago."[15]

But despite the mayor's plea, federal aid was not forthcoming.

At the first session of the convention, in his address of welcome, Cermak spoke of the nation's plight. "In her stress and suffering, America is turning to us for leadership and relief," he declared. "Millions of hungry men and women and children have pinned their hopes upon this convention."

Cermak declared that his public career had been influenced "by the philosophies of Jefferson, Jackson, Cleveland, and Wilson" and admitted that he was thrilled to be part of a gathering that would be choosing the next president of the United States. In his welcoming address, Cermak did not give a hint about his preference. But within the Illinois delegation he made it known that he was for anyone but FDR. Although Cermak was close to Smith, Roosevelt suspected that the mayor of Chicago favored Ritchie.[16]

1 9

—

KINGFISH

N INE DAYS BEFORE the Democratic convention, the National
Farmer Labor Party sought to draft Huey Pierce Long, the
flamboyant senator from Louisiana, as its 1932 presidential nominee.
"We figure he is the only man in the United States who has got nerve
enough to go out and try to remedy present chaotic conditions," said
Roy M. Harrop, chairman of the leftist party's executive committee. For
the vice presidency, the party slated the aging reformer Jacob J. Coxey,
a household name in the 1890s as the general of "Coxey's Army," the
first national crusade against unemployment. Although he hoped to be
president one day, Long declined this invitation. "What is the use being
the head of a party," he asked, "if you don't have anybody to rule?"[1]

But Long, who was a brilliant orator and populist hero, still intended
to help remake the Democratic Party in Chicago. At thirty-nine, he
was a champion of the powerless and had accumulated more power at
the state level than anyone in American history. "There may be smarter
men than me," Long said, "but they ain't in Louisiana." Long adopted

the nickname of the "Kingfish" after the smooth-talking hustler on the *Amos 'n' Andy* show. As governor of Louisiana from 1928 to 1932, he rocked the power elite by increasing taxes on corporations, including the big oil companies that had long dominated the state. He reduced property taxes and public utility rates, doubled the number of charity hospitals, and for the first time provided free schoolbooks to every child in the state. Long also opened free night schools where 175,000 adults learned to read and write, and he constructed a new campus for Louisiana State University, which he transformed into one of the South's premier institutions of higher education. Huey built eighty-five hundred miles of new roads, bridges across every major river in the state including the Mississippi, a thirty-four-story state capitol in Baton Rouge, and a new governor's mansion.[2]

In the process, he enriched himself and became a virtual dictator. Huey had 10 percent deducted from the salaries of public employees and kept the proceeds. He bragged that the Louisiana legislature was "the finest collection of lawmakers money can buy." While holding public office, Long collected huge legal fees from special interests. "I am still a partner in a law firm," he told *New York Times* political correspondent Arthur Krock, "and the boys cut me in on the receipts. There ain't a corporation doing business in Louisiana that will employ any law firm but ours, provided they can get us to represent them." Huey used the state militia and law-enforcement agencies as his private police force. It was part of his legend that the Kingfish had two men abducted for threatening to expose one of his extramarital affairs. One of them was later placed in a straitjacket by Long's henchmen and confined to a mental institution. The man later wrote a book called *Kidnapped by the Kingfish*. "A man who has the gift for power gets his means and his ends mixed up," said Robert Penn Warren, whose 1946 novel, *All the King's Men*, is based on Long.[3]

Prohibited under state law from succeeding himself, Huey was elected in 1930 to the U.S. Senate but would not give up the governor's office and did not take his legislative seat until January 1932. As his gubernatorial successor, the Kingfish chose his bumbling sidekick Oscar K. Allen, which meant that Long still ruled. On his arrival in Washington, Huey attracted more attention than any new senator in more than a generation. He declined to serve on committees and ignored the tradition that freshmen legislators were silent. With the Depression as his issue, Long used the Senate floor as his forum to appeal to the discontented. "Share the wealth," he demanded. In the spring of 1932, he introduced a resolution that would place a $1 million limit on annual incomes and a $5 million limit on inheritances.[4]

With his cherubic face and boundless energy, Long struck John Dos Passos as "an overgrown small boy." A. J. Liebling of *The New Yorker* remembered him as a most unusual character: "A chubby man, he had ginger hair and tight skin that was the color of a sunburn coming on. It was an uneasy color combination, like an orange tie on a pink shirt."

"He had great intellectual capacity. He had a tremendous emotional and psychological drive. His ambition knew no bounds and he was completely ruthless," recalled Marquis Childs of the *St. Louis Post-Dispatch*. "As an infighter he had the resourcefulness and cunning of a tiger. It was fascinating to watch him on the Senate floor skating circles around men with slower and far more orthodox minds."[5]

From his first day in the Senate, Huey was looking ahead to the Democratic convention. He talked then about supporting a fellow southerner for the presidential nomination, listing as possibilities House Speaker John Nance Garner, Senator Pat Harrison of Mississippi, and Senate minority leader Joseph T. Robinson. As for the front-runner, the Kingfish told reporters: "Governor Roosevelt wouldn't have a chance. He failed with Cox and that should end him."

Long soon became disillusioned with his list of southerners because of their conservatism. He later hinted that he would support Alfred E. Smith and urged the liberal Republican senator George W. Norris of Nebraska to seek the presidency. Burton K. Wheeler of Montana, a Democratic progressive and among Long's few friends in the Senate, lobbied him to support FDR. "After Long took his seat in the Senate, I was determined to line up his potent support in my campaign to get nominated," Wheeler recalled. Over dinner at the Congressional Country Club, Long listened to Wheeler's arguments and replied: "If Norris will tell me he's for him, I'll be for him." Norris, who had bolted his party to back Smith in 1928, confided to Huey that he now favored Roosevelt. "I don't like your son of a bitch," the Kingfish told Wheeler, "but I'll be for him."[6]

What clinched his decision, Long later told the Bronx County Democratic leader Edward J. Flynn, was that he had interviewed the other contenders including Smith, Baker, Ritchie, and Byrd. "He had made up his mind that he would have none of them," Flynn remembered. "He had no intention of calling on Roosevelt because should he do so and be disappointed, he would have no one to support at the convention."

As he detrained in Chicago from the Capitol Limited, a reporter asked Huey if he would be interested in the Democratic vice-presidential nomination. "I wouldn't be vice anything," the freshman senator from Louisiana declared. "I'd rather be the biggest man in a little village than the second biggest man in a great city. Huey Long stands second to nobody."

That included Senator James Hamilton Lewis. "I'm gonna outdress that pink-whiskered son of a bitch in his own town," he confided to Turner Catledge of the *New York Times*. For the convention, Long had four suits made by his New Orleans tailor and brought a trunk of new clothes to Chicago that included numerous summer trousers and flashy neckties. On his arrival, Huey strutted in a white-flannel double-breasted suit with pearl buttons, crimson tie and crimson handkerchief, two-toned shoes, and a straw hat.[7]

"The Kingfish was never a shrinking violet and he aroused the most violent likes and dislikes," recalled James A. Farley. "His followers idolized him while to others his habits of swagger and bluster made him obnoxious and odious to an intense degree. By a twist of fate, Huey suddenly held the center of the stage. The eyes of the nation were turned his way, and he loved it."

At the Dearborn Street station, he was met by his security detail of four Louisiana troopers. According to Long's biographer T. Harry Williams, the state policemen were made honorary Chicago police officers at the senator's request, which gave them the authority to carry weapons. "The Senator knew that his rough tactics made him a likely target for assassination," recalled Krock. "This is why he moved about with bodyguards, armed with sawed-off shotguns, in his automobile, at public assemblages, and adjoining his private quarters. But I saw no evidence that the possibility obsessed him."

While in Chicago, Long worried about such a threat. Anne Pleasant, the wife of a former governor, hated the senator with whom she had clashed earlier that month in Baton Rouge. When Mrs. Pleasant got into an argument with a statehouse clerk, Huey nearly had her ejected. "I can't have a drunken, cursing woman in the capitol," he told Mrs. Pleasant. She replied that Long had no right "to put a taxpayer out of the capitol." According to a state policeman, Mrs. Pleasant had a handgun in her purse and was acting strangely. Long, who found out that she had once been treated for mental illness, ordered his security detail to keep her under surveillance during the convention.[8]

Long had no qualms about using force. When a delegate disrupted a meeting of the Credentials Committee, the Kingfish turned to committee chairman John S. Hurley and exclaimed: "I can give you a man to take care of that man, brother, if you want to." Hurley did not take him up on this offer.

The Louisiana senator made at least one public threat during the convention. As seventeen-year-old Harry F. Byrd Jr. walked into the lobby of the Congress Hotel, he encountered a red-haired man in a white linen suit waving his arms and shouting, "Where's Governor Byrd? I'm gonna kill him!"

Long was incensed because the elder Byrd had aligned himself with a rival delegation in a credentials dispute. "Three nights later, Father received a call from Long while my uncle, the late Admiral Richard E. Byrd, and I were with him," the younger Byrd recalled. "Long asked Father to come to his suite immediately. Dick asked Father not to go. 'It's too dangerous,' Dick said. 'You don't know what that fellow will do. He has already threatened to kill you.'

"My father insisted on going to see Long. But Dick said that unless Father phoned within ten minutes to report that everything was all right, he would get a pistol from the hotel detective and go immediately to the Long headquarters. My father called back in ten minutes. There was nothing to be concerned about, he said. Huey merely wanted to support him for Vice President."[9]

Long, whose slogan, "Every man a king," was inspired by a line in William Jennings Bryan's 1896 "Cross of Gold" speech, styled himself as among the Great Commoner's populist heirs. William Jennings Bryan Jr., who had never met Huey, presented him during the convention with a gold fountain pen that had been given to the late secretary of state by the schoolchildren of Mexico. "I have been carrying on Bryan's policies in the United States Senate," Long told reporters. "That's why he gave it to me."

As a leader of the Roosevelt forces, Long worked behind the scenes to discourage favorite-son movements in the restless Arkansas and Mississippi delegations. When the senator called on his friend Alfalfa Bill Murray, he awakened the Oklahoma governor and caught him in his pajamas. "You're the farmer's candidate, aren't you?" Huey asked. "Most farmers are up before this time of day." The Kingfish offered to put on another pair of pajamas and talk politics, but Alfalfa Bill dressed while they discussed the convention.

"He dwelt upon the virtue in the possible candidacies of everybody except Roosevelt and himself, even suggesting me as a candidate. He understood the favorite-son game," Long later wrote. "I soon saw that I was fencing with a past master in politics. Had I listened to him very long he would have been at work to make a favorite-son candidate out of me."

While Alfalfa Bill was shaving, a room-service waiter brought his breakfast. "Absent-minded as I sometimes am, I ate some of the breakfast and left," Huey recalled. "We had a lot of banter and fun," Murray said afterward. "There might have been a few cuss words, but it was all in fun."[10]

Smith manager John J. Curtin of Brooklyn confronted Long and accused him of breaking an agreement to support the former governor's renomination. The Kingfish denied making any such commitment and then ripped into Smith for favoring a sales tax. "I am for the redistribution of all the wealth of the United States," Huey added, "and that's what Roosevelt stands for." He was of course exaggerating FDR's economic views.[11]

For the moment, Long had a more compelling reason to be allied with Roosevelt. A rival slate headed by three former Louisiana governors contested Huey's slate. Without the support of Roosevelt's majority, he was in jeopardy of being kicked out of the convention. "Just before the national convention," Wheeler recalled, "Huey telephoned me that he had hand-picked his delegates and told them to be for Roosevelt without the formality of a state convention."

Long told Wheeler that his slate had been challenged. "What should I do about it?" he asked. Wheeler suggested a fallback strategy. "I told him the national convention would frown on his unorthodox methods," he recalled in his 1962 memoir *Yankee from the West*. As the Montana progressive knew, many delegates in Chicago welcomed a chance to humiliate his brash friend.[12]

Long decided to send a third delegation to Chicago. "The Unterrified Democrats of Louisiana are going to have a convention tomorrow," Huey told his aide Robert Brothers, "and you're their leader. They will meet in the Capitol. I have the banners made and a band hired. March into the Capitol and take over."

This burlesque convention did not help the Long cause. The new delegation, chaired by former lieutenant governor Fernand Mouton, voted to support state senator Jules Fisher of Louisiana for the presidency and state representative George Delesdernier for vice president. "If elected," the latter wisecracked, "I will graft every dollar I can." Fisher pledged to move the nation's capitol to a little village on the Gulf Coast. Laughing all the way to Chicago, their announced slogan was "Gin Fizzes, No Beer."

By fielding this third slate, Huey showed his contempt for the rival delegation headed by the men he scorned as has-beens. "They're always contesting down in Louisiana," he said with a twinkle in his eye. "Those fellows are all like the Irishman who woke up drunk in the graveyard one morning and said, 'It's resurrection morning and I'm the first one to rise.'"[13]

In the face of this challenge, Long needed the support of FDR delegations in other states. Before the convention, Farley wanted to know if

Louisiana would be following the unit rule, which committed all twenty delegates to Roosevelt. "We vote as a unit on everything," the Kingfish replied.

At a meeting of the Roosevelt delegates, Long got carried away. "It really sickened me," recalled FDR fund-raiser Frank Walker. "Very blatantly he boasted of having stuffed the ballot boxes in the state of Louisiana elections. He made capital of this, and bragged about it, stating that it was very helpful in carrying elections down there. He said he always made sure that there were enough ballots to win elections actually in the ballot boxes before the polls were officially open. All this he stated openly, in the presence of the entire group of approximately sixty-five delegates, and it didn't seem to bother Huey in the slightest."[14]

On hearing that Roosevelt had given up the fight to drop the two-thirds rule, Long did not surrender. At a meeting of the Rules Committee, he used Mayor Richard L. Metcalfe of Omaha as his front man in sponsoring a resolution that would suspend the two-thirds rule after the sixth ballot and provide for nomination by a simple majority on succeeding roll calls. "It's the Republican press that is leading the fight to retain the two-thirds rule," Huey asserted. "While the Republicans are nominating their candidate by majority rule, they want the Democrats to keep the two-thirds rule."

Former senator Atlee Pomerone of Ohio protested that departure from the century-old rule would endanger Democratic prospects in the November election. "The origin of the two-thirds rule was to protect slavery," Long shot back. "We stood by slavery 100 years and the two-thirds rule was part of that program." Long also noted that Roosevelt, in calling off the fight, had endorsed a rule that would prevent a deadlocked convention.

Farley had been caught off guard. When the committee approved the resolution advocated by Long, Roosevelt was accused of trickery. The opposition alleged that the rules were being changed in the middle of the game. After consulting with FDR, Farley issued a statement disavowing the committee's action. J. Bruce Kremer, the Rules Committee chairman, who favored the rules change, finally withdrew the resolution at Farley's insistence. "The long headache was over," Farley remembered. "We had cleared another hurdle that might have proved disastrous."[15]

With the support of Roosevelt's majority, Long believed that his delegation would ultimately prevail. The pro-FDR slates from Minnesota and Puerto Rico were also being contested. Long stirred up another controversy when he declined to appear before a subcommittee hearing of the case. "There has been no resolution passed by the National Democratic Committee, so far as I know, that allows anyone to select any subcommittee for this purpose," he wrote Democratic National Committee chairman John J. Raskob. The challenged delegations from Minnesota and Puerto Rico joined the Kingfish's rebellion. Although Jouett Shouse insisted that the hearing would go forward, the boycott worked.[16]

The case then went before the full Democratic National Committee. In his opening argument, former Louisiana governor Jared Sanders said that Long had been cited for violating party guidelines at the last national convention. The courtly Sanders testified that his slate had followed procedure in choosing delegates at a state convention while Huey had vetoed legislation that would have assured more fairness in delegate selection and had once again circumvented the rules. The contest, he argued, came down to a choice between "elected" and "selected" delegates. On his side, Sanders proclaimed, were the "decent and clean Democrats of Louisiana," which included "every living former governor of the state" except the Kingfish. The former governor ridiculed Mouton's delegation as Long stooges who were chosen at "a mock convention."

Mouton responded with a comedy routine. "There are three kinds of fishes here," he quipped, "the Kingfish on one side, the ex-fishes on the other, and I am the little fish." As the state insurance commissioner, Mouton was a senior member of the Long organization. Yet he insisted, "I am with you fellows 100 percent to get the scalp of the Kingfish." Mouton, a French-speaking Cajun, chortled that he was withdrawing Delesdernier's candidacy for vice president because he had asked a number of delegates to second his nomination "and all of them told me, 'I can't pronounce the name.'"

Huey, who had written Mouton's script, jovially claimed that he was up against both the Sanders and Mouton slates. "I'd like to put them both out," he declared. "I have no entente cordiale with either one of them."

Then he got personal. Sneering at his old adversary, Long said that it had been twenty-four years since Sanders had been elected governor. "And he ain't never going to be again, either! You needn't worry about that." The Kingfish said that Sanders had a faulty memory. "You are never going to get through with your Louisiana contests," he told the committee, "because the people of Louisiana are not going to elect this set to public office, and they are going to have to come to Chicago to get recognition. They can't get it in Louisiana. They have had their chance, and they have been beat, beat, beat down there in every kind of election." He gloated that Sanders had failed three times in races for the U.S. Senate.

"That is true," Sanders acknowledged.

"Certainly," Huey retorted. "Whatever I say is going to be true."

With his arms waving, the Kingfish stated that his delegation had more legitimacy because it included both of the state's senators, eight congressmen, the sitting governor, and the mayor of New Orleans. "That is the kind of delegation we brought up here—men elected by the people," he said. As for Sanders's allegation that he had abused his veto authority, Long offered this explanation: "There were 1,100 bills clogging the Legislature. What did I do? How did I get rid of them? Why I had my floor leader rise and move the passage of every one of them, and then I vetoed them."

Huey conceded that he had pledged to sponsor legislation providing for the selection of 1932 presidential delegates by popular vote or by the 104-member state central committee. But when his opposition sought to impeach him, the Kingfish changed his mind about the preferential primary. "They didn't want to wait that long for me. They got up a proposition to impeach me as governor," he recalled. "We beat that impeachment, finally, and then I ran for the United States Senate."[17]

In a surprisingly close ballot, Long took this round. By a vote of fifty-five to thirty-two, his delegation was seated. The Minnesota delegation had been approved with seventy-one votes. A dozen southern members of the national committee had voted to oust Huey from the convention. The senator's vitriolic remarks and the comedy act of his burlesque slate had reduced the hearing to a theater of the absurd. "Perhaps their tactics amused some people," Farley recalled, "but they disgusted a lot of delegates and in that way lost considerable support for Huey."

The Sanders delegation then took its challenge to the Credentials Committee and, if stopped there, vowed to go before the full convention. "I'll support your delegation on one condition—that you quit your clowning," Roosevelt floor manager Arthur F. Mullen bluntly told the Kingfish.[18]

Huey took the advice. But it did not make him any less controversial. An overflow crowd packed the Gold Room of the Congress Hotel on Monday night when the Credentials Committee began hearing arguments on the Louisiana delegation. It was another stormy meeting. Sanders, opening the debate, reported that for more than fifty years Louisiana had chosen national convention delegates at a state convention. When the Kingfish abandoned this tradition in 1928, Sanders said that Long's slate was uncontested and thus seated. This time, the former governor said, Huey should be held accountable for breaking the rules.

Long was applauded and jeered when he took the platform, and he said that the heckling was all right with him. But he expressed the hope that his followers would show more courtesy when the other side spoke. As Huey began speaking, he was interrupted. "Did your State Committee call a convention this year?" asked a California member of the panel. Long paused and tried to go on with his remarks. But the Californian would not let him off the hook and the Kingfish answered: "No."

In another arm-waving performance, Long declared that he alone represented the people of his state and had every right to choose the delegation. The committee went into executive session at 12:45 a.m. and debate raged on until nearly three in the morning. A motion to seat each of the rival delegations and split their votes was narrowly defeated. Long said that he would rather be thrown out than accept this compromise. By a vote of thirty-four to seventeen, the Credentials Committee voted to seat Huey's delegation. But no sooner had the vote been announced than the opposition served notice that the fight was going to the floor of the convention. "Ordinarily," reported H. L. Mencken, "a contest before the Credentials Committee has little repercussion on the floor. The committee solves its problem as best it can and the convention follows its lead, with maybe a half hour or so of formal oratory. But this time there was at least one contest that stirred

the convention, and that was the one between Huey Long and his enemies in Louisiana."[19]

FOR THE ROOSEVELT forces and their opposition, this was the first
critical vote of the convention. As the most controversial figure in
American politics, Long had at least as many enemies as friends in
Chicago. Once Huey declared for FDR, the Stop Roosevelt delegations from Massachusetts to California united in support of the
Sanders slate. After his retreat on the two-thirds rule, FDR suddenly
looked vulnerable and the opposition had new life. "If we lost on any
of the tests we were through," recalled Farley, "and we knew it."[20]

Arguing the case against Long, Scott W. Lucas of Illinois made a
solid presentation. A World War I veteran and downstate lawyer, Lucas at forty was the national judge advocate of the American Legion
and a forceful debater. A former semiprofessional baseball player and
avid sportsman, he once killed three ducks with a single shot. Like the
Kingfish, Lucas was a sharp dresser who favored double-breasted
suits. And like Huey, he had a zest for political combat. Lucas reminded the delegates that Long had been put on notice in 1928 for violating party guidelines yet had ignored this reprimand. He noted that
the Sanders delegation had been chosen by a state convention on a population basis. "My friends, we believe from the voluminous record of
inescapable facts presented before this committee," Lucas stated, "that
the methods applied by the seated delegation from Louisiana are dicta-
torial, illegal, unwarranted and a direct challenge to the fundamental
principles of this republic."

When Long strode to the rostrum, he weathered a storm of boos and
catcalls. Cermak had packed the galleries with anti-Roosevelt partisans
and the opposition hissed from the floor. "Don't applaud me! Don't

applaud me!" Huey taunted and they became even more outraged. "My time is limited and I don't want applause." He later confided, "I knew they were booing but I also knew the people down in Louisiana, hearing all that noise over the radio would take my word for it that it was applause."[21]

Speaking rapidly in a strong clear voice, Long explained that he had followed the rules and cited Louisiana state laws and court decisions to support his case. "He had on a table behind him a pile of lawbooks that he had sent up from Louisiana, and frequently he would pause and ask an assistant to hand him one of the books," T. Harry Williams disclosed in his Long biography. "He would open it, obviously to a marked page, and without reading would quote from it, sometimes several paragraphs."

Under state law, Long said that the central committee had acted within its authority in choosing the delegation of which he was the chairman. He referred to the gathering called by the Sanders slate as a "rump convention." "This is not a contest over the law," he said. "They knew that if they had held this convention in time for us to have gone to court we would have got out an injunction against them to keep them from coming here with that kind of fiasco."

Huey also cited the 1928 rules of the Democratic National Committee stating that the delegates from several states, including Louisiana, "must be elected by their legally qualified state committees." With a tone of amusement, he noted that "we have a gentleman from Illinois telling you to unseat the men in Louisiana" chosen "under the same process as the at-large delegates from Illinois." Why, the senator asked, should Louisiana be held to a different standard? By the end of his remarks, Long had the crowd on his side.[22]

A hush came over Chicago Stadium as the roll call began. Long got the forty-eight votes of Alabama, Arizona, and Arkansas. Then

California cast forty-four votes against him and the balloting stayed close. Half of the Roosevelt delegates in Iowa and Maine voted to unseat the Kingfish. So did the entire FDR slate from North Carolina. New York, Ohio, Illinois, Indiana, Maryland, New Jersey, Massachusetts, Rhode Island, Texas, and Virginia were against Long. Despite their friendship, Murray had his Oklahoma delegation vote against Huey. But against all this opposition, the Roosevelt coalition survived this test. Farley delivered big-time for his Louisiana ally. The final vote was 638 to 514 to seat the Long delegation. A shift of sixty-three votes would have produced a different outcome. Pennsylvania, which passed to poll its delegates, gave Long a majority late in the roll call when it cast fifty-five votes for his slate. "To Huey Long goes the credit of being the first to split the party and get 'em acting like Democrats," Will Rogers wrote in his column. "I'll bet when judgment day comes things will go on unusually quiet till all at once there will be the blamedest fight and it will be over what to do with Huey."

A jubilant Long grabbed the Louisiana standard, jumped up on a chair, and waved his arms in triumph as Pennsylvania announced its vote. After this roll call, the pro-Roosevelt Minnesota delegation won its fight for permanent seating. Then, Senator Thomas Walsh of Montana defeated Jouett Shouse for the permanent chairmanship by a vote of 626 to 528. "To me the most vital moment of the convention," Farley wrote in his diary, "was the seating of Huey Long's delegation."[23]

20

ROLL OUT THE BARREL

ORE THAN ANY issue since the Civil War, Prohibition had torn apart the Democratic Party. William Jennings Bryan, the three-time presidential nominee, championed the rural crusade. In 1916, he declared, "The prohibition issue is here, and here to stay until the saloon is driven out of the United States." By the eve of World War I, twenty-six states, mostly in the South and West, had gone dry. In the spring of 1918, the Great Commoner, as Bryan was known, became president of the National Dry Foundation, a coalition that included twenty-eight organizations including the Federal Council of Churches. By January 1919, three-fourths of the states had ratified the Eighteenth Amendment prohibiting the "manufacture, sale or transportation" of alcoholic beverages. A year later, Prohibition went into effect. "Let the world rejoice," Bryan proclaimed. "The greatest moral reform of the generation has been accomplished."[1]

William G. McAdoo succeeded Bryan as leader of the party's rural Prohibitionists. For more than a decade, southern and western

Democrats clashed on this issue with the party's eastern wing led by Alfred E. Smith and Albert C. Ritchie. "It is the one topic uppermost in the minds of people in every section and both parties," Frank R. Kent of the *Baltimore Sun* reported. "There is no other question capable of emotionally disturbing the voters."[2]

Roosevelt, who viewed Prohibition as "a red herring," avoided the issue as much as possible and in this clash of the absolutes deftly managed to stay on good terms with both sides. As a young state senator he compiled a 100 percent voting record with the Anti-Saloon League and sponsored the league's local-option measure. His voting record in Albany was more reflective of his upstate constituency than his personal views. At the 1920 Democratic convention, he joined Smith in helping to defeat a proposed dry plank in the party platform. His reputation as a moderate dry was among the reasons FDR was selected for the vice presidency on the Democratic ticket headed by the wet James M. Cox. He made no public comment about the issue in this campaign but privately endorsed the "splendid results" of the antisaloon amendment and assured southern drys that Cox would enforce the law. As early as 1923, he suggested that the bitterly divisive issue could be settled with a national referendum. "The wets are feeling so cocky," he wrote a wet friend, "that they believe they could carry it—the drys are so sanctimoniously satisfied that they ought not to be afraid of the issue being put to a popular vote."[3]

Roosevelt, trying to have it both ways, suggested to Bryan that the referendum would be the ultimate vindication for the Great Commoner's righteous cause. "New York State is not nearly as wet a state as some Democrats try to make out," he confided to Bryan. "The City of New York and certain other cities like Buffalo and Albany are undoubtedly in favor of light wines and beer, but the rural sections would, in my judgment, vote heavily against much or even any, modification of the Volstead Act."

Smith and Roosevelt had long differed on this policy question. In 1923 when the New York legislature voted to repeal the state's Prohibition-enforcement law, FDR wrote Smith: "I am mighty sorry for the extremely difficult position in which you have been placed over this darned old liquor question." Roosevelt advised a veto but Smith signed the repeal act and called for the legalization of beer and wine. As manager of Smith's bid for the 1924 presidential nomination, Roosevelt was bewildered by his candidate's refusal to modify his stance. When FDR pressed Smith to make a public pledge that he would enforce the law of the land, Roosevelt got nowhere. FDR believed that Smith as the 1928 Democratic presidential nominee doomed his chances by embracing repeal. In his gubernatorial campaign that year, he loyally backed Smith but distanced himself from the Prohibition issue.[4]

By 1930, after a decade of unprecedented lawlessness and corruption, a large and growing number of Americans questioned the wisdom of what President Hoover described as a "noble experiment." Across the nation, more than two hundred thousand illegal speakeasies replaced the old saloons, and organized crime accumulated massive profits. More than five hundred thousand arrests failed to discourage people from buying a cocktail or glass of beer. State and federal law-enforcement agencies often worked in tandem with the racketeers. During the twenties, 706 agents were fired from the Treasury Department and another 257 were prosecuted for taking bribes. The federal government admitted its inadequacy to enforce the law. At his first Governors Conference, Roosevelt asserted that states should assume more of the burden in enforcing Prohibition. In 1930, as a candidate for a second term, FDR called for repeal of the Eighteenth Amendment and recommended a new amendment giving states the option of going wet or dry.[5]

As Roosevelt maneuvered for the presidency, he forged alliances with southern Prohibitionists and blocked national chairman John J. Raskob's misguided attempt to have the Democratic National Committee endorse the repeal of the Eighteenth Amendment. By taking this stand against Smith and Raskob, he effectively positioned himself in the South and the West. "Until this moment," Cordell Hull recalled, "all the prohibition population of the country, including those who did not desire to make prohibition a partisan issue, had been clearly against the Smith-Raskob group. From this date on, these forces looked with either favor or much less disfavor on Governor Roosevelt. . . . All or most of those opposed to the Smith movement were gradually and ultimately to turn to Roosevelt as the most effective way of killing off Smith."

FDR, though nominally for repeal, told the dry camp that he would rather not have a liquor plank in the platform. "Franklin D. Roosevelt has declared for repeal, to be sure, but he inspires little fear or hatred among the drys," Ray Thomas Tucker reported in *The Mirrors of 1932*. "They suspect that, once in the White House, he will make no move to endanger the dry laws. They believe that his history and background incline him to little more than political sympathy with the wets."[6]

But Roosevelt took heat from southern allies when he reiterated his call for repeal. He also proposed giving states the freedom to choose and generating public revenue by selling liquor through state agencies. Daniel C. Roper, who had spent months lining up dry support, felt betrayed. "Roper told me over the telephone," Robert Woolley wrote the old Wilsonian colonel Edward M. House, "that he is afraid the reaction throughout the South and the West would be such as to destroy the Governor's chances for the nomination." The old dry Josephus Daniels lamented to Hull that Roosevelt had sold them out. "I am unable to see what alternative there is except chaos and anarchy," Hull answered. "It is in the light of this situation that I feel justified in driving ahead in an effort to be of some aid in organizing the right-minded and right-thinking forces around Roosevelt."[7]

FDR could not ignore public opinion. By the spring of 1932, the country had turned against Prohibition. *The Literary Digest,* which conducted a straw poll of more than 4.6 million Americans, found popular majorities for repeal in forty-six of the forty-eight states. By slender margins, Kansas and North Carolina were the holdouts. In a similar poll taken in 1930, these states and Arkansas, Oklahoma, and Tennessee produced dry majorities. Only 40.43 percent favored repeal in 1930, compared with 30.46 percent for Prohibition, and 29.11 percent for modification. According to the 1932 poll, 73.5 percent of the American public favored repeal. "The case for prohibition is increasingly debatable," conceded dry activist Stanley High. "Any doubt on that point ought to be dispelled by the *Literary Digest* poll—which the drys are inclined too lightly to dismiss."[8]

The British statesman Winston Churchill, visiting the United States in 1932 for the first time in three years, was struck by the shift in public attitudes about Prohibition. "On the former occasion many championed it with vigor or at least defended it with conviction," Churchill observed. "But now, in 1932, I could find scarcely a voice raised in defense of such a system. Indeed, on every side in a score of states, among the dominant figures of American life, there was a fierce and universal disdain for the principle of prohibition."

In June, as the conventions neared, the dry forces were on the run. John D. Rockefeller Jr., a lifelong teetotaler whose family had bankrolled the Anti-Saloon League, made the surprise announcement that he favored repeal. "It is my profound conviction that the benefits of the Eighteenth Amendment," Rockefeller said, "are more than outweighed by the evils that have developed and flourished since its adoption."[9]

North Carolina, one of only two remaining dry strongholds in the *Literary Digest* poll, suddenly shifted. Senator Cameron Morrison of

North Carolina, a leading Prohibitionist, fell to a wet challenger. "I am willing to die for prohibition," said Morrison. In the dry state of Florida, Congresswoman Ruth Bryan Owen, daughter of the Great Commoner, was defeated for renomination by an opponent who favored repeal. The elder Bryan had carried the Sunshine State in all three of his presidential campaigns. Following the defeat of his niece, Nebraska governor Charles W. Bryan urged the Democratic convention to declare a moratorium on Prohibition.

But it was an issue that compelled attention. "Here we are in the midst of the greatest crisis since the Civil War," the philosopher John Dewey noted, "and the only thing the two national parties seem to want to debate is booze."[10]

At the Republican convention, the Hoover administration pushed through a compromise plank recommending a new amendment that would give states the option of allowing liquor under federal control. A minority plank introduced by Senator Hiram Bingham of Connecticut called for straight repeal of the Eighteenth Amendment. Cheered on by the pro-wet galleries, Bingham asked the GOP to give the people "a chance to vote cleanly" on repeal. "It was evident that the sentiment of the convention was overwhelmingly for repeal," Arthur Krock reported in the *New York Times*. "But the word had been passed down the line from the White House." By a close vote, the Bingham plank was rejected. The Republican *New York Herald Tribune* commented that Hoover's victory had been achieved "at a ruinous cost in disappointed hopes and outraged convictions."

FORMER STATE DEPARTMENT official Breckinridge Long, who would be among Roosevelt's floor managers in Chicago, expressed concern about the high-profile roles of dry advocates in their campaign.

Long questioned FDR's selection of Barkley and Walsh as temporary and permanent convention chairmen and the recommendation of Hull to chair the Resolutions Committee. There was also speculation about the Tennessee senator as a vice-presidential nominee.

"Much of Frank's strength in the political organization comes from what is known as the dry section of the country. The persons now in positions of responsibility in those sections were elected before the enormous trend against prohibition became evident," Long wrote privately. "Consequently they are still dry. . . . It is natural that these men, now prominent in Roosevelt's behalf, should be considered by the rest of the country as leading exponents of what is now apparent as a losing cause."

Long warned that the front-runner's identity with the drys could "do a good deal to distract from the fine and definite position Roosevelt himself has taken and may easily be construed or propagandized as straddling."[11]

SMITH AND RITCHIE, whose strategists outmaneuvered Roosevelt on the two-thirds rule, now wanted a showdown over the party's most divisive issue. If FDR sought to prevent a strong repeal plank, Smith would seize this opportunity to inflame passions and rally the party's wet majority. Roosevelt's forces were so worried about losing this roll call that his allies proposed breaking another tradition. Roper introduced a plan to change the order of business and place the selection of a candidate ahead of voting on the platform. After bitter debate, the Rules Committee adopted Roper's plan by a three-vote margin. "This is a part of their program of pretense and deceit," alleged Thomas D. Lyons of Oklahoma. "They want to get these nominations made ahead of a storm which will break out on the floor over certain planks in the platform."

In the face of this criticism, the Roosevelt camp backed down. Having already lost the two-thirds rules change, Farley wanted to avoid another contentious battle. If the Rules Committee, controlled by Roosevelt's men, was split over this procedural issue, Farley did not want to risk a floor vote. At his insistence, Roper withdrew his resolution. The convention program would follow long-standing tradition.[12]

WHILE GIVING NO public hint of his strategy, Roosevelt had also decided that he would not contest Smith over the Prohibition plank. Following the Republican convention, he spoke with advisers about incorporating the minority Bingham plank into the Democratic platform. Hull, anticipating that his Prohibitionist views could be a liability for Roosevelt, turned down the chairmanship of the Resolutions Committee. On the Tennessee senator's recommendation, FDR chose former senator Gilbert M. Hitchcock of Nebraska, a wet, to lead the platform-writing committee. Walsh, a staunch Prohibitionist, had modified his position and now favored a referendum. So did Barkley, who had been among the chief sponsors of the Eighteenth Amendment. As Roosevelt went over the keynote speech with the senator, he asked how the Kentuckian would approach the liquor question. "I'm going to say," Barkley replied, "that the Democratic convention ought to put in its platform a plank advocating the submission of an amendment to the people repealing the Eighteenth Amendment."

"I think you can go further than that," Roosevelt said. "I think you ought to come out flatfooted yourself for repeal of the Eighteenth Amendment."[13]

It was the highlight of Barkley's two-hour speech. "Two weeks ago in this place, the Republican party promulgated what it called a plank on the Eighteenth Amendment," Barkley said. "It is not a plank. It is a promiscuous agglomeration of scrap-lumber." Cheering and laughter broke out. "Dr. [Nicholas Murray] Butler condemns it because it is dry; Senator Borah because it is wet," the keynoter gleefully noted. "The American people condemn it because it is neither."

Then Barkley declared, "This convention should recommend the passage by Congress of a resolution repealing the Eighteenth Amendment of the Constitution." As the galleries roared their support with passionate enthusiasm, the delegations of forty states from New England to California paraded through the crowded aisles. The organist struck up the "Maine Stein Song," "How Dry I Am," and "Happy Days Are Here Again."

But not everyone was in a holiday mood. Governor John Pollard of Virginia resisted the efforts of a half dozen young women to pin on his lapel a button reading "My vote goes wet." The Prohibitionist Pollard told them: "I can't compromise with principle just to oblige." Hal Brennan of Laredo, former state commander of the American Legion, gripped the Texas banner and would not allow it to be carried in the parade. W. L. Rea, an old-time Texas Ranger, drew a thick .45 caliber pistol from a hip holster when other delegates jostled him into the parade. "I've brought this along today," Rea said, spinning his gun by its trigger guard, "and it'll make me boss of this delegation. Nobody's going to push me around and if I don't want to parade, I won't be parading." A Chicago police officer approached the old ranger and took his pistol. "All right," Rea agreed. "My boys here understand me now."

Governor Martin S. Conner of Mississippi, fiercely protective of his state's banner, kept it out of the wet parade. The Carolinas, Arkansas, Virginia, Kansas, and Bryan's Nebraska sat out the demonstration. But for fifteen minutes, the cheering throng ruled.[14]

Even before this demonstration, the momentum had been building for straight repeal. Senator David I. Walsh of Massachusetts claimed the support of twenty-three delegations for straight repeal. "The way in which repeal sentiment grew steadily in volume, like a huge snowball gathering size as it went along," Farley later wrote, "seemed almost unbelievable even to those men and women who had been battling doggedly for years to end the prohibition regime."

THE ORIGINAL MAJORITY plank, written by Cordell Hull and supported by six of the nine members of the Drafting Committee selected by Roosevelt, advocated submission of repeal to state conventions and pledged federal enforcement in states that voted to remain dry. "This agreement seemed to be generally acceptable until about the time the convention opened," Hull recalled. "Then suddenly the wet forces from the big cities started a movement to write a plank in the platform making prohibition a party question. Wet leaders with whom I had reached my agreement proceeded to forget about it and joined the rapid procession toward an anti-prohibition plank."

On Wednesday, June 29, Senator Hitchcock called the Resolutions Committee into executive session for this unfinished business in the Rose Room at the Congress Hotel. For more than four hours, wets and drys fought it out. Hull pleaded for the adoption of the subcommittee's plank, making the argument that Prohibition would upstage the economy as a Democratic issue if the convention voted for straight repeal. David Walsh countered that the American people were demanding a simple, forthright declaration for repeal. In the first roll call, Hull's majority plank was defeated by a vote of thirty-five to eighteen. Soon afterward, the Walsh plank was substituted as the majority plank by a vote of thirty-five to seventeen. As the committee deliberated, the next session of the full convention had been delayed from noon to three, and then finally to seven.

Hull vowed to fight on. But Farley tried to talk him out of it. By conceding on the repeal plank, Roosevelt meant to deny Smith his best chance to swing the convention. Farley urged Hull not to give Smith this opportunity. "I felt I should make a statement setting out the minority views and the record of what had happened," Hull remembered, "although it was manifest that a wet plank would be adopted."[15]

At the Wednesday night session, Senator Hitchcock got a polite reception as he read the Democratic platform that criticized the Hoover administration, pledged a 25 percent reduction in federal spending, while at the same time promising unemployment relief, and the creation of jobs through public works projects. But when he announced, "We advocate the repeal of the Eighteenth Amendment," the great hall shook to the rafters as more than twenty thousand men and women stood, shouted, tossed hats into the air, and paraded through the crowded aisles. "It was the first time since dealing in intoxicating beverages became a federal offense," F. Raymond Daniell reported in the *New York Times,* "that a great national party had come out flatly for repeal and immediate modification, and the delegates and paying guests hailed the wet platform declaration much as the crowds in the cities hailed the news of the armistice in 1918."[16]

The cheering stopped as Hull went to the rostrum and began speaking for the minority plank. The galleries started booing and shouted him down. Finally, Senator Walsh of Massachusetts, author of the majority plank, stepped to the microphone and asked the hecklers to show respect to their opponents. In his opening argument, Hull noted that the minority plank at the beginning of the week had been favored by 85 percent of the delegates. Some started crying "No" in response to the senator's assertion. Hull added that it would be a mistake to adopt a straight repeal plank after only a few hours of debate. "Twelve years!"

shouted a man in the galleries with a loud voice. Throughout this ordeal, the courtly Hull remained calm. "I ask you Democrats to be quiet and listen to this," he said, "because we may realize later on that it is more important than we now think." He argued that the party would be setting an unfortunate precedent if it got into the business of endorsing constitutional amendments.

Hull, setting the stage for the most dramatic exchange of the convention, noted that Smith in his 1928 presidential nomination acceptance speech had endorsed resubmission. "There was laid down that the people, not one party, not one segment, but the people as a whole," said Hull, "should be permitted to say whether an amendment to the Constitution should be voted up or down."[17]

Then it was Smith's turn. As the Happy Warrior stepped into the spotlight and took the rostrum, he was overwhelmed by the tumultuous demonstration. This hero of the cities stood smiling as the delegates and galleries cheered and shouted for more than ten minutes. While bathing in this acclaim, he drank two glasses of water and split another with Senator Walsh. When the organist began playing, "The Sidewalks of New York" in what H. L. Mencken described as "an almost terrifying manner, with every stop wide open and a ton or so of extra weight on the safety valve," many delegates started marching through the stadium in the convention's most spontaneous parade. "Even Smith seemed surprised by the reception, and there was moisture in his eyes," Claude Bowers later wrote.[18]

Smith did not disappoint the faithful. "I desire to make a few corrections in some of the statements made by Senator Hull," the former governor said in his rasping Lower East Side voice. "Of course the fact that the Senator only found out in the last three days that there was sentiment in this country for repeal is just too bad." A great howl rose from the floor and waves of laughter rocked the mezzanine and balconies.

"There is absolutely nothing that the convention can do about that," Smith declared, "except to possibly extend sympathy." As for Hull's contention that "it was an innovation in the conduct of our national politics to have a party declare in favor of an amendment to the Constitution," Smith suggested otherwise. "What about the income tax, Senator? Didn't we declare as a party in favor of that?" The galleries roared again. "What about the direct election of United States Senators? Did we not as a party declare in favor of that? And if I am not mistaken, the Senator was a delegate to one of those conventions and voted for that."

The former governor ridiculed Hull's attempt to use Smith's 1928 position as an argument for the minority plank. "That was four years ago—did the Senator agree with me four years ago?" Smith taunted. "He did not." The crowd broke into loud applause and cheering. "And because I happened to be four years ahead of my time, just look at what happened to me."

Without mentioning Roosevelt by name, Smith made an unmistakable reference to the front-runner's difficulty with this issue. "If there is anything in the world today that the American people dislike it is a dodger," Smith asserted. "The time has thoroughly passed when you can carry water on both shoulders, when you can be wet when you are among the wets and dry when you are among the drys, invoking always that quiet little subterranean passage whereby you hope to ease by when nobody is looking."[19]

The convention voted 934 to 213 in favor of Smith's plank. "It was still too early to say who the nominee would be," Emily Smith Warner recalled, "but Father had at least won this victory though the fight had been a long one and had been begun against heavy odds." Roosevelt, who had long disagreed with Smith on this issue, showed pragmatism in staying out of the floor fight. When the convention voted for repeal, FDR declined comment. "Early this morning," Arthur Krock reported in the *New York Times*, "the Democratic party went as wet as the seven seas."[20]

21

STALEMATE

T HE MOMENT HAD arrived. On the Thursday afternoon of June 30, Senator Thomas J. Walsh banged down his gavel to open the nominating session of the 1932 Democratic National Convention. It looked like an Independence Day pageant. Hundreds of American flags waved from the steel girder rafters and four miles of red-white-and-blue bunting adorned the balconies. In the corners of the vast stadium, larger-than-life portraits of Thomas Jefferson, Andrew Jackson, Grover Cleveland, and Woodrow Wilson evoked images of the party's glory days.

More than three thousand delegates and alternates settled into two acres of red undertaker chairs. Roosevelt's camp, which dominated the Committee on Arrangements, gave favored seating to their allies. Alabama, Louisiana, and Minnesota were in the front row. "Remembering the old adage of the one bad apple in the barrel, we put California behind New York and both of them a half-mile away from Texas," Arthur Mullen later wrote. "We left New York and New Jersey together, but took Illinois away from them both."[1]

*   *   *

THE GALLERIES BELONGED to Mayor Anton J. Cermak. "Delegates could not get tickets for their wives. Public men of high standing and influence were denied admission to the hall," reported Willis J. Abbot of *The Christian Science Monitor.* "Persons who had bought tickets found them useless." Cermak had ten thousand tickets printed and through the police department determined who was allowed into the convention. Jouett Shouse, seeking to pack the mezzanine and balconies with anti-Roosevelt partisans, gave Cermak thousands of tickets. An incensed Mullen got none but protested and finally obtained a hundred passes for FDR's camp. But above the floor, Cermak ruled. "I am controlling things," the mayor said, "all the way down the line."

With the two-thirds rule still in effect, the outcome was far from certain. Campaign manager James A. Farley had predicted a quick victory so many times that the Associated Press nicknamed him "One-Ballot Farley." But as the vote approached, he spoke with less certitude. "If we don't make it on the first roll call," Farley said, "we will on the second or third." According to his public estimate, Roosevelt would have more than seven hundred votes on the first ballot.[2]

FORMER JUDGE JOHN E. Mack, delivering the first nominating speech, noted that Roosevelt "comes into this convention with the greatest number of states behind him in the history of the Democratic party—the North, the East, the South and the West—the great Central States of the Midwest. There never was a candidate who appealed to the whole country as this man has." In a bland performance, Mack was generous in his treatment of the competition. "Great indeed," he marveled, "is the party which has within its ranks such illustrious candidates."

Massachusetts governor Joseph B. Ely, nominating Smith as "a modern Andrew Jackson," responded in a different tone. Without naming Roosevelt, Ely ridiculed him as a "doubting, equivocating, polite gentleman." Then he brought up the health issue. "We as Democrats will find it difficult to impress a nation with the advisability of a change," Ely asserted, "unless our nominee is a man of action, virile, and rugged personality. . . . To win requires a man who can take the blows both physically and mentally without retreating a single inch." Roosevelt listened in anger and disbelief. "Only two people overstepped the bounds of decency at the convention: Frank Hague and Ely," he confided to Felix Frankfurter.[3]

SMITH ALSO HAD a grievance. Angered by speculation that he was about to quit and release his delegates, the former governor accused Roosevelt's men of subterfuge. "I am not only going to stick but I am going to be nominated," he declared. Although Farley denied that FDR's camp was peddling this rumor, Smith believed otherwise.

"I am informed that newspapers today throughout the country carried headlines and newspaper articles creating the impression that I am about to withdraw as a candidate for the nomination for president. Nothing could be further from the truth," the former governor insisted. "I have spent a large part of my career with newspapermen. I found them always to be fair. I wish I could say as much about the adherents of one of the candidates, who today have been passing the world around that I am withdrawing, or that I concede the nomination of anyone on the second, third or any other ballot.

"Nothing is to be gained by small tactics or mean tactics in a big game. This line of information is designed to deceive the whole country,"

Smith concluded. "Enthusiasm for a cause has deadened their sense of fair play."[4]

Yet Smith had been doing the same thing to Roosevelt. In a blunt conversation with New York secretary of state Edward J. Flynn, he predicted the slippage of Roosevelt's lead and ultimate collapse of his presidential fortunes. "I believe this was the conviction not only of Smith, but of almost all the others who aspired to the nomination," Flynn remembered. "They all thought there would be a stalemate, and each was hoping to be the beneficiary of the expected disintegration of Roosevelt's strength."

As the delegations of thirty-four states and six territories joined the floor demonstration for FDR, each state standard bore posters of Roosevelt declaring that he was "for progressive government." Giant FDR banners unrolled from the balconies and organist Al Melgard burst into "Anchors Aweigh." Because of his wartime service as assistant secretary of the navy, Roosevelt had chosen the navy anthem. Louis Howe and Flynn, listening to the convention from Howe's suite, thought the music was much too solemn. "That sounds like a funeral march," Flynn told Howe. "Why don't we get something peppy for them to play, like "Happy Days Are Here Again?" Howe agreed and sent word to the stadium.[5]

Originally written for the 1929 Hollywood musical *Chasing Rainbows*, this snappy tune brought new life to the floor demonstration and would forever be identified with Roosevelt. As Melgard rolled into another round of "Happy Days," new banners sprouted up and more delegates snake-danced and shouted.

Tall and athletic Jimmy Roosevelt, the candidate's oldest son, grabbed the New York standard from the side of John F. Curry. The Tammany leader made no objection, F. Raymond Daniell reported in the *New York Times,* as young Roosevelt "charged down the aisles like a sophomore storming the goal posts of a rival college after his team had won." After watching this from the family box, Franklin Jr. leaped over the rail and joined his older brother.

In a shrewd move by Farley, fans with Roosevelt's picture on both sides were distributed throughout the floor. Although the stadium had primitive air-conditioning, the huge klieg lights for the newsreels made it a hothouse. By the time of the floor demonstration, even Mayor Cermak and Alfalfa Bill Murray were staying cool with FDR. "Looking out over the floor of the convention," the *New York Times* observed, "it seemed at first glance that a miracle had happened—that the Democrats had all agreed on Roosevelt without so much as a debate, let alone a roll-call."[6]

AFTER SENATOR TOM CONNALLY of Texas nominated John Nance Garner as "a man of the people" and "field marshal of the armies of the democracy," more than a thousand marchers paraded through the aisles. Will Rogers, carrying the Oklahoma flag, joined in. Melgard swung into "The Eyes of Texas," followed by "The Old Gray Mare." McAdoo, immaculate in a white linen suit, marched with daughter Ellen, and Melgard began playing "California Here I Come." Malvina Passmore, a striking Houston woman in a red dress, stood on a chair on the platform, waved two Lone Star flags, and got a rousing ovation when she sang "Dixie" to the accompaniment of the mighty organ.

Smith, though, had the longest and most tumultuous demonstration aided by three bands and the clanging of fire bells. As Ely finished his speech, Melgard rolled into "The Sidewalks of New York" and the immense throng in the galleries cheered and shouted for more than an hour. Former mayor John F. Fitzgerald of Boston, known as "Honey

Fitz," stepped to the rostrum and led the convention in singing his trademark tune "Sweet Adeline" then swung into "The Sidewalks of New York." When the spotlight focused on Catherine Dunn Smith, the former governor's wife, the crowd roared. "The Smith demonstration was the realest thing in the convention," said the Kansas editor William Allen White.[7]

BALTIMORE MAYOR HOWARD W. JACKSON, a Ritchie supporter, moved for a three-hour dinner recess, noting that the radio broadcast of the convention was about to end. Ritchie favored the delay expecting that his parade would be the loudest and largest of the evening session. On the platform Roosevelt allies broke into a heated argument over Jackson's motion. "When I started I was leading this thing—and we're going through," snapped J. Bruce Kremer of Montana. Floor leader Mullen wanted the dinner break. Farley, worried that the delay could slow FDR's momentum, sided with Kremer. Overruling them, Senator Walsh asked for a voice vote, which was inconclusive. Walsh then asked each side to stand and the motion carried.

During the recess, all sides hustled for votes. In the penthouse of a Gold Coast apartment building, former Ohio governor James Cox huddled with Jersey City mayor Frank Hague and Henry Breckinridge, Byrd's floor leader. Under an informal agreement, the Smith forces and the favorite sons vowed to stick together until the convention deadlocked and the Roosevelt bandwagon stopped. Smith was then expected to withdraw and allow the coalition to unite behind a single candidate. The Cox strategy would then push Ritchie until the convention drafted Baker. "We are all right," a coalition leader told Frank R. Kent, "if they don't buy us."[8]

Roosevelt was offering up the vice-presidential nomination. If a favorite-son candidate dropped out of the coalition, a switch to FDR could stampede the convention. Governor George White of Ohio, ambitious for the vice presidency, had fifty-two votes pledged to his favorite-son candidacy. "The capture of such a large delegation would have been sufficient to ensure nomination," Farley later wrote. But White did not have the authority to barter. Cox, the dominant figure in Ohio Democratic politics, was using White to hold the delegation for Baker. In removing himself from contention for the vice presidency, White said that he was "observing the spirit of the understanding" between Cox and Baker.

Before returning to the convention hall, Farley stopped at the Sherman House and conferred with Garner floor manager Sam Rayburn. At a previous meeting, Farley had suggested the House Speaker as a possible running mate for FDR. "Now this time," said Farley, "I know positively that we can bring about his nomination for second place on the ticket."

Rayburn asked what Farley wanted.

"Have the Texas delegation record its vote for Garner on the first ballot," he replied, "and then before the result is announced switch to Roosevelt. I feel certain that some state will make the break after it becomes apparent that the Governor has a big majority, and Texas might as well be first."

"Hell, no," the congressman answered, "we've got a lot of people up here who've never been to a convention before, and they've got to vote for Garner a few times."

In the event of a deadlock, Rayburn wondered how many ballots Roosevelt's lines could hold without breaking. "Three ballots," Farley said, "four ballots, and maybe five."

"Well, we just might let the convention go for a while," Rayburn replied, "even if we are interested in the vice-presidency, and I'm not saying that we are."[9]

The largest crowd in the history of political conventions attended the evening session. All of the twenty-two thousand seats were filled and another five thousand were wedged into standing room. Outside on Madison Street, fifteen thousand stood on the sidewalk and listened to the booming public-address system. An enterprising youngster scaled a fire escape, lowered it to the ground, and allowed fifty people to crash the gate. When the doors were ordered closed by the fire marshal, two U.S. senators were denied admission.

AS THE CONVENTION resumed, Senator Carter Glass nominated Byrd, comparing him to the great Virginians Patrick Henry and Thomas Jefferson. "What Byrd did for Virginia," said Glass, "he would do for the country if nominated by this convention." The Richmond Blues National Guard regiment's band, in their white-and-blue War of 1812 uniforms, kicking off the Byrd demonstration, struck up "Carry Me Back to Old Virginia" before swinging into "Dixie." A group of Richmond debutantes released a flock of "white doves of peace" that were actually pigeons. These birds fluttered in the spotlights, then ascended to the rafters and perched over the heads of uneasy delegates. Admiral Byrd, Governor Pollard, and General Billy Mitchell led the Virginia contingent through the aisles, and the delegations of eleven states joined the procession.

Howe had tried for weeks to win over Byrd. Given FDR's close ties to Admiral Byrd and cordial relationship with the former governor, Howe regarded Virginia as their best hope for a breakthrough. At this session of the convention, Farley sought out Admiral Byrd and "offered the vice-presidential nomination to his brother Harry." The polar explorer, instructed to reject any offers from Roosevelt's camp, told Farley that he "would not interfere" with his brother's strategy. Robert

Jackson, secretary of the national committee, approached the admiral and proposed another deal. If Virginia would switch its votes, Jackson promised that FDR would nominate the admiral as the next secretary of the navy. Jackson said years later that Richard Byrd seemed interested. "But Harry embarrassed me," Jackson recalled, "by saying he had considered me a friend who should have known he would never be a party to so contemptible a maneuver."

"I couldn't deliver them," the former governor told Jackson, "and I wouldn't if I could."[10]

Governor Ritchie was then courted. From the beginning of the week, Breckinridge Long kept in touch with the Maryland governor's camp. "I told them I was authorized to approach Ritchie and to say we would like to see him vice president," Long later wrote. "It was on an 'if' basis. I would make him an offer to throw our whole support to him, if he would place himself at our disposal and withdraw in Roosevelt's favor when we said the word." James Roosevelt reported in the *Boston Herald*, "There is a strong movement on foot to get Governor Ritchie of Maryland to agree to become the running mate of Roosevelt. If such an arrangement is consummated, the Smith wing of the party may very easily be reconciled to the support of a Roosevelt-Ritchie ticket." Senator Pat Harrison of Mississippi, predicted that "Roosevelt, Ritchie and repeal," would be a winning combination.

At the convention hall, Farley had Mayor Jackson of Baltimore deliver the message that FDR was offering Ritchie the vice-presidential nomination, "if he would withdraw as a candidate for the presidency."

But for Ritchie, it would be all or nothing. His allies, including Bernard M. Baruch and Chicago Board of Trade president Peter Carey, were putting on the blitz. William T. Kemper, Democratic national committeeman from Missouri, received more than one hundred telegrams on Thursday urging Ritchie as an alternative to FDR.[11]

As the great demonstration for him began that night, the black, gold, red, silver, and white colors of the Maryland State flag waved throughout the galleries and more than a hundred "Win with Ritchie" banners dominated the floor. The Richmond Blues and the organ played "Maryland, My Maryland," and confetti rained from the balconies. "It's all over now!" a Ritchie partisan shouted. A single banner proclaimed, "Jefferson, Jackson, Cleveland, Wilson and now Ritchie." Mayor Cermak, who liked Ritchie, held a Maryland flag in his hand as he led Illinois delegates into the demonstration. "This country is getting sick and tired of government by a stuffed shirt," declared Richard F. Cleveland, son of the late Democratic president, in seconding Ritchie. "The circumstances of the time constitute a solemn call to arms. The long fight back to economic stability calls for a man who is used to the stress of battle. With pride Maryland offers such a leader."

While Ritchie watched near the speaker's platform, Farley sauntered over and put his hand on the governor's shoulder. "Bert, it's a great demonstration," Big Jim said, "but it doesn't mean a thing. We have the votes and that is what counts."

Smiling and shrugging his shoulders, Ritchie conceded, "Maybe you're right."[12]

Huey Long did not share Farley's confidence. The Louisiana populist thought FDR had folded too soon in the two-thirds rule fight and worried that his lead was slipping. From the convention hall, he telephoned Roosevelt in Albany. "Hello, Franklin—this is the Kingfish," he said.

"Hello, Kingfish, how are you?" Roosevelt answered.

"I'm fine and hope you are," said Huey. "I have a suggestion for you which will clinch the nomination."

Roosevelt gave him full attention.

"I think you should issue a statement immediately," said Long, "saying that you are in favor of a soldiers' bonus to be paid as soon as you become President."

"Well," replied Roosevelt, "I'm afraid I cannot do that because I am not in favor of a soldiers' bonus."

"Whether you believe in it or not," asserted the Kingfish, "you'd better come out for it with a strong statement, otherwise you haven't got a chance for the nomination."

Roosevelt thanked Long for his suggestion but said that he could not endorse the bonus.

"Well," said Huey, "you are a gone goose."[13]

Since Roosevelt had a majority of the delegates, Farley could decide whether to go directly into the balloting after the nominating speeches or seek an adjournment. "I was nearer the point of mental and physical exhaustion that night than at any time during the convention," he later wrote. "The nervous strain during this period of suspense was very close to the limit of physical endurance." After midnight, he escaped to his tiny hideaway office, stretched out on a cot, and summoned lieutenants to determine their next move. "I remained on the cot, too weary to get up, and questioned each one of them," he reminisced. "The verdict was that delay was dangerous; that time was bound to work for the opposition; that the only sensible course was to insist upon a ballot that night before adjournment."

FARLEY TELEPHONED ROOSEVELT and informed him of this tactical decision. "Go to it, Jim," the governor replied.[14]

In an effort to stall the balloting, the anti-Roosevelt forces extended the nominating festivities to their greatest possible length. Banker Melvin Traylor, nominated by Chicago Democratic leader Mike Igoe, watched his fifteen-minute demonstration from a favored seat near the speaker's platform. "If through any unforeseen circumstance Traylor is nominated," Paul Y. Anderson wryly observed in the *St. Louis Post-Dispatch*, "he is expected to run on the platform that his bank is still open. Several southern delegates who have experienced difficulty in cashing checks here joined spontaneously in the Traylor parade."

Frank Scofield, Traylor's campaign manager, created a stir when he told reporters that a man claiming to be a Roosevelt supporter had of- fered him $10,000 in exchange for the Illinois favorite-son's with- drawal. Farley dismissed this allegation as "ridiculous." R. G. Dunham, Traylor's floor manager, attributed the bribe attempt to "an interloper or someone who butted in and didn't have anything to do with any- one's campaign."

This hoax notwithstanding, Roosevelt wanted Traylor out of the race. Like the other favorite sons, the Democratic banker could have traded his delegates for the vice presidency. Farley had encouraged speculation about this possibility. Robert Jackson, on Roosevelt's be- half, proposed another deal. If Traylor dropped out in FDR's favor, the Chicago executive would be the next secretary of the Treasury. Traylor declined, confiding that he could not afford the pay cut.[15]

At 3:00 a.m., Alfalfa Bill Murray was nominated and the "Girls' Kiltie Band" led a fourteen-minute demonstration. Murray, sitting with the Oklahoma delegation, stood and waved as delegates across the stadium gave him a rousing ovation. Huey Long, on the speaker's plat- form, motioned his delegation into the parade. Oklahoma native Will Rogers, galloping through the aisles, quipped that he was glad Chicago's schoolchildren weren't exposed to this spectacle. "They would never again have asked, 'What's the matter with the country?' "

As the session dragged on, Farley cut the number of seconding speeches. Some but not all of Roosevelt's allies yielded their moment on the speaker's platform. "I learned on this occasion," Farley later wrote, "that a thorough-going Democrat will give you his support, his loyalty, his vote, and his money—but never his radio time." The crowd laughed and cheered Huey Long as he called for an end to the seconding speeches. "I call upon all supporters of Governor Roosevelt to omit all seconding speeches," said Josephus Daniels, "and hasten the vote."[16]

While John W. Davis slept in his first-row seat on the speaker's platform, several photographers moved in for a close-up. When the 1924 presidential nominee awakened, the newsmen lowered their cameras. Davis recognized what was up and in mock exhaustion dropped his head on the shoulder of another delegate. The photographers set their cameras only to have Davis lift up his head. After repeating this prank, he turned his attention to the business of the convention. The New Yorker then dozed off again and the flashbulbs popped.

Before the balloting, Senator Connally twice sought to adjourn the convention. The first motion was defeated on a standing vote. Soon afterward, Connally tried again and demanded a roll call. "There was no point in going further until we were all rested," the Texas senator recalled, "so I took the floor and made a motion that we adjourn." By this time Hague and other Stop Roosevelt leaders wanted the balloting to start. "They had come to the conclusion that if the convention were kept in continuous session, the delegates would tire and drop," Connally said. Massachusetts, which at first voted for the motion, switched after Hague came out against it. In the end, only California, New York, Oklahoma, and Texas backed Connally's motion.[17]

The flamboyant George Preston Marshall of Washington, D.C., who would soon bring professional football to the nation's capital, made the last pitch. "Perspiring delegates, I am closing the show," declared Marshall. "This is the finish. There is one thing that I would like to say to you. We haven't got a vote in the District of Columbia, but there are certain people in the District who have ideas. We have to do one thing that no one else in this convention hall has to do—we have to live with the next President. We have to live with the nominee, and we have lived next door to a man that we know is worthwhile living with. I second the nomination of Albert Ritchie."

At 4:28 a.m. clerk Patrick J. Haltigan stepped to the microphone and began the first roll call. Most of the galleries were empty and large areas of the floor were abandoned. "The convention looked like a shambles," Farley later wrote. But he knew that a call for adjournment would be interpreted as another retreat by FDR's forces and still held out hope for a first-ballot decision. Howard Bruce of Maryland, a Ritchie strategist, estimated that the Stop Roosevelt bloc would receive about 484 votes on the first ballot, more than enough to deadlock the convention.[18]

Surrounded by family, Roosevelt listened to the radio from a comfortable chair in his study at the Executive Mansion in Albany. In the seclusion of his suite at the Congress, Smith stacked quarters next to the pay radio and dropped in another coin when the radio clicked. Garner, who did not listen to the nominating speeches, slept soundly in the apartment of his Washington hotel.

The first ballot took almost two hours. Former Alabama governor William Woodward Brandon, announcing twenty-four votes, started the Roosevelt bandwagon. Early in the roll call, Garner pulled nearly even with FDR when McAdoo cast California's forty-four votes. Mullen was most worried about possible defections in the District of Columbia, Iowa, Minnesota, and Mississippi, where "the balance was precarious" and Roosevelt could lose these entire delegations under the unit rule. Walsh rejected a demand from Smith supporters to poll the Iowa delegation, noting that the delegation had been instructed to vote for Roosevelt. When Ritchie's camp challenged the unit rule in the District of Columbia, Walsh dismissed their claim. Thomas Quinn, a Ritchie supporter in the Minnesota delegation, objected to his state's voting for Roosevelt as a unit and produced a telegram from the State Democratic Central Committee of Minnesota releasing delegates from previous instructions. "The Chair cannot recognize any authority in the Democratic Committee of the State of Minnesota," Walsh replied, "to annul or recall a resolution of instructions given by the state convention." All of the above rulings might have gone the other way if Shouse had been the presiding officer. "Thanks to his [Walsh's] rulings, we held intact the unit voting in those states which had instructed for it, and where it helped us," said Mullen.[19]

When New York was called, Curry requested a poll of the delegation. For what purpose, asked Walsh? "I am unable to give the full vote," the Tammany leader replied. Walsh then asked the clerk to proceed with the poll. Until this moment, Curry had yet to declare his preference for the nomination. Curry had never been close to Smith but voted for the former governor as the coalition's best chance of keeping the delegation beyond FDR's reach. Another factor in Curry's support of Smith was that the first-ballot vote would keep the former governor from opposing Tammany's slate in the next municipal election. Their native state voted sixty-five for Smith and twenty-eight for Roosevelt. Mayor Walker left the stadium in the early morning hours and slept across the street in the back seat of a limousine. When he returned to the hall, Walker walked to the New York standard and asked for recognition.

"The Mayor of New York is recognized," said Walsh.

"Mr. Chairman," said Walker, "I hear that in my absence an alternate voted on my name. May I ask the privilege of casting that vote myself at this time?"

"The delegate has that right," answered Walsh.

With Roosevelt sitting in judgment on corruption charges, Walker loudly announced, "I desire that my vote be cast for Alfred E. Smith." The convention throngs cheered his defiance.

Grateful for Walker's support, Smith resented the defection of former allies. "Ed, you are not representing the people of Bronx County in your support of Roosevelt," Smith told Bronx leader Edward J. Flynn. "You know the people of Bronx County want you to support me."

Flynn conceded this point but noted that he committed to Roosevelt at a time when Smith had removed himself from the race. "It was an extremely painful interview," Flynn recalled. "My friendship with Smith had been much longer and more intimate than my friendship with Roosevelt."[20]

Senator James Reed got all thirty-six Missouri votes when the roll was first called. Thomas J. Pendergast, the Kansas City boss, Reed's longtime ally, vowed to stand by his man "regardless of the outlook." In his memoirs, Farley claimed that Pendergast covertly backed Roosevelt. But Flynn regarded the Kansas City boss as a leading member of the Stop Roosevelt movement. There is also evidence that Roosevelt disliked Pendergast for supporting Reed in Chicago. What is clear is that at the end of the first roll call, a dozen Missouri votes switched to Roosevelt. This woke up the galleries and provoked jeers and booing.

At a caucus of the Missouri delegation, Reed had to fend off a motion by a Roosevelt supporter to exclude him from the room. "I am not here begging the vote of any delegate," the former senator shot back. "If my record of service for the Democratic party does not entitle me to the support of the delegation, and if any delegate is willing to violate the instructions of the state convention, I will not beg him to vote for me."[21]

The first ballot showed Roosevelt with 666 votes; followed by Smith, 201; Garner, 90; White, 52; Traylor, 42; Byrd, 25; Reed, 24; Murray, 23; Ritchie, 21; and Baker, 8. Farley leaned back and looked over the floor to see where the anticipated bandwagon rush would begin. But Missouri was the only state that had given more votes to FDR. "I was so sure the opposition lines would break that the disappointment was almost more than I could bear," Farley recalled. "Nothing happened. Not a single delegate shifted. Two years of tireless work seemed headed for political oblivion."

After the first roll call, Walker's lawyer John J. Curtin approached Mullen with an offer to swing the New York delegation behind Roosevelt if the governor pledged to drop the Seabury charges. "I didn't even take up the proposition with Roosevelt," Mullen later wrote. "I figured that we were going to get through without New York, and in the national election Jimmy Walker would be more of a liability than an asset to us."[22]

As the second ballot got under way, Farley looked to Cermak.

The Chicago mayor controlled the fifty-eight votes of Illinois and also the thirty votes of Indiana. During the all-night session, he devoured a jar of homemade pickled lamb's tongues and plotted strategy with Stop Roosevelt allies. "Cermak shared the lead in attempts to swing votes, preferably for Al Smith or Ritchie, but for anyone to beat Roosevelt," former mayor Carter H. Harrison, an FDR man, later wrote. "The game was to steal votes, if only for a ballot or two, and so secure a break in our ranks."

Cermak smoldered when Harrison and former governor Edward Dunne, who sat near him in the Illinois delegation, stood and cheered for Roosevelt. "Tell 'em to shut up and use some sense," the mayor told Chief Bailiff Al Horan. "Didn't I put them on the delegation?"

"You ought to have known better," Horan replied. "You can't shut 'em up. They're too tough. That's one time you slipped, Tony."

"Yeah," said Cermak, "that's one time I slipped."

Farley pleaded with Cermak, knowing that the mayor had the votes to put Roosevelt over the top. "Had Illinois come over," Farley remembered, "there is no doubt in my mind that under the customary practice at national political conventions, the vice-presidential nomination would have gone to that state. Certainly I would have done everything possible to bring it about." If Cermak had made this deal, it is probable that Traylor would have gone on the ticket. Another possibility would have been Lewis. Although Cermak had been embarrassed by J. Ham's disavowal of his favorite-son candidacy, his ascension to the vice presidency could have opened up a senatorial seat for the mayor. Cermak, Farley later wrote, "had everything in his hands at that moment—national prominence, possibly the Senate which he had his eyes on."

As a leader of the coalition that produced the deadlock, Cermak had no intention of helping Roosevelt. After listening to Farley's arguments, Cermak insisted that the delegation could not switch to another candidate without a caucus. Farley knew better, "but could do nothing."[23]

Both sides were scrambling. A Roosevelt supporter in the Ohio delegation, former state chairman W. W. Durbin, demanded a poll of the Buckeye State. White took all fifty-two votes on the first ballot. The only defection when delegates were polled was Durbin's half-vote for Roosevelt. Another large state, Pennsylvania, showed little change when its delegates were polled. Roosevelt had received forty-four of the Keystone State's seventy-six votes on the first ballot and got the same number of votes when his supporters demanded the poll. Two Ritchie supporters fought for nearly an hour for their release from the District of Columbia's unit rule but Walsh said the rule was binding and counted them for Roosevelt. Hague sought to break open the Iowa and Michigan caucuses, where the shift of a few votes under the unit rule could cost FDR an entire delegation.

On the second roll call, Roosevelt gained eleven votes. Six were from Missouri, where FDR and Reed each received eighteen votes. Pendergast still voted for Reed, but Kemper assured Roosevelt's camp that most of the Missouri delegation would ultimately switch to FDR. Roosevelt also picked up two votes in Indiana, and single votes from New York and North Dakota. Farley had been holding a few votes in reserve to offset possible defections. The second ballot showed Roosevelt leading with 677.75 votes followed by Smith with 194.25 votes and Garner with 90.25 votes. On this roll call, Murray cast Oklahoma's twenty-two votes for his pal Will Rogers. Farley was again disappointed that the opposition lines were holding firm.

"No candidate having received the two-thirds of the entire number of votes," declared Walsh, "there is no choice."

Mullen then moved for adjournment, but the opposition leaders protested. "We have been held here all night at great inconvenience," said Dudley Field Malone of New York, "and we are prepared to stay here all day."

When Walsh called for a voice vote, it was inconclusive. Stepping back from the microphone he summoned Mullen. "Walsh told me that he was afraid we'd lose the motion if it went to a vote," Mullen later wrote. If the Stop Roosevelt forces won this test, they would have momentum going into the third ballot. As a Smith ally demanded a roll call, Mullen withdrew his motion.[24]

"Watch this one closely," Farley told Bob Jackson as Walsh began the third ballot. "It will show whether I can ever go back to New York or not."

Roosevelt narrowly averted disaster. Senator Pat Harrison of Mississippi, advised by FDR's men that the convention would adjourn, returned to his suite at the Congress Hotel when he turned on the radio and heard the beginning of the third ballot. Harrison hurriedly put his

clothes back on and took a cab to the convention hall. Governor Martin
S. Conner, a Baker supporter, was on the verge of stripping his state's
twenty votes from Roosevelt. Harrison returned just in time to keep
Mississippi in line by a single vote. "Had that delegation broken, Roosevelt could never have been nominated," Arthur Krock recalled years
later, "because he would have gone down so far that Ritchie or Baker
would have come up."[25]

Flynn credited Huey Long with holding Arkansas and Mississippi
for Roosevelt on the third ballot. "There had been a good deal of quar-
reling among the delegates from these two states. We had been informed of this and were extremely fearful lest the delegates should
abandon the unit rule and scatter their strength," Flynn remembered.
"We were afraid that if other states saw Arkansas wavering they might
follow suit. It was clear to me then, and it is clear now, that if that had
happened, the Roosevelt candidacy would have suffered immensely."

According to Flynn, Long was recruited by Roosevelt's camp to
prevent Arkansas and Mississippi from breaking away. "We put the entire responsibility on Long," Flynn said. "Huey went out on the floor
of the convention and got to work. He threatened. He cajoled. He bullied the two senators concerned—Robinson and Harrison. He shook
his fist in Harrison's face and bellowed, 'If you break the rule, you so-
and-so, I'll go into Mississippi and break you!' "[26]

From all accounts, Long played an important role in protecting Roosevelt's southern flank. But Flynn may have overstated Long's dealings
with Harrison and Robinson. Farley and Frank Walker said that Harrison on his own held Mississippi in line. As for Robinson, he and Long
had not spoken in months. During the convention, with the Senate still
in session, the Arkansas Democrat stayed in Washington. With Robinson staying away from Chicago, Long filled the leadership void in the

Arkansas delegation. "There is no question but that without Long's work," said Flynn, "Roosevelt might not have been nominated."

On the third ballot, Roosevelt picked up only five votes, while Garner gained ten, and Smith dropped four votes. "Still the break failed to come," lamented Farley. After keeping the nomination from Roosevelt for a third consecutive ballot, a Tammany leader gloated, "He's sunk and we hope he stayed that way." Indiana University law school dean Paul McNutt, chairman of the Hoosier delegation, added: "The Roosevelt vote was disappointing."[27]

At 9:15 a.m. the convention finally adjourned until Friday night. Delegates were flooded with thousands of telegrams from across the nation urging Baker's nomination. Walter Lippmann began circulating a petition among prominent Democrats calling on the convention to draft Baker. "The way out of the danger of a deadlock is not only open, but it is attractive," Lippmann wrote. "For all through these various delegations there is an astonishingly strong though quiet conviction that the party can unite on a man who is stronger than any of the leading contenders. That man is Newton Baker of Ohio. My impression is that he is the first real choice of more responsible Democrats than any other man, and that he is an acceptable second choice to almost every one."[28]

After the third ballot, Mullen vowed that Roosevelt would fight on. "We have taken a new poll of our rockbound strength," said FDR's floor leader, "and it convinces us that 650 of our delegates will stay here until Roosevelt is nominated or until hell freezes over. If the emissaries of corrupt interests continue to halt the nomination of the man who is clearly the choice of the majority of the party, we shall speak out. We will denounce the damnable hypocrisy of the people who misrule New York City, Jersey City and Chicago, coming here to stand behind Mr. Smith in an effort to seize the power in the nation or else throw the party on the rocks."

At Roosevelt headquarters, there was a sense that this could be the beginning of the end. The odds against FDR's nomination were now five to one. Marion Dickerman would never forget the gloom and despair. Farley admitted that the Roosevelt lines could not be expected to hold. "There was no joy in the Roosevelt camp," Raymond Moley later wrote. "It seemed probable that when the convention was resumed and another ballot taken, a pretty general crack-up of the Roosevelt forces would occur. There was no great liking for the Roosevelt movement on the part of a good many state leaders, and at the first sign of weakness it would crumble."[29]

Rexford G. Tugwell of Columbia University, Moley's associate in the "Brain Trust," and Harry Hopkins, director of New York State's Temporary Emergency Relief Administration, felt that Roosevelt had been stopped. Basil O'Connor, FDR's law partner, was already talking about taking retribution against those responsible for his friend's loss. "We'll have the governorship six months more anyhow," he said, "and boy, will we make those damned Tammany fellows wish they hadn't played this game!"

At 5:20 p.m., alone in his Executive Mansion study, Roosevelt telephoned Baker in Cleveland. "It now looks as though the Chicago convention is in a jam and that they will turn to you," FDR said. "I will do anything I can to bring that about if you want it."

A surprised Baker told FDR that he should not concede "on the basis of any such information as I have." As this conversation indicated, Roosevelt knew that the nomination might be lost. But he urged delegates to hold firm.[30]

"I am in this fight to stay," Roosevelt pledged in a telegram. "This is a battle for principle. A clear majority of the convention understands that it is being waged to keep our party as a whole from dictation by a small group representing the interests in the nation which have no place in our party.

"My friends will not be misled by organized propaganda by telegrams now being sent to delegates. Stick to your guns. It is clear that the nation must not and shall not be overridden. Now is the time to make clear that we intend to stand fast and win."[31]

2 2

SWITCH

ITH BAKER GAINING momentum, Joseph P. Kennedy sensed that Roosevelt's vulnerability might be turned into an advantage. As one of the few Wall Street speculators to get out of the stock market before the Great Crash, he was the toughest and shrewdest of FDR's men. The tall, red-haired financier had a fortune estimated at $100 million and was among Roosevelt's more generous contributors. This campaign marked his debut on the national political stage. "Roosevelt was a man of action," Kennedy recalled. "He had the capacity to get things done. . . . I knew what he could do and how he did it, and I felt that after a long period of inactivity we needed a leader who would lead."[1]

Before heading for Chicago, Kennedy conferred with Roosevelt in New York and discussed strategy. "I had admired the skill with which he engaged in light banter with the Governor," Arthur Krock later wrote, "without overstepping the limits of the deference appropriate in the circumstances." Krock was in Kennedy's Chicago hotel suite when his telephone call was put through to William Randolph Hearst at San Simeon.

While in the movie business, Kennedy developed a friendship with the press lord and stayed frequently at the Hearst castle. Although a generation older, W. R. had much in common with the founding father of the Kennedy dynasty. Both were outsiders with a lust for power and social acceptance. Just as Hearst once aspired to the presidency, the younger man now dreamed of becoming the nation's first Irish Catholic president. And like the publisher, this grandson of Irish immigrants was an economic conservative and isolationist. In the spring, Kennedy had made a "business trip" to California that included a stop at San Simeon.

On the Friday morning of July 1, with the convention deadlocked, Kennedy telephoned Hearst and urged him to break the stalemate.

Addressing the publisher as "W. R.," Kennedy warned that Baker was more than a threat. As the power behind the Garner candidacy, Hearst had influence over the California and Texas delegations. Garner had gained support on the third ballot and had second-choice support in at least a half dozen other states including New York. W. R. felt obligated to support the House Speaker for at least several more ballots.

"Do you want that man Baker running our country," asked Kennedy, "that great defender of the League of Nations, that ardent internationalist whose policies you despise? No, of course you don't. But that's just who you're going to get if you keep holding out your delegates from Roosevelt, for if the convention cracks open, it'll surely be Baker. And then where will you be?

"If you don't want Baker, you'd better take Roosevelt," Kennedy argued, "because if you don't take Roosevelt, you're going to have Baker."

"All right. Is that my choice?" asked Hearst. "Could I get Ritchie?"

"No, I don't think so," Kennedy replied. "I think if Roosevelt cracks on the next ballot, it'll be Baker."

"All right," W. R. said. "I'll turn to him."[2]

Soon afterward, Hearst placed a call to his aide Joseph Willicombe in Chicago with new instructions. Willicombe then relayed this message to George Rothwell Brown. "Mr. Hearst has a request to make of you," said Willicombe. "He wants you to go to Speaker Garner and say to him that he is very fearful that on the next or some subsequent ballot delegations will desert Roosevelt," Willicombe said. "Mr. Hearst is fearful that when Roosevelt's strength crumbles it will bring about either the election of Smith or Baker. Either would be disastrous."[3]

The decision would be Garner's alone.

In Room 1702 at the Congress Hotel, Louis McHenry Howe had pushed himself beyond the limit. Coughing and wheezing from chronic asthma, Roosevelt's lieutenant nearly passed out. "He looked like death," recalled Marion Dickerman. "It was just terribly hot in Chicago, and in those days, you know, nothing was air-conditioned excepting movie theaters and drugstores. Jim told me he wondered if Louis could live through the convention, and I wondered, too. The only part of him that seemed absolutely alive were the eyes. They seemed to blaze out of their sockets. He was in his shirtsleeves, of course, with the collar open, and that scrawny neck seemed scrawnier than ever. His shirt was soaked with sweat. It clung to his thin arms and bony chest. Every now and then he doubled over, coughing in the most horrible way, though that didn't keep him from smoking one cigarette after another."

Shortly before noon Farley came into the suite, stretched out on the carpet next to Howe and suggested a way out of the stalemate. "I told him that in my opinion Texas was the best bet and that it was my intention to stake everything on bringing over the Lone Star State," Farley recalled. "He agreed that it looked like the only course to pursue."[4]

At Farley's request, Senator Pat Harrison tracked down Garner campaign manager Sam Rayburn and arranged a meeting in Harrison's suite. "This would be technically neutral territory and, more important, it wouldn't attract the attention of the press, as would a meeting of this kind in Garner or Roosevelt headquarters," Harrison's friend George E. Allen said. Before Rayburn arrived, Farley asked the senator: "What shall we offer them?"

Without hesitation, Harrison replied, "Anything they want."

Still tired from the all-night session, Farley fell asleep in his chair and was snoring. Allen, with whom Harrison was sharing the suite, suggested that Farley take a nap on his bed until Rayburn arrived. "I did," Farley later wrote, "and, according to George, immediately resumed my snoring."

Rayburn brought Silliman Evans, manager of Garner's headquarters at the Sherman House. "Without wasting much time on shadowboxing, we got down to business," Farley recalled. "There was no disguising the fact that we had to have the Texas delegation to ensure victory for the Roosevelt cause." Farley again proposed Garner for the vice presidency in exchange for his delegates. Harrison urged Rayburn to make this deal. "Neither Sam nor Silliman needed much convincing. They were both realists in politics and saw the situation exactly as it was," Farley said. Although Rayburn did not make a commitment, he seemed responsive. As the meeting broke up, Rayburn told Farley: "We'll see what can be done."[5]

On the eve of the convention, Senators Harry Hawes of Missouri and Key Pittman of Nevada proposed a Roosevelt-Garner ticket. Hawes telephoned Roosevelt in Albany and asked if Garner was an acceptable running mate. "Senator, that would be fine," FDR replied. "The Governor of New York and the Speaker of the House from Texas—clear across the country." Roosevelt then told Hawes to get in touch with Farley. "We have had a talk with interested parties and we can say no more," Pittman and Hawes wired Senator Tom Connally at the Sherman House. "All believe that strongest ticket will be Roosevelt and Garner."[6]

Neither Hawes nor Pittman had talked with the House Speaker. On learning of their effort, an angry Garner rebuked Hawes for sending out telegrams implying that he was ready to quit the presidential race. Once the convention deadlocked, Garner's nominator Tom Connally suggested to Mullen that Texas Democrats might be open to a deal. "We're not going to drop Garner unless we have some consideration for him," Connally said. "How about making it definitely Garner for vice president?"

Mullen favored Garner but did not have the authority to make this commitment. Soon afterward, he brought Farley to the Texas senator. "I told them immediately that Texas wouldn't come over to Roosevelt unless we had absolute assurance that Garner would be the vice-presidential nominee," Connally said.

"We'll do that," Farley pledged.

"That isn't enough," Connally said. "I don't want any old political assurance. I need your personal assurance as man to man that if the Texas delegation comes over to Roosevelt, you'll nominate Garner for vice president."

When Farley agreed, Connally promised to take the offer to Garner.[7]

Farley next worked the California delegation. Santa Barbara publisher Thomas M. Storke and Los Angeles millionaire Hamilton Cotton, McAdoo's closest friends in the delegation, conferred with Roosevelt's manager in the rear bedroom of his suite. "Boys, Roosevelt is lost unless California comes over to us on the next ballot," Farley said. "I am eighty-seven votes short, and I cannot hope to get them unless you switch to Roosevelt on the fourth ballot."

Storke replied that California would eventually go to Roosevelt, but "we felt we owed it to Garner to go along with him for at least another ballot or two."

"Then Newton D. Baker will be nominated," Farley predicted. "He is the interests' candidate, and you will be playing squarely into their hands if you wait. I tell you, unless California comes over on the fourth ballot, Roosevelt is lost and Baker will win!"

Storke asked how Baker could take the nomination.

"Five midwest states that have been held in the Roosevelt column by the unit rule—Minnesota, Iowa, the two Dakotas, and Mississippi—will break and scatter on the fourth ballot," Farley said.

Storke and Cotton argued that it was premature for California to make this switch. "What does Mac want?" Farley asked. "Will he go as vice president?"

The Californians said McAdoo had no interest in going on the ticket.

"Then," Farley asked, "how about Ambassador to the Court of St. James? Or Secretary of the Treasury?"

"Mr. McAdoo wants nothing and is expecting nothing," Storke said. "He cannot be made a party to any deal."

But when Farley asked if McAdoo would support Garner for the vice presidency, the Californians answered in the affirmative.

"All right, then, let's make it Roosevelt and Garner," Farley said. Storke and Cotton agreed to seek McAdoo's support for switching the Golden State's delegation.[8]

McAdoo still had White House ambitions of his own. "We discovered that our friend from California treasured the idea that we didn't have all the votes we claimed," Robert Woolley reported to Colonel House, "and that, a deadlock resulting, a dark horse could walk away with the nomination—he being the dark horse."

During the all-night session, Breckinridge Long sought to negotiate with McAdoo but became suspicious of his agenda. "McAdoo would not come along," Long later wrote. "McAdoo was still in a trading mood but with himself in the picture and his own fortunes to be benefited."

McAdoo called his ally at San Simeon and asked for another shot at the presidency. Hearst had supported Wilson's son-in-law in 1924 and was now running him for the Senate. If California and Texas were going to switch their votes, it should not necessarily be for Roosevelt, the former presidential contender argued. But W. R. replied that McAdoo's time had passed.[9]

Meanwhile, George Rothwell Brown conferred with Garner in the Speaker's hideaway office. "Mr. Hearst is fearful that the nomination will go either to Baker or Smith, unless you throw your strength to Roosevelt," Brown said. "He regards Baker as an internationalist and a reactionary. If Smith should be nominated, we will have the fight of 1928 all over again, with the party torn asunder, and all hope of electing a Democrat gone."

"Say to Mr. Hearst that I fully agree with him," Garner replied. "He is right. Tell him I will carry out his suggestion."

Garner thought the convention would be making a mistake if it rejected FDR and nominated Baker. "Compromise candidates don't win presidential elections," he said. "Garfield was the last one who did, and he won in a very close popular vote."

At about 3:00 p.m., the House Speaker telephoned Rayburn. "Sam, I think it is time to break this thing up. Roosevelt is the choice of the convention," Garner said. "He has had a majority on three ballots. We don't want to be responsible for wrecking the party's chances. The nomination ought to be made on the next roll call."

Before making his announcement, Garner sought more information. "Mr. Garner was willing and really wanted the California-Texas delegations to be released," Rayburn later wrote, ". . . but there were some other things that had to be done before release was made."

Late in the afternoon, Rayburn reported back to the Speaker. "Smith's bloc was standing firm. Roosevelt could not break into other delegations, and Mississippi and some other states were about to desert him," Garner later told Bascom Timmons. "Feelers showed that California would go to Roosevelt if I released the delegates. Texas would not, unless I went on the ticket with the New York governor. . . . If Texas and California did not go to Roosevelt on the fourth ballot, Rayburn thought the convention was in for a deadlock."[10]

As the Texas caucus assembled at the Sherman House, Rayburn faced a rebellion led by Amon G. Carter, publisher of the *Fort Worth Star-Telegram*. Although the Lone Star state had only forty-six votes, Texas sent 180 delegates to Chicago with each having one-fourth of a vote. At the meeting called by Rayburn, 105 delegates were rounded up. If the other seventy-five delegates had attended the caucus, Carter might have succeeded in holding the delegation. Many of these absent Texans were out working other delegations to win votes for their favorite son.

"Amon Carter and the bunch were raising hell," Rayburn said years later. "Amon was attending his first convention and running around, saying he had talked to this one and that one. He was going to nominate Garner whether he had the votes or not."

Rayburn, anticipating a close vote, turned over the gavel to Silliman Evans and left the room to place another call to Garner. "I got him right away," he recalled. "I knew somebody would challenge my releasing the delegation."

It was a brief conversation. "Do I have permission to release the Texas delegation now?" asked Rayburn.

"Yes," replied the House Speaker.

"Do you release the Texas delegation now?"

"Yes," Garner answered.[11]

As Rayburn hurried back to the meeting, he ran into McAdoo, who had called a meeting of the California delegation. "What are we going to do?" the Golden State's chairman asked. "We will vote for Jack until hell freezes over if you or he says so."

"I told him Garner had just released the Texas delegation, and in my opinion we were going for Roosevelt," Rayburn said. Since the House Speaker had withdrawn his candidacy, Rayburn suggested that California should join Texas in switching to FDR. It was his understanding that the West Coast delegates were legally bound to Garner and could not support another candidate without his consent.[12]

McAdoo had a different recollection. As the chairman of the California delegation, he felt that the caucus was obligated to Garner only if he remained in contention. "It was obvious to me that there was no chance to nominate Garner since Roosevelt had polled within eighty-seven votes of the required two-thirds. I was well aware of the effort which was being made . . . to tie up one-third of the convention and produce a deadlock which it was hoped by its proponents would defeat Roosevelt and result in the nomination of some other candidate," he later wrote. "I realized that if the convention could be deadlocked in this manner we would have a repetition of the disastrous 1924 Madison Square Garden Convention and that it would result in the defeat of any Democrat who might be nominated."

If California did not swing to Roosevelt on the next ballot, McAdoo believed that FDR's support would crumble as his own lines had in 1924. He had never liked Roosevelt but their political views were similar and his election would mean the return of progressive government for the first time in two decades. Most of McAdoo's longtime allies were already in Roosevelt's camp and presumably would have influence in a Roosevelt administration. If Roosevelt was stopped, McAdoo believed that the convention would turn to Baker or Smith. By making his move on the next ballot, McAdoo could take out his revenge on those old rivals, establish California's Democratic Party as a national political force, and have his own moment of glory as the party's once and future kingmaker.[13]

On his return to the Texas caucus, Rayburn's voice broke as he announced that Garner was releasing his delegates. Even with the House Speaker's instructions, Rayburn had difficulty persuading his caucus to abandon their favorite son. "John is out," Rayburn said. "He asks me to thank all of you from the bottom of his heart for your loyalty."

An indignant partisan shouted, "We don't care what John wants. We are with him and we are going to stick!" A motion was made that Texas stay with Garner. W. A. Tarver of Austin then moved that the caucus should switch to Roosevelt and that all previous motions should be tabled. Carter urged his fellow Texans not to desert their state's top Democrat.

"You're not deserting him," Rayburn shot back. "He doesn't want your votes. He wants you to be released."

After impassioned debate, the motion to support Roosevelt carried by a vote of fifty-four to fifty-one. "We quit too soon," lamented Carter, "We realized that Garner's only chance for the presidential nomination lay in a deadlock. I felt we had a horse all saddled up for a two-mile race, but one of the jockeys pulled him up at the quarter-mile post. We had a chance of a lifetime to nominate a President from Texas, but a few of our friends were just a little weak-kneed."[14]

At about 6:00 p.m. McAdoo conferred in his penthouse with a Smith delegation that included former New York Supreme Court Justice Daniel F. Cohalan and federal judge T. Martin Manton. The Smith camp urged California to stick with Garner through the sixth ballot. If they succeeded in blocking Roosevelt, McAdoo asked what would happen next. Smith's men had no answer. McAdoo said that he might be willing to support a compromise nominee but would not "go up a blind alley." He suspected that Smith intended to swing to Baker. The New Yorkers reiterated that they did not know where the coalition was headed. "He thereupon told them he was through with the 'combination,' and considered himself a free agent," Brice Clagett recalled, "clearly indicating that meant support for Roosevelt."[15]

"It is inexplicable how Mr. Smith ever believed that Mr. McAdoo and Mr. Hearst would make common cause with him merely to accomplish one of Mr. Smith's personal desires," Krock later wrote. "So long as their involved state seemed greater to them than to Mr. Smith's, they went along. But as soon as they perceived that only the Smith interest was being served, they broke the very fragile connection."[16]

Daniel C. Roper told McAdoo that unless California and Texas switched to Roosevelt on the fourth ballot that his old rival Baker was headed for the presidency. Still resentful of Baker's closeness to Wilson, McAdoo was ready to deal. "I'll do this only upon certain assurances that he [Roosevelt] must give me through you and no one else," McAdoo told his longtime ally. He wanted control of federal patronage in California, an assurance that Garner would be the vice-presidential candidate, and that McAdoo could veto the nominees for secretary of state and secretary of the treasury. "After I explained the situation to Howe, he put through a call to Albany and located Governor Roosevelt," Roper said. "I took the telephone and explained the conditions. . . . Governor Roosevelt gave me the required assurances over the telephone."[17]

Another reason McAdoo chose Roosevelt is that the New York governor was the most progressive of the Democratic contenders. "He has much the same feelings about Wall Street, the 'interests,' and the 'greedy corporations' that the progressive Democratic senators who have managed the Roosevelt campaign here express in the Senate," wrote Frank R. Kent. "He is and has always regarded himself as a progressive Democrat and it was to have been expected that with Garner unavailable he would have swung to Roosevelt in preference to Ritchie, Baker, Byrd or any other Eastern conservative."[18]

Like Rayburn, McAdoo met stiff resistance. After talking with Storke and Cotton, McAdoo scheduled a caucus meeting in the Sherman House at 7:00 p.m. The doors were locked and only delegates or their alternates were allowed in the room for this surprise "eleventh hour" caucus. Throughout the preliminary fights and presidential balloting, they had voted against Roosevelt and many were reluctant to switch. As McAdoo opened the meeting, he said that the delegation should discuss what course it should take in the presidential balloting. "He told us," Storke later wrote, "there were reasons to believe that changes might occur shortly in the key delegations—Smith's and Roosevelt's—and that if one or the other showed signs of collapse or made significant gains, what should be the California policy?"

While not expressing his own preference, McAdoo signaled that he favored Roosevelt by calling for an end to the deadlock. He noted that a prolonged stalemate would jeopardize the party's chances of recapturing the White House. When McAdoo invited comments from the floor, some Garner partisans were in a fury. A large number preferred to stay with Garner, while others argued for Roosevelt and the Bay Area delegates suggested Smith as a second choice. The meeting soon turned into a shouting match. "McAdoo," shouted a delegate from San Diego, "you are attempting to betray us!"

Grace Bryan Hargreaves, daughter of William Jennings Bryan, rose and brutalized McAdoo. "We came here to nominate John Nance Garner and no one else," she yelled. "I am ready to stay right here in Chicago until we nominate John Nance Garner!"

McAdoo turned pale, stiffened his back, and clenched his fists but would not respond to this criticism. His pragmatic appeal had been rebuked. Instead of achieving consensus, he was now confronted with a runaway delegation. If the vote was splintered, the convention could be headed for a fifth ballot. McAdoo would not risk polling the delegation. "It will never be known how the California delegation would have voted in that caucus," Storke later wrote. "No vote was ever taken. Personally, I would estimate that more than half would have insisted on staying with Garner for at least one more ballot. Perhaps fifteen might have gone over to Smith. Possibly a majority favored Roosevelt. The only certain judgment of the situation was that unanimity was impossible."

John B. Elliott, Democratic leader of Southern California, offered a resolution proposing a steering committee of four delegates headed by McAdoo with the authority "to determine when, and to whom the vote of California should go in the event of a switch from John Nance Garner."

When the delegates approved the resolution, McAdoo named Elliott, Democratic national committeewoman Nellie Donohue of Oakland, and C. C. McPike of San Francisco as the other members of the committee. As the caucus broke up and the Californians headed for Chicago Stadium, the steering committee met in McAdoo's penthouse suite and quickly decided to join Texas in switching to Roosevelt on the fourth ballot. "This was kept in the strictest secrecy," Storke wrote years later. "Our California delegation was never polled on this issue, either in caucus or on the floor."[19]

Smith did not believe the first rumors about the California and Texas switch. "It can't be," he said. "I have McAdoo's personal promise to the contrary." After trying vainly to reach McAdoo, Smith then called Baruch. "Bernie," he said, "your long-legged friend has run out on us, just as I thought he would."

"Why, Al, you must be mistaken," replied Baruch.

"No, I ain't mistaken," Smith said. "You'll find out."

Baruch sought to contact McAdoo. Soon afterward, the New York financier called back Smith. "Well, Al, I guess you're right," Baruch said. "He's in caucus now and wouldn't come out to see the man I sent down."

Smith then telephoned Garner at his hotel apartment in Washington. He reached Ettie Garner. "Mrs. Garner, this is Alfred E. Smith," he said, "and I would like to talk to the Speaker."

She replied that Garner had gone out for a few minutes but said that her husband would be glad to talk when he returned. Thirty minutes later, Smith tried again but the call went to the front desk. "Yes, Governor," the clerk answered, "I'll get the Speaker for you. I know just where he is."

Smith waited for what seemed an eternity. Finally, the clerk returned. "Governor," he said, "I'm awfully sorry. I thought I knew where the Speaker was, but I can't find him." That was unfortunate, the Happy Warrior said, because he did not have much time and had important business to discuss with Garner.

"Look here, Governor," the clerk confided. "I'm a friend of yours and I'm going to tell you the truth. He's up on the roof eating dinner, but he doesn't want to talk to you."[20]

Smith now understood that his comeback was doomed.

"I meant no discourtesy to Smith," Garner later explained. "I knew he was in a bitter, last-ditch fight in which I did not intend to take part. I decided it was best for me to talk only to Sam Rayburn, Amon Carter or some other members of the Texas delegation. There was no reason to talk to outsiders. If Roosevelt had called, I would not have taken that one, either."[21]

By remaining in the race, Smith had unwittingly become Roosevelt's ally. "The failure of the opposition," wrote H. L. Mencken, "was the failure of Al Smith. From the moment he arrived on the ground it was apparent that he had no plan, and was animated only by his fierce hatred of Roosevelt, the cuckoo who had seized his nest. That hatred may have had logic in it, but was impotent to organize the allies."

William Allen White, a veteran observer of national political conventions, felt that Smith had a chance to strengthen the anti-Roosevelt forces by withdrawing after the third ballot. "He could have given Ritchie enough votes to deadlock the convention for a ballot or two and then the South and West would have led the parade to Baker," said White. "Smith certainly displayed the talents of a provincial politician."[22]

Hague sought to keep Garner in the race by offering him New Jersey's thirty-six votes on the fourth ballot. Shouse said that Smith himself was prepared to support Garner.

Farley had gotten word that Baker's forces had wrested control of the Mississippi delegation, and there were threats of possible defections in North Carolina and Iowa. After confirming that the Texas and California delegations would be switching, Farley went to Curry's suite at the Blackstone "in the hope that they would see the light and join the bandwagon procession." The Tammany leader and Brooklyn's Mc-Cooey turned down Farley, asserting that Roosevelt had been stopped.

As they headed for Chicago Stadium, some of Roosevelt's closest associates had not been told about the Garner switch. Rexford G. Tugwell and Harry Hopkins, who shared a cab, looked as if they were going to a wake.[23]

Lela M. Stiles, Howe's assistant, quietly delivered an envelope from her boss to Cermak not knowing its contents. As she got to the mayor's suite, Stiles remembered: "I was admitted by a suspicious-looking man who stepped aside to let two other men carrying a tub of ice going in. I told the man I had to see the Mayor, that I had a message from Roosevelt headquarters, and was to wait for an answer. He snatched the letter from my hand and ducked through the door where the ice had gone and I heard loud, excited voices.

"I never saw His Honor, but in about ten minutes the same man came out and laid an envelope in my hand. I dashed back by the same route I had come—stairs, elevators, elevators, stairs, until I reached 1702, where Louis and Farley waited. I passed the message to them." Stiles later realized that she had informed Cermak about the Garner switch.

At the stadium, the political correspondent Thomas L. Stokes was in the Scripps-Howard convention bureau when he learned that Garner had released his delegates. Stokes strolled into the lobby and saw Mayor Hague standing alone. "I took particular delight in telling him the news," Stokes recalled. "He frowned and dismissed my information with a wave of his hand."

"Aw, that's just a newspaper report," said Hague.

"It happens to be true," Stokes replied.[24]

McAdoo almost failed to get to the stadium. Shortly before the evening session was to begin, the chairman of the California delegation stepped off the curb in front of the Sherman House and got into the backseat of his official limousine. As he sped past City Hall, the gleaming marquee of the Palace Theater, and the screeching tracks of the El, the former Treasury secretary was right on schedule. But about a mile from the hotel, on the Near West Side, the chauffeur came to an abrupt stop and informed McAdoo that his limousine had run out of gasoline. With the car stalled in the middle of the street, traffic was blocked and scores of drivers began honking their horns. Since the limousine had been provided by Cermak's hospitality committee, McAdoo would always believe that the gasoline had been siphoned from the limousine to make him late for the critical fourth ballot.

A Chicago policeman then offered McAdoo a ride on the back of his motorcycle. "McAdoo in desperation climbed aboard," said Storke. "However, he could not keep his long, gangling legs from scraping the pavement so, after going a hundred yards or so, he had to dismount."

The cop hailed a taxi for McAdoo and, with his siren running, escorted him to the stadium. By the time he arrived, the fourth ballot had already begun and the pro-Smith galleries were loudly jeering Arizona's vote for Roosevelt. Finally, Chairman Walsh banged down his gavel and called for order. "The tenseness of the scene we found there is almost indescribable," Moley later wrote. "The Chicago politicians had apparently been planting great numbers of leather-throated mugs in the galleries for the purpose of shouting down the Roosevelt delegates on the floor. . . . One almost had a sense of impending physical violence."[25]

If it had not been for this prolonged booing that delayed the roll call, McAdoo might have arrived too late. In the absence of the chairman, California could not have recorded its vote and would have lost its turn. If that had happened, there was always the possibility of defections from southern and midwestern Roosevelt delegations. But as McAdoo took his seat, Arkansas was casting eighteen votes for FDR.

Amon Carter of Texas approached McAdoo and pleaded with him to stick with Garner for at least two more ballots, stating that it was too early to "desert" their candidate. If California stayed with Garner, Carter predicted that Texas would do the same. "He believed that Garner could eventually be nominated," McAdoo later wrote. "Amon was very vigorous in stating his position but I told him that the strategic move to end the threatened deadlock was for California to switch to Roosevelt on the fourth ballot; that we had decided to do exactly that and could not change the plan."

During his hectic ride to the convention, McAdoo scribbled Walsh a note. "Please recognize me when California is called, Tom," McAdoo wrote. "You will not be disappointed."[26]

When the Golden State was called, McAdoo answered: "I request the chair's permission to explain California's vote."

After Walsh agreed to give him the spotlight, McAdoo mounted the platform. As he approached the microphone, he whispered to a long-time ally: "Now, I'll square myself." He had a score to settle with Smith, who had thwarted his presidential hopes at Madison Square Garden. McAdoo, wrote H. L. Mencken, "came so close to getting the nomination that the memory of its loss must still shiver him."

"He relished the opportunity of settling with an old enemy," said Clinton W. Gilbert. "Under the circumstances, any other politician would have remained in the background. . . . But McAdoo is the kind of man who never lets prudence deprive him of the fullest satisfaction of paying off an old score."

Yet for the presidential son-in-law who had spent two decades in pursuit of the White House this appearance was bittersweet. "I knew that his ultimate ambition had been killed as surely as had been Al Smith's," Arthur Mullen wrote afterward. "If the convention had gone into deadlock, he might have had a chance at the nomination for what-ever it would have been worth at the time. As well as any one there, he knew that he was tolling the bell for his own funeral."[27]

A hush came over Chicago Stadium as McAdoo began speaking. "California came here to nominate a President of the United States," he said. "She did not come here to deadlock this convention or to en-gage in another disastrous contest like that of 1924.

"In my great state, where the Democratic Party has increased its registration this year 143 percent, we believe that the interests of the people of the United States will be best conserved by a change from a Republican to a Democratic administration. We think that a useless contest on this floor, long prolonged, would only lead to schisms in the party that could not be cured, perhaps, before the election. Sometimes, in major operations, where skillful surgery is required, the life of the patient may be destroyed if there is unnecessary delay. We believe, therefore, that California should take a stand tonight that will bring the contest to a swift and, we hope, satisfactory conclusion—a stand which will promote party harmony, a stand which we take with the utmost unselfishness and regardless of individual views or personal consideration—a stand prompted by our belief that when any man comes into a Democratic National Convention with the popular will behind him to the extent of almost seven hundred votes," McAdoo said as the pro-Smith galleries shouted him down.

Standing tall and smiling, McAdoo greatly enjoyed the fireworks he had sparked. The standards of more than thirty Roosevelt states were brought in front of the speaker's platform and Melgard struck up "Happy Days Are Here Again" followed by "California Here I Come." A Texas banner joined the parade. "It's all over," exclaimed Huey Long.

As the men and women in the balconies thundered their disapproval, Walsh tried vainly to restore order. After prolonged booing, Walsh turned to Cermak. "I appeal to the Mayor of the City of Chicago and to the citizens thereof," he said. "If he or they have any regard whatever for the honor of their city, he will silence this disturbance in the gallery."

The booing turned into cheers as Cermak stepped to the microphone. "Let me appeal to my friends in the galleries," he said. "The Democratic National Committee was kind enough to come to our city with this great wonderful convention. You are their host. Please act like their host. Please, I appeal to you, allow this great gathering to go back home with nothing but pleasant memories of our city."

But when McAdoo returned to the podium, the Smith partisans booed even louder. "I want to thank the galleries for the compliment they have paid me," McAdoo shot back. "The convention wants to know, for the guidance of future Democratic conventions, whether or not this is the kind of hospitality that Chicago accords its guests. I intend to say what I propose to say without regard to what the galleries or anybody else think."

McAdoo noted that his delegation had come to Chicago as supporters of "that great Texan" Garner: "We have lost not one whit of the love and respect in which we hold that great statesman. He is worthy of the highest place that you could give him, but he hasn't as many votes as Mr. Roosevelt. Mr. Garner himself is in accord with the position I take.

"The great state of Texas and the great state of California are acting in accordance with what we believe to be best for, first for America and next for the Democratic party," he said. "I want to cause no wounds. Those of 1924 were created against my wish."

Then he declared, "California casts forty-four votes for Franklin D. Roosevelt."[28]

Listening to the radio broadcast in Albany, Roosevelt expressed his gratitude. "Good old McAdoo!" By announcing that Texas would also be making this switch, the veteran of the Wilson years had broken the deadlock.

Within minutes, Cermak returned to the platform and announced the withdrawal of his favorite son Traylor. 'It is our great happiness now," the Chicago mayor said, "to cast our votes with our neighboring state, Indiana, whose consent I have from the chairman of that delegation. We have been authorized to say to you that they have joined us and we now cast our vote jointly for the next President of the United States—eighty-eight votes for Franklin D. Roosevelt."

Smith went into a fury when Cermak broke ranks. Shortly after the convention, the mayor of Chicago had an unpleasant meeting with the former New York governor. "Smith became overcome with anger," according to the mayor's biographer Alex Gottfried. "He shouted and swore and ranted about Cermak's disloyalty."

But Cermak made a pragmatic choice and led a stampede of the favorite-son states. Governor Ritchie personally announced Maryland's switch to Roosevelt. Through spokesmen, former senator Reed of Missouri, Governor White of Ohio, and Alfalfa Bill Murray of Oklahoma released their delegates. Near the end of the roll call, Governor Byrd strolled to the podium and released his delegates to Roosevelt.

The Massachusetts, New Jersey, and Rhode Island delegations backed Smith until the end. Sixty-three members of the New York delegation stuck with their former governor. Smith declined comment on Roosevelt's triumph.[29]

State Senator Herbert E. Hitchcock, the sixty-three-year-old chairman of the South Dakota delegation, had the honor of making Roosevelt the nominee when his state's ten votes put FDR over the required 766 votes. "I dashed to the headquarters room on the gallery floor and got Albany on the telephone," Farley recalled. "I then experienced the greatest thrill of a lifetime of politics—the privilege of congratulating Franklin D. Roosevelt on his nomination for the Presidency of the United States."

In the final tally announced by Walsh, FDR got 945 votes, followed by Smith with 190.5 votes, and a scattering of votes for favorite sons. "Franklin D. Roosevelt having received more than two-thirds of all the delegates voting," said Walsh, "I proclaim him the nominee of this convention."

A handful of key players turned the tide. As Farley noted in his diary, Kennedy's telephone call to San Simeon was important. So were

Farley's negotiations with Rayburn. Hearst and McAdoo were also critical. Shouse blamed the latter. "If McAdoo had not broken the pledges he made," Shouse wrote Baker, "Roosevelt would not have been nominated. On the fourth ballot there would have been serious defections from his ranks with the result that some other nominee would have been certain. That nominee would have been either you or Ritchie."[30]

Farley said that Garner alone had the authority to release the Texas and California delegations. "The anti-Roosevelt coalition broke up at the appropriate point when California and Texas went over to the majority," Lippmann wrote in the *Herald-Tribune*. "The Garner delegates had no good reason for separating themselves from the other Roosevelt states in the South and West."

In later years, other Democrats wrote memoirs taking excessive credit for Roosevelt's nomination. As Basil O'Connor wryly commented to FDR: "Of the 56,000 Democrats alleged to have been in Chicago, undoubtedly 62,000 of them arranged the McAdoo shift."[31]

23

WINGS

I N A BREAK with tradition that symbolized a new era, Roosevelt
announced that he would fly to Chicago to accept the 1932 Democratic presidential nomination. It had been the custom dating back to
the first half of the nineteenth century for the standard-bearer of a major political party to be formally notified in his hometown two months
after the convention. A dozen years earlier FDR had delivered his vice-
presidential acceptance speech from the front porch of his Hyde Park
mansion before a cheering crowd. "In abandoning the tradition,"
Arthur Schlesinger Jr. has written, "Roosevelt was responding to what
he perceived as a passionate popular hope for a bolder temper in national affairs."

Roosevelt had played it coy when the press had asked about rumors
that he might go to the convention by plane. "Now, I'll tell you what
I'm going to do," he said as reporters pulled out their notebooks. "I'm
going to bicycle out to Chicago.

"I'm going to get one of those quintets—you know, five bicycles in a row.

"Father will ride in the first seat and manage the handlebars. Jim will ride second, then Elliott, then Franklin Jr., and then John.

"Sam [New York Supreme Court Justice Samuel I. Rosenman] will follow—on a tricycle."

Roosevelt—enjoying the speculation—laughed heartily.[1]

The adventurous fliers Charles A. Lindbergh and Amelia Earhart had excited the American people with their courage and daring. As the first presidential candidate to fly, Roosevelt also captured the public imagination. In 1932, air travel was still considered hazardous. It had been just a year since Knute Rockne of Notre Dame, the nation's most celebrated football coach, died in a plane crash. "Airplane travel still seemed an unnatural act, and it wasn't a good bet statistically either," Thomas Petzinger Jr. wrote in *Hard Landing*, his book about the history of the airline industry. "People flying in 1930 were roughly 200 times more likely to be killed than the passengers of forty years later. Navigation aids were rudimentary: pilots often followed railroad tracks, until one too many of them failed to notice the approaching tunnels."[2]

American Airways, which then had one flight a day between Albany and Cleveland, made special arrangements for the Roosevelt flight. "The planes then on the route were not safe enough. They were also too cramped," recalled Goodrich Murphy, who was then general traffic manager for American Airways in Albany. Special arrangements were made to have a Ford Tri-Motor brought to Albany from the Dallas–to–Los Angeles line. "It was a primitive airline in those days, and people were scared to fly," said Murphy. "To get a governor on a plane might help spread a little confidence. That's why we were willing to go to so much trouble."

Within the Roosevelt camp, the historic flight was a topic of intense debate. FDR decided to take the plane because it would be the quickest way to get to Chicago and would avoid delaying the convention more than another day. Howe, Roosevelt's son-in-law Curtis Dall, and Dutchess County neighbor Henry Morgenthau Jr. argued that he should not put himself at risk. "Many delegates were jittery," recalled Howe's aide Lila Stiles. "Suppose something happened in this hour of victory. Some even called the Governor." Roosevelt had no such concerns. As assistant secretary of the navy, he had made several trips in naval aircraft. Although he had not been in the air since World War I, Roosevelt had been impressed by advances in aviation technology and believed that the trip to Chicago would get his campaign off to a flying start. "He knew the value of drama in public office and in public relations, and he understood the psychology of the American people of 1932," Rosenman said two decades later. "He wanted to let people know that his approach was going to be bold and daring; that if elected he would be ready to act—and act fast. It was in that spirit that the whole trip to Chicago was conceived."[3]

When Roosevelt told one of his secretaries, the thirty-one-year-old Grace Tully, that he wanted her to be on the flight, she hesitated. "It was another tough decision for me," she later wrote. "I had never flown, I was not sure how good a traveler I would be in the air—and I had made no will. I talked about it at length with mother that night—until nearly 2:00 a.m. to be exact—but I knew from the beginning that I was going."

Others in the thirteen-member Roosevelt party included his wife, Eleanor, and their sons Elliott and John, Rosenman, executive assistant Guernsey Cross, secretary Marguerite A. "Missy" LeHand, state troopers Earl Miller and Gus Gennerich, pilots Ray D. Wonsey and Fred Clark, and airline official Max Pollet, working the flight as steward. Rosenman, who had misgivings about this flight, was surprised that

FDR had assembled a party of thirteen. "We knew his superstitions," Rosenman later wrote. "He disliked lighting three cigarettes on a single match, or having thirteen at a table, or starting a voyage on the thirteenth."[4]

The Ford Tri-Motor had a capacity of fifteen passengers. One of the wicker seats had been removed to give Roosevelt more room. An airline mechanic made a small desk for FDR to write on and also installed a typewriter table so that the secretaries could work during the flight. When his motorcade drove to the Albany airport, his car stopped under one of the aircraft's giant wings. A wooden ramp had been constructed to make it easier for Roosevelt to get on and off the plane. He was carried into the cabin backward.

"It's a perfect day, isn't it?" FDR told the small crowd that had come to watch his departure from the airport that had until recently been a cow pasture. Roosevelt, who was often superstitious about the weather, knew that reports were less than favorable.

The Ford 5-AT Tri-Motor, often referred to as the "Tin Goose," weighed thirteen thousand pounds, had a wingspan of seventy-seven feet, was almost fifty feet long, and could fly at top speeds of 110 miles an hour. A sturdy and reliable all-metal aircraft with a corrugated aluminum exterior, the 5-AT had been introduced by Ford in 1928. It had three propellers and engines, low-pressure tires for landing on rough surfaces, and a swiveling tail-wheel with a shock absorber. "With its fixed landing gear, exposed air-cooled engines, and boxy shape," aviation historian R. G. Grant has written, "it exemplified the problems of drag that designers were trying to identify and fix in the late 1920s."[5]

At 8:25 a.m., the plane taxied down the runway, then slowly ascended into the leaden sky and sailed into the west. Under the best of conditions, this aircraft was seldom comfortable. And on this flight, the weather was not optimal. "It was a bleak day with strong winds blow-ing from the west, slowing our speed and making the flight a bumpy one," Tully said. "The plane was not insulated as effectively as today's transports and it was both noisy and cold. Johnny became sick soon after the take-off and spent most of the trip in the tail end."

Shortly after the plane departed, a storm shut down the Albany airport. If Roosevelt had scheduled a later takeoff, the charter aircraft probably would not have left. Weather forecasts given to the pilots just before takeoff predicted heavy rain and thunderstorms. "It was a rough ride along that Mohawk Valley," Murphy said. "Flying up against the prevailing winds at that low altitude was rough, and that Ford was a balloon. It had a light loading per square foot and rode like a blimp."[6]

Along the route, short-wave radio messages alerted upstate New York residents to the progress of the Roosevelt plane and many rushed to local airstrips to catch a glimpse of the historic flight.

At an altitude of fifteen hundred feet, the silver plane flew south of Utica and just north of Syracuse. Roosevelt read congratulatory messages, pointed out landmarks to his sons, and appeared to be enjoying himself. James Kieran of the *New York Times,* attempting to scoop the competition, chartered a single-engine red Cessna in Albany and tried unsuccessfully to keep up with the larger and faster Roosevelt plane.

The pilots considered an emergency landing in Rochester. Despite plans to fly over clouds, the charter flew under them. Airport officials in Rochester made preparations for the charter to land. It was hazardous for the Tri-Motor to fly in bad weather because some of the instruments were located on the outboard engines and pilots had to look out the side windows to read them.

"There were storms all around us," said Pollet. "We checked over the train connections, and were prepared to take care of the party if we had to land."[7]

But the Roosevelt charter kept going. The plane landed at Buffalo for refueling at 11:06 a.m. and stayed on the ground for thirty-eight minutes. Everyone on the plane except FDR got off and stretched their legs. "The trip was pretty bad from Albany to Buffalo," Eleanor later acknowledged.

During this layover, Roosevelt telephoned congratulations to Harvard law professor Felix Frankfurter on his nomination to the Supreme Judicial Court of Massachusetts. "I haven't been able to tell you how happy I am that you got your big chance," he said. "I wish it were the Supreme Court of the United States—that's where you belong."

Frankfurter had already declined the nomination but later wrote FDR: "I couldn't tell you about it when we talked because I was under the obligation of silence." Massachusetts governor Joseph B. Ely, who still wanted Frankfurter on the bench, had asked him to refrain from public comment. In this conversation with Roosevelt, Frankfurter urged him to make peace with the Smith wing of the party. "I have an important suggestion that I want to put to you at once," he said. "I wish you would write a rather personal note to Governor Ely, asking him to come down to see you as soon as his public business permits. You could say that you are asking him to do what you would have done if fate had reversed the roles."

"There is a limit to what a fellow will do to turn the other cheek," FDR replied.

"But I wish you would write him, not as governor but as national committeeman," suggested Frankfurter. "Remember he is that."

"Yes, that's true," Roosevelt said. "But he must be an awful ass."

Frankfurter persisted. "You really can afford to take the initiative with Ely," he said. FDR took the advice and Ely would campaign for him that fall throughout New England.[8]

Meanwhile, in Chicago, Roosevelt daughter Anna and her brothers

James and Franklin Jr. were in the American Airways radio room listening to messages from the chartered plane. While their father was in Buffalo, the young Roosevelts expressed concern that the weather bureau had issued storm warnings between there and Cleveland. "In the hall that day," recalled Bowers, "I found many of his friends apprehensive, fearing an accident." In the press section, newspapermen began speculating who might take Roosevelt's place if the plane went down.

At 11:44 a.m. the Roosevelt plane left Buffalo to the southwest along the shoreline of Lake Erie. "Strong head winds delayed us, and made it a very rough flight," Rosenman later wrote. "Once, between Buffalo and Cleveland, I looked up from my work toward the Governor, and what I saw convinced me that here indeed was a man of steel nerves, who could shake off worry and excitement and deliberately take rest when necessary." Roosevelt was sleeping soundly.

Soon afterward, Pollet served a luncheon of chicken, cream-cheese and olive sandwiches, fresh fruit, ice cream, and chocolate cake. "Every one did full justice to the lunch," Pollet said.

After this meal, Roosevelt worked with Rosenman on the final draft of the acceptance speech. "With each radio report, we were falling further and further behind schedule," Rosenman later wrote, "and more and more paragraphs came out of the acceptance speech. This lopping off of material on which we had worked so long and so hopefully was a painful process. I know that there were some jewels dropped on the airplane floor that day."[9]

Landing in Cleveland at 1:43 p.m., Roosevelt waved from the passenger window to a cheering throng of five thousand people. "I am launching a new progressive ship of state in adopting this most modern form of transportation," FDR said in a message read over the radio.

Newton D. Baker declined an invitation from the acting mayor of Cleveland to be a member of the official welcoming committee. "I had some very important engagements this morning that could not be shifted," Baker said. "I'm very, very much occupied." When asked whether he would support FDR, Baker would not comment.

Smith also shunned Roosevelt. As FDR headed toward Chicago, his defeated rival boarded a special train for the return trip to New York. "Had he been better advised," Bowers said, "he would have remained to greet the victor." Smith gave no indication whether he would support FDR. Before embarking on his flight, Roosevelt was asked if he expected to get together with Smith. "I certainly hope so," FDR said. At the urging of a mutual friend who boarded the former governor's train, Smith did not openly attack FDR.[10]

While Roosevelt sat in his plane as it was refueled at the Cleveland airport, delegates in Chicago headed to the stadium to choose a vice-presidential nominee. McAdoo wanted to go on the ticket but Roosevelt would not alienate the Smith wing of the party by selecting their bitter adversary. On Saturday morning, Baruch went to Roosevelt headquarters at the Congress Hotel and touted Ritchie. Farley replied that the Maryland governor had missed his chance.

Senator Burton K. Wheeler of Montana, Roosevelt's first supporter among the western progressives, hoped to become his running mate and did get some consideration. "He wanted the vice-presidential nomination desperately," said Frank Walker. "He had never quite recovered from the sting of his defeat when he was the vice-presidential candidate with the elder La Follette on the Progressive ticket in 1924. In my opinion, his being passed over in 1932 was what originally soured Wheeler on Roosevelt. He never was wholeheartedly for him after that."[11]

Governor George H. Dern of Utah, who played a key role in delivering the Rocky Mountain region to Roosevelt, openly sought the vice-presidential nomination and had the backing of four western delegations.

Some of Roosevelt's earliest allies, including partisans of Wheeler and Dern, urged Farley to summon a meeting for the selection of the vice-presidential candidate.

But Roosevelt would not delegate this responsibility.

Even before the California and Texas switch, Roosevelt had expressed a preference for Garner. After the nomination was secure, "Cactus Jack" was the only defeated contender to send him a congratulatory telegram. "My mind was fully made up," Farley later wrote, "that Speaker Garner was entitled to the nomination if he wished to accept, and with the aid of several others, I had already started the job of swinging the entire Roosevelt strength behind his candidacy."

Garner would always deny that he sought the vice presidency. "I didn't want the thing—I had an important office—and if I hadn't been nominated for Vice President, I might be Speaker today," he said in 1957. Following the convention, he said that his reputation as a shrewd trader "would not be helped by trading the second most important office in the nation for one which in itself is almost wholly unimportant."

But there is evidence that Garner actually did want to go on the ticket. His wife, Ettie, approached Rayburn about this possibility. "Sam," she told the Texas congressman before the convention, "Mr. Garner tells everybody that he's not a bit interested in the vice presidency. I happen to know better. But don't let him know I told you."[12]

As Rayburn left for Chicago, Garner brought him into his confidence. For the first time in his three-decade House career, he was thinking about retirement. "There might be a chance for me to be nominated for Vice President," he said, "and it might be a nice way for me to taper off my career by spending four years presiding over the Senate."

Within Roosevelt's camp, Flynn objected to Garner's selection. "I was not against him personally, but I had my doubts because of the fact that he came from the South—from Texas in particular. My reason for this was that the main support for Smith was largely among Irish Catholics," said Flynn, the son of Irish immigrants. "They felt keenly that Smith had been defeated in 1928 because of his religion. They knew also that Texas, which was normally overwhelmingly Democratic, had gone for President Hoover. I felt, therefore, that if a candidate were named from Texas, Catholics would use this as an excuse for opposing the national ticket.

"I urged this point very strongly in my talks with Roosevelt. I pointed out that the feeling among Catholics was intense, and that the smart of the defeat in 1928 had not died out," Flynn added. "I said that this feeling ought to be allayed by nominating someone who was not from the South, but from the West or Midwest."[13]

Roosevelt, though, regarded Garner as the strongest possible choice. As the first Democrat to preside over any branch of the federal government in more than a decade, "Cactus Jack" had great prestige in the party and leadership credentials. As for the argument that he had no appeal beyond the Solid South, Garner had demonstrated in California that he would strengthen the ticket in the West. Finally, Roosevelt felt that he owed the House Speaker for releasing his delegates and breaking the deadlock. Once Farley recommended the Texan, FDR instantly approved. "He wouldn't have anyone else," Garner recalled years later. "He made them nominate me for Vice President. His managers did it."[14]

House majority whip John McDuffie of Alabama appealed for party unity in his speech nominating Garner. McDuffie observed that Republicans had been counting on dissension and discord to split the Democratic Party. "Let the country understand today there is happiness in the Democratic household," he declared. "We have had our differences, Democrats often differ, but Democrats are good sports."

McDuffie commended Roosevelt for selecting "the outstanding

Democrat in the American Congress" for the second slot. "John N. Garner is a red-blooded he-man," said McDuffie. "I am proud to enter the name of this son of Texas as a running mate for the son of the Empire State."

While the convention awaited Roosevelt, Chairman Walsh filled the time by allowing thirty-seven seconding speeches for Garner. "We sent the soldiers to Texas in 1836," said Huey Long, "and we delight to second the nomination of Garner."

Boston mayor James Michael Curley added comic relief and annoyed the pro-Smith Massachusetts delegation by appearing on the platform to second Garner's nomination as a delegate "from the beautiful island of Puerto Rico." Curley wryly noted that it was "an old Spanish custom to do something for the 'forgotten man,'" referring to himself. The mayor gloated at his home-state rivals and danced a jig as he passed the Massachusetts delegation on his return to the convention floor.

When the convention nominated Garner by acclamation, FDR expressed confidence in his running mate's "splendid ability" and noted that their friendship dated back to the Wilson administration.[15]

By 2:54 p.m., the Roosevelt plane was back in the air for the final leg to Chicago. While heading west along the south shore of Lake Erie, FDR dictated a radiogram to Cermak: "Sorry strong head wind makes us a little late. But it is a delightful trip and we are getting a fine view."

In response to several written questions from American Airways, Roosevelt described the service as "excellent and very comfortable." FDR said that he had confidence in the future of aviation and predicted "a definite and probably gradual growth." While still over Ohio, pilot Wonsey briefly interviewed Roosevelt over the radio: "How do you like the trip, Governor?"

"Fine," said FDR. "It's my first in a big cabin ship like this. When I was in the Navy Department, we had only open planes."

By the late afternoon, the bone-shaking vibration and thundering noise had worn down the Roosevelt entourage. All had received cotton balls to use as earplugs to mute the deafening roar of the three engines. As on most flights of this era, motion sickness was a problem. Tully and Rosenman complained of discomfort. John Roosevelt had been airsick from the time the plane left Albany. Even Pollet, a veteran of commercial air travel, was stricken during the long flight "but managed to stave off any serious illness and to carry on in my work."[16]

While flying over northeastern Indiana, the pilot radioed that the air was bumpy and the passengers had been shaken up. "Father has done a lot of flying and he won't mind that," James Roosevelt chuckled in the American Airways radio room. "He's a good sailor."

Jimmy and his two siblings were evacuated when a gasoline fire of unknown origin broke out in the hangar on the south end of Chicago's Municipal Airport. Several airplanes in the building were pushed out of the path of the blaze and the flames were quickly extinguished.

At the Stadium, Chairman Walsh cut short the Garner demonstration with the announcement that the Roosevelt plane was ten miles west of South Bend and would be approaching Chicago within twenty-five minutes.

A crowd of more than ten thousand party faithful had gathered at Chicago's Municipal Airport for their new leader's arrival. At 4:30 p.m., Walter Butterworth of the National Broadcasting Company made this announcement: "The plane bearing Governor Franklin D. Roosevelt has successfully outridden adverse weather conditions and is now circling the airport in Chicago." The American Airways plane first appeared as "a mere speck in the sky that grew larger and larger" as it approached.

Moments later, the NBC reporter was back on the air: "The most beautiful ship has glided down to the ground, bearing Governor

Roosevelt. . . . They are getting everybody off the runway. I am going to ask the engineer now to open up the microphone wide so that you can hear the voice of the motors."[17]

As the beaming Roosevelt emerged from the plane, he stood tall on the flag-draped ramp, conveying the image of athletic vigor. The crowd gave him a hero's welcome, surging over a fence meant to hold them back, and drowning out his words with earsplitting cheers and applause. It was unheard of for a political figure to attract such cheering throngs. Ordinary people were attracted to him in the same way that they thrilled to Babe Ruth and Charles A. Lindbergh. F. Raymond Daniell of the *New York Times* reported, "The scene on the field was like that at one of the Long Island airports on an occasion such as the arrival of a transatlantic flier."

"He gave aviation the biggest boost it ever had," Will Rogers declared in his column. "Took his family and flew out there. That will stop those big shots from thinking their lives are too important to the country to take a chance on flying."

In the crush of the crowd, Roosevelt's glasses were knocked off but not broken. Someone picked them up and returned them to the candidate. But another FDR admirer grabbed the candidate's hat as a souvenir. "When they knocked his glasses off and stole his hat," Daniell recalled, "he knew the campaign was on."[18]

When someone from the crowd asked Roosevelt how he had liked the flight, he replied "fine." Another voice urged him to make up with Al Smith. "I'll do that," FDR jovially replied. FDR embraced his sons James and young Franklin, but daughter Anna and daughter-in-law Betsy had trouble navigating through the crowd. "Hey you!" a photographer snarled at the Roosevelt women. "Get back out of the way!"

"They're only members of the family," said a friend.

"I know," the photographer replied, "but can't they wait a minute?"

As Farley approached his side, Roosevelt clutched his hand. "Jim, old pal—put it right there—great work." Howe, leaving Suite 1702 for the first time in a week, also worked his way through the crowd and shared in this moment of triumph.

Mayor Cermak, who had held elective office for thirty years, had never seen a more demonstrative crowd. "Chicago considers it a great honor," he said, speaking into the microphone, "to be the first of the cities of this Union to receive the next President of the United States."

"I am very glad to visit Chicago," replied FDR, "but personally to be welcomed by you, one of my very old friends. I am very happy about what has happened in Chicago this year and I am very confident that your prophecy about the result is going to be proved."[19]

George Gaw, the city's greeter, who had sent his big white car for FDR, had ordered some planes to fly out and escort the presidential candidate's plane into the airport. "Somehow the little fleet became confused up there in the blue," recalled Stiles, "picked up a mail plane by mistake, and escorted it grandly into the landing. The face of the aerial postman, when he alighted amid all this pomp and splendor, was something to behold."[20]

As Rosenman got out of the plane, Moley informed him about the latest dispute within the Roosevelt camp. "You've got to do something about this," he said. "Louis [Howe] has read the acceptance speech, and he says it's terrible. He stayed up all last night and dictated a brand-new one; and he is going to try to get the Governor to deliver it instead of the speech which you telephoned in last night. I have tried to tell him now how foolish that would be, but it's no use; he is over there talking to the Governor about it now."

Roosevelt, Howe, and Farley were seated in the back of Mayor Cermak's seven-passenger white Cadillac convertible. "I squeezed into the car," James Roosevelt remembered, "and immediately there began one of the most incongruous performances I ever have witnessed. Louis had strong objections to part of Father's proposed acceptance speech and he began arguing with him even as the car was rolling in from the airport. Pa listened to him with one ear, argued back out of the side of his mouth—all the while smiling and waving at the wildly cheering crowds. Finally—and it was one of the few times I ever heard him get really rough with Louis—Pa suddenly exploded: 'Dammit, Louie, I'm the nominee!' " [21]

As Roosevelt drove through the blue-collar neighborhoods of the Southwest Side, he was warmly greeted from the sidewalks and plant gates by tens of thousands of workers in overalls and shirtsleeves. Kids playing sandlot baseball interrupted their game and rushed to the street, shouting "hooray for the next president." Roosevelt sped past Northerly Island where the "Century of Progress" 1933 World's Fair exhibition halls were nearing completion. "As I was driving along the Boulevard a few minutes ago," he told a crowd in Grant Park, "we passed the World Fair buildings and I asked Mayor Cermak: What date does the fair open?

"He told me that it was next summer and I said that God willing I'll be here to help you open it," said Roosevelt. "I am on my way to the convention to help my fellow Democrats close the most successful convention in many years."[22]

After a brief stop at the Congress Hotel, Roosevelt headed for the Stadium. Facing the nation for the first time as the standard-bearer of the Democratic Party, Roosevelt delivered a formal address as the occasion required but also spoke directly to the American people about how he would respond to the greatest crisis since the Civil War. FDR rejected all but the first page of the orthodox Howe speech and used the Rosenman text written in collaboration with Moley. Roosevelt had already declared his intention to be a progressive president and in this speech he would transform the Democratic Party into an instrument of social change. "Throughout the nation there was clear understanding that if Roosevelt were elected there would be a new kind of thinking in Washington," said Rosenman. "It was a discussion of progressive government and liberal thought, the interdependence of all groups in the economy, prohibition, public works to provide employment, reforestation for better use of land and to provide employment. . . . federal responsibility for the relief of unemployment distresses, and the right of all people to a more equitable opportunity to share in national wealth."[23]

When Roosevelt appeared on the rostrum, wearing a blue suit with a rose in his lapel, the organist struck up "Happy Days Are Here Again," and the crowd of more than twenty thousand leaped to their feet for an ovation that lasted more than ten minutes. "The convention was only lukewarm to the Governor up to that time," Richard L. Strout reported in *The Christian Science Monitor*. "Governor Roosevelt had the votes but not the enthusiasm. His appearance changed all this. His trip by airplane shattered tradition as did his mere presence before the convention. Finally a burst of applause announced his arrival. There appeared in the speaker's rostrum a big man—a smiling, happy man—who spoke informally and permitted humor to run through his address. There is little doubt that his winning personality bolstered his hold at that time."

"Roosevelt the crusader was unveiled before the enraptured delegates and before a reporter who has his emotional sprees and still a few heroes in spite of many disappointments. America had long waited for a hero. So had I," said Thomas L. Stokes of Scripps-Howard newspapers. "There he stood. Roosevelt on the stump still stirs me as he stirred me that day when he appeared before the Chicago convention. Then I first knew that characteristic toss of the head. Then I first knew that confidential look with the upraised eyebrow he gives his audience when he has delivered a thrust, succeeded by the slow grin as the audience catches it and tosses it around in laughter."

Through the live network coverage, Roosevelt also showed his mastery of a new medium that had become a dominant force in American culture. On this night, across the land, many ordinary people were listening to him for the first time. "He was the first great American radio voice. For most Americans of this generation, their first memory of politics would be of sitting by a radio and hearing that voice, strong, confident, totally at ease," David Halberstam has written. "It was in the most direct sense the government reaching out and touching the citizen, bringing Americans into the political process and focusing their attention on the presidency as the source of good."[24]

In opening his remarks, FDR made reference to his long flight. "I regret that I am late," he said, "but I have no control over the winds of heaven and could only be thankful for my navy training." The crowd roared.

Roosevelt also thanked delegates for extending the convention another day "for I know well the sleepless hours which you and I have had." This appearance, he acknowledged, "is unprecedented and unusual, but these are unprecedented and unusual times. I have started out on the tasks that lie ahead by breaking the absurd traditions that the candidate should remain in professed ignorance of what has happened for weeks until he is formally notified. . . . Let it be from now on the task of our party to break foolish traditions. We will break foolish traditions and leave it to the Republican leadership, far more skilled in that art, to break promises."

After a decade of conservative leadership, Roosevelt served notice that his party would once again stand for democratic values. "As we enter this new battle, let us always keep present with us some of the ideals of the party: The fact that the Democratic Party by tradition and by the continuing logic of history, past and present, is the bearer of liberalism and of progress," he said. "This is no time for fear, for reaction or for timidity. And here and now I invite those nominal Republicans who find that their conscience cannot be squared with the groping and failure of their party leaders to join hands with us; here and now, in equal measure, I warn these nominal Democrats who squint at the future with their faces turned toward the past, and who feel no responsibility to the demands of the new time, that they are out of step with the party."

Roosevelt left no doubt about his commitment to the political left. "The people of this country want a genuine choice this year," he said, "not a choice between two names for the same reactionary doctrine. Ours must be a party of liberal thought, of planned action, of enlightened international outlook, and of the greatest good to the greatest number of our citizens."

Under his administration, Roosevelt pledged that the federal government would "assume bold leadership in distress relief" and "a continuing responsibility for the broader public welfare." In a strong clear voice, he then explained that the nation was at a turning point.

"Never before in modern history," he said, "have the essential differences between the two major American parties stood out in such striking contrast as they do today. Republican leaders not only have failed in material things, they have failed in national vision, because in disaster they have held out no hope, they have pointed out no path for the people below to climb back to places of security and of safety in our American life.

"Throughout the nation, men and women, forgotten in the political philosophy of the government of the last years look to us here for guidance and for more equitable opportunity to share in the distribution of national wealth.

"On the farms, in the large metropolitan areas, in the smaller cities and in the villages, millions of our citizens cherish the hope that their old standards of living and of thought have not gone forever. Those millions cannot and shall not hope in vain.

"I pledge you—I pledge myself to a new deal for the American people. Let us all here assembled constitute ourselves prophets of a new order of competence and of courage. This is more than a political campaign; it is a call to arms. Give me your help, not to win votes alone, but to win in this crusade to restore America to its own people."[25]

EPILOGUE

F RANKLIN D. ROOSEVELT captured the presidency in November with the largest vote in history and forged a new coalition that dominated American politics for more than a generation. FDR would go on to win a record four terms as the nation's chief executive and held office until his death in April 1945. For his bold leadership in the Great Depression and World War II, he is usually ranked with George Washington and Abraham Lincoln on the short list of great presidents.

In a time of deepening gloom, Roosevelt gave Americans hope. With his cigarette holder, self-assured smile, and that magnetic voice, he was always larger than life, a symbol of optimism and confidence. Breaking with the nineteenth-century tradition of limited national government, he understood that the disadvantaged could no longer depend on the kindness of strangers. Under his leadership, the federal government promoted the general welfare. From the sharecroppers of the Mississippi Delta to the landless farmers of the Dust Bowl and migrant workers of California, Roosevelt embraced the "one third of a nation" that was "ill-housed, ill-clad, ill-nourished." His humanity is reflected in the novels of John Steinbeck, the songs of Woody Guthrie, and the art of Ben Shahn.

SUPREME COURT JUSTICE William O. Douglas said, "He was in a very special sense the people's President because he made them feel that with him in the White House they shared the presidency." The political columnist Joseph Alsop, a Roosevelt cousin, said that FDR's greatest accomplishment was that he "included the excluded."

As Labor secretary Frances Perkins observed, "There was a bond between Roosevelt and the ordinary men and women of this country. He was profoundly loyal to them. Even when good reasons were presented for not carrying out such a program that would be beneficial to them, he would examine, appreciate and even understand the arguments against a project, but persist."

The New Deal provided relief for the hungry, shelter for the homeless, Social Security for the elderly, and millions of jobs for the unemployed through the Civilian Conservation Corps, National Youth Administration, Works Progress Administration, and other alphabet agencies. During the 1930s these workers constructed highways, bridges, subways, and airports. Roosevelt built the Tennessee Valley Authority that provided low-cost power to the nation's poorest region and brought rural America into the modern age through the Rural Electrification Administration. His farm loan programs saved tens of thousands of family farms from foreclosure. Through tax reform he brought about the largest redistribution of income in American history and was scorned by wealthy conservatives as "a traitor to his class." In fact, he rescued the nation from economic disaster and saved American capitalism. Roosevelt protected investors and established regulations over Wall Street through the Securities and Exchange Commission. He abolished child labor, established the minimum wage, and signed laws that guaranteed workers the right to collective bargaining and to organize unions. His policies would lift millions of Americans into the middle class.

Admiral Samuel Eliot Morison, in *The Oxford History of the American People*, described Roosevelt's program as "a new deal of old cards, no longer stacked against the common man. Opponents called it near-fascism or near-communism, but it was as American as a bale of hay—an opportunistic, rule-of-thumb method of curing deep-seated ills."

"Roosevelt tried to make it clear," added the historian Henry Steele Commager, "that every person in the United States—male or female, white or black, child or adult, citizen or non-citizen—is part of our society and has a right to all the rights extended to 'persons' by the Constitution. No one part of the nation—geographical or social—can suffer without hurting the welfare of the whole."

In foreign policy, he led what was still an isolationist nation to the leadership of the free world. At a time when the leaders of other western democratic nations were following the dangerous policy of appeasement, FDR alerted the American people to the threat of Axis aggression. Returning to Chicago in October 1937 for what became known as his "Quarantine Speech," he condemned the brutal regimes of Nazi Germany and Imperial Japan. "Nations claiming freedom for themselves deny it to others," he said. "If those things come to pass in other parts of the world, let no one imagine that America will escape, that it may expect mercy, that this Western Hemisphere will not be attacked. . . . It seems to be unfortunately true that the epidemic of world lawlessness is spreading."

Roosevelt prepared the nation for war and provided crucial aid to Great Britain. As FDR's biographer Conrad Black has written: "Without Roosevelt's strategic insight and tactical expertise, it would not have been possible to bring such powerful and decisive assistance to Britain and Canada in 1940 and 1941, when the future of civilization depended on their ability to resist Hitler."

In his 1941 State of the Union message, Roosevelt took on the isolationists. "Those who would give up essential liberty to purchase a little temporary safety deserve neither freedom nor safety," he said. FDR then outlined his vision of "a world based on four essential human freedoms." Beginning with the traditional American principles of freedom of speech and religion, Roosevelt added "freedom from want" and "freedom from fear." These democratic values defined the Allied cause in World War II and also were the ideals that inspired the creation of the United Nations.

As the great communicator of his time, Roosevelt was the first chief executive to shape and influence public opinion through the new medium of radio. His fireside chats were immensely popular and politically effective. "He gave the impression of speaking to every listener personally, like a sympathetic, authoritative, and omniscient friend," the journalist John Gunther has written. "You could practically feel him physically in the room."

He was the most eloquent of American presidents and so vividly expressive that his great speeches are still remembered. In his first inaugural address, he assured Americans that "the only thing we have to fear is fear itself." Speaking before a crowd of one hundred thousand at Philadelphia's Franklin Field in 1936, he summoned his countrymen to "a rendezvous with destiny."

In contrast with the somber and aloof men who preceded him in the White House, Roosevelt sparkled with life. The newsreels showed him wearing an Indian war bonnet at a Boy Scout camp, teasing his granddaughter, hosting a picnic at Hyde Park for the King and Queen of England, tossing out the first ball at the World Series, and greeting coal miners in West Virginia. "He had not a personality," Arthur M. Schlesinger Jr. observed, "but a ring of personalities, each one dissolving on approach, always revealing still another beneath."

Roosevelt not only won the presidency four times but his party won all seven congressional elections from 1932 through 1944. Since the Civil War the Democrats had been in the minority but Roosevelt built a diverse coalition that transformed his party into a majority. This coalition included younger voters, union households, family farmers, African Americans, Jews, Catholics, white southern Protestants, liberal intellectuals, and the impoverished. He united the rural and urban wings that had long divided the Democratic Party, brought organized labor into the party's ranks, and got blacks to abandon their allegiance to the party of Lincoln. If the Democratic Party had nominated another candidate at Chicago in 1932, it is highly unlikely that Newton Baker or Albert Ritchie would have had comparable success.

Although Roosevelt's health became an issue at the Chicago convention, he outlived most of his rivals, including Alfred E. Smith, Newton D. Baker, Albert C. Ritchie, James A. Reed, J. Hamilton Lewis, and Melvin Traylor. John Nance Garner, the most durable of the 1932 contenders, left the vice presidency after two terms and returned to the Rio Grande Valley where he died in 1967 at ninety-seven.

Two of the major figures at the convention were later slain by assassins. While visiting with Roosevelt at a Miami park, Mayor Anton J. Cermak was shot in February 1933 by Joseph Zangara whose bullet had been meant for FDR. Huey Long, who broke with Roosevelt soon after the inauguration, hoped to run against him in 1936. But Long was assassinated in September 1935 at the state capitol in Baton Rouge by the son-in-law of a political enemy.

New York mayor James J. Walker, faced with the threat of possible removal from office by Roosevelt, quit in September 1932. His resignation was welcomed at Hyde Park because it spared FDR an unpleasant decision. Walker could have been prosecuted on corruption charges. But Roosevelt had always liked the dapper mayor and gave him a pass. Kansas City Democratic boss Thomas J. Pendergast and Boston mayor James Michael Curley, who were among the more colorful figures at the Chicago convention, were not so lucky. Pendergast and Curley were prosecuted by Roosevelt's Justice Department and did prison time. Both blamed FDR for their legal troubles.

Louis McHenry Howe, Roosevelt's confidant and friend, lived at the White House until his death in 1936. If it had not been for the selfless dedication of this extraordinary man, FDR might have retired from public life after being stricken with polio.

James A. Farley, FDR's campaign manager, became Democratic national chairman and postmaster general, serving in both positions until 1940. The most skillful political professional of his generation, Farley would have been successful in any era. After helping FDR remake the party in his own image, Farley resigned from the cabinet and as party chairman when Roosevelt decided to seek a third term.

Edward J. Flynn, who stayed in the Bronx as Democratic leader, remained among Roosevelt's closest advisers and served in the first administration as regional administrator for the National Recovery Administration's public works program. Succeeding Farley as Democratic national chairman in 1940, he managed Roosevelt's last two presidential campaigns.

William Gibbs McAdoo was elected in the fall of 1932 as a Democratic senator from California. Despite his critical role in breaking the convention deadlock, Roosevelt never forgave him for supporting

Garner in the California primary. But FDR honored his pledge to name McAdoo ally Daniel C. Roper as secretary of commerce.

Thomas J. Walsh, whose rulings as permanent chairman of the Chicago convention helped Roosevelt win the nomination, was slated to become attorney general in the new Democratic administration with the promise of a future appointment to the Supreme Court. But Walsh died just before FDR took office. He was seventy-four years old.

Alben W. Barkley, temporary chairman of the convention, became Senate majority leader in 1937 and served in that position for a decade. During the Republican-controlled 80th Congress, he served as minority leader. In 1948, Harry Truman chose him for the vice presidency.

Sam Rayburn, Garner's floor leader at the 1932 convention, became House majority leader in 1937 and Speaker of the House in 1940, a position that he held longer than any other man. Rayburn served as permanent chairman of three Democratic National Conventions and also promoted Lyndon Johnson's rise to power.

Cordell Hull, who played an important role for Roosevelt at the Chicago convention, served for eleven years as secretary of state. Despite this record tenure, he was not the major architect of foreign policy. Roosevelt kept that role for himself. George H. Dern, disappointed at being passed over for the vice presidency, was named in 1933 as secretary of war and became one of the hardest-working members of the cabinet. Still in office, he died in 1936.

William Randolph Hearst contributed generously to Roosevelt's campaign in the fall of 1932 and also used his newspapers and newsreels to promote FDR. But Hearst quickly became disillusioned with the New Deal, which he labeled the "Raw Deal." In the next three presidential elections, his newspapers supported Roosevelt's unsuccessful opponents.

Joseph P. Kennedy, whose courtship of Hearst helped deliver the nomination to FDR, was rewarded with appointments as the first chairman of the Securities and Exchange Commission and, later, as ambassador to Great Britain. But Kennedy broke with Roosevelt over the administration's foreign policy. Although the ambassador never ran for elective office, in 1960 he helped his son John win the presidency.

Harry F. Byrd, who would have been Baker's vice-presidential choice, was appointed to the Senate in 1933 when Roosevelt named Virginia senator Claude A. Swanson his secretary of the navy. Byrd remained in the Senate for thirty-two years, serving for his last decade as chairman of the Finance Committee. His son Harry Jr. succeeded him in the Senate.

Burton K. Wheeler, though disappointed at being passed over for the second slot, supported most of the New Deal's progressive measures and campaigned for Roosevelt again in 1936. But he held the successful bipartisan opposition to FDR's effort to expand the Supreme Court in 1937. An isolationist, he opposed Roosevelt's efforts to aid the Allies and alleged that FDR's foreign policy "will plough under every fourth American boy." After Pearl Harbor, he supported the war.

Following the Chicago convention, Tammany Hall's John F. Curry further alienated himself from Roosevelt by seeking to block FDR's choice of Herbert Lehman as his gubernatorial successor. Curry also denied slating for a full judicial term to Supreme Court Justice Samuel I. Rosenman, FDR's friend, and excluded Farley as a member of the city's delegation to the 1932 New York State convention. In April 1934, Curry paid for these mistakes when he became the first Tammany leader to be voted out of office by the Executive Committee.

Smith in 1934 joined John J. Raskob and Jouett Shouse in founding the conservative Liberty League. After Roosevelt's election, none of them ever supported another Democrat for the presidency. Of the

Smith bloc at the 1932 convention, only Frank Hague of Jersey City became a major Roosevelt ally.

Earl Dickerson, who presented the NAACP's plank at the 1932 convention, was elected to the Chicago City Council in 1939 and in 1941 was named by Roosevelt as a member of the President's Committee on Fair Employment Practices. Although Roosevelt made the slightest of commitments to civil rights and did almost nothing to end segregation, he named more blacks to office than his predecessors and opened up the Democratic Party to African Americans. For the first time, at the 1936 Democratic National Convention in Philadelphia, blacks had full status as delegates.

Following his dramatic flight to the 1932 convention, Roosevelt returned to New York by train and would go by railroad that following winter to his inauguration in Washington. He did not travel by plane again until the 1943 Casablanca conference with Winston Churchill and Charles de Gaulle. And this was the first time that a sitting president had flown. There were reminders after FDR's 1932 flight that aviation was still hazardous. Will Rogers, who had praised Roosevelt for his boldness in flying, was killed in a 1935 plane crash with the famous pilot Wiley Post. Amelia Earhart, cheered by thousands on her return to Chicago in June 1932, died in a plane crash five years later.

Among the reasons that few conventions since 1932 have had great drama is that Roosevelt abolished the two-thirds rule. Since 1936 a Democratic presidential candidate has needed only a simple majority to win the nomination. Only twice since then has a Democratic convention gone beyond the first ballot. At the 1952 convention in Chicago, the reluctant Illinois governor Adlai E. Stevenson was drafted for the presidential nomination on the third ballot. Four years later, when Stevenson won a second nomination in Chicago, he stirred great excitement by allowing the convention to choose his running mate. After a spirited contest, Estes Kefauver edged out John F. Kennedy on the second ballot. This is the last time that either of the major political parties has gone beyond the first roll call.

Roosevelt chose Chicago Stadium as the site for the 1940 and 1944 Democratic conventions. When he did not want to formally declare his candidacy for a third term, a voice from a tiny basement room of the stadium shouted "We Want Roosevelt!" into the public-address system and worked the crowd into a frenzy. It was the voice of Chicago sewers commissioner Tom Garry, following the script of Mayor Edward J. Kelly. In 1944, Roosevelt was nominated a fourth time and with his approval the delegates dropped Henry A. Wallace from the ticket and replaced him with Harry S. Truman.

A half century later, the stadium was torn down to make way for a parking lot. But we will always have the memories of the Roosevelt era. Happy days were here again.

NOTES

CHAPTER 1: THE MAN WHO WASN'T THERE

1. William Braden, "FDR's Chicago Connection," *Chicago Sun-Times*, January 31, 1982; Frank Freidel, *Franklin D. Roosevelt: The Ordeal*, 80; Earland Irving Carlson, *Franklin D. Roosevelt's Fight for the Presidential Nomination, 1928–1932*, 35.
2. Mark Sullivan column, *Raleigh News and Observer*, June 19, 1932; Frank Sullivan, "On to Chicago," *New Yorker*, June 4, 1932; Raymond Moley, *After Seven Years*, 27.
3. Lela Stiles, *The Man Behind Roosevelt*, 169; James A. Farley, *Behind the Ballots*, 121; Alfred B. Rollins, *Roosevelt and Howe*, 341; Ralph G. Martin, *Ballots and Bandwagons*, 310.
4. Frank R. Kent, "The Great Game of Politics," *Baltimore Sun*, June 20, 1932; William Allen White column, *Louisville Courier-Journal*, June 29, 1932; Statement by James A. Farley on status of the Roosevelt campaign, June 10, 1932, JAF Papers; Louis M. Howe, 1932 Democratic National Convention file, LMH Papers.
5. Farley, *Behind the Ballots*, 111; Edward J. Flynn, *You're the Boss*, 90–91.
6. Editorial, *New York World-Telegram*, June 10, 1932; Farley, *Behind the Ballots*, 129.
7. Howe to FDR, June 3, 1932, LMH convention file; Rollins, *Roosevelt and Howe*, 334–335; *New York Times*, June 28, 1932.
8. FDR to Farley, June 26, 1932, JAF Papers; Grace Tully, *FDR: My Boss*, 50–51.
9. Frank R. Ken, "The Great Game of Politics," *Baltimore Sun*, June 24, 1932; John Callahan letter, and FDR to C. E. Broughton, June 22, 1932, Wisconsin preconvention file, Democratic National Committee manuscripts.
10. "Governor Roosevelt Seems Calm," Associated Press report from Albany, June 29, 1932.

CHAPTER 2: CHICAGO 1932

1. Alex Gottfried, *Boss Cermak of Chicago*, 241; Emmett Dedmon, *Fabulous Chicago*, 335; *Scarface: The Shame of a Nation*, produced by Howard Hughes, directed by Howard Hawks, screenplay by Ben Hecht, 1932.
2. *Official Proceedings, 1932 Democratic National Convention*, 482; Don Hayner and Tom McNamee, *The Stadium*, 19.
3. David Lowe, *Lost Chicago;* William G. Shepherd, "Fair for Tomorrow," *Collier's*, September 17, 1932; *Official Proceedings*, 478–485.
4. Anton F. Cermak to FDR, December 24, 1931, Illinois preconvention file, DNC; Robert H. Ferrell, *FDR's Quiet Confidant*, 65; *Official Proceedings*, 489–494.
5. Walter Trohan, *Political Animals*, 44; FDR to William Arnold, June 3, 1932, Illinois preconvention, DNC.
6. George Murray, *The Legacy of Al Capone*, 169; Gottfried, *Boss Cermak*, 58.
7. James Doherty, "Cermak Story Is Oil for the Lamp of Sonny," *Chicago Tribune*, March 24, 1946.
8. Cermak to FDR, December 7, 1928 and November 26, 1929, Illinois preconvention file, DNC.
9. T. H. Watkins, *Righteous Pilgrim*, 247; "World's Fair Mayor," *Time*, April 13, 1931; Mauritz A. Hallgren, "Chicago Goes Tammany," *Nation*, April 22, 1931; Claude W. Gilbert, "Czech Reign," *Collier's*, January 7, 1933.
10. Murray, *Legacy of Al Capone*, 169; Gottfried, *Boss Cermak*, 245, 275, 299.
11. Virgil Peterson, *Barbarians in Our Midst*, 157; Gottfried, *Boss Cermak*, 298.
12. Gottfried, *Boss Cermak*, 418; FDR to James C. Bonbright, March 11, 1930, governor's personal file; Elliott Roosevelt, *The Roosevelt Letters, Volume Three, 1928–1945*, 52–53; Carlson, *Roosevelt's Fight*, 333.

CHAPTER 3: FRONT-RUNNER

1. Freidel, *The Ordeal*, 204; FDR to Robert W. Bingham, September 29, 1931, Bingham Papers.
2. James F. Byrnes to FDR, November 12, 1928, South Carolina preconvention file, DNC.
3. Tully, *FDR My Boss*, 4.
4. Roy V. Peel and Thomas C. Donnelly, *The 1932 Campaign: An Analysis*, 60–61; Freidel, *Franklin D. Roosevelt: The Triumph*, 204–205; *New York Times*, March 30, 1931.
5. Rollins, *Roosevelt and Howe*, 61; Carlson, *Roosevelt's Fight*, 20–21; Ferrell, *FDR's Quiet Confidant*, 61–62; Memorandum of Josephus Daniels interview with Frank Freidel, FDRL.
6. Flynn, *You're the Boss*, 84.
7. John B. Kennedy, "Jim the Salesman," *Collier's*, September 17, 1932; Hugh Bradley, "An Elk on a Tour," *American Mercury*, September 1932; James A. Farley cover profile, *Time*, October 31, 1932; Red Smith, *To Absent Friends*, 236; Raymond Moley, *27 Masters of Politics*, 107.
8. Farley, *Behind the Ballots*, 81–83.
9. Farley to FDR, July 6, 1931, JAF Papers.
10. Scott Bullitt to Farley, July 10, 1931, Washington State preconvention file, DNC; Oswald West to Farley, August 9, 1931, Oregon preconvention file, DNC.
11. Farley to Louis M. Howe, July 11, 1931, JAF Papers; Farley to FDR, July 11, 1931, JAF Papers.
12. Farley, *Behind the Ballots*, 86–87; Howe to Edward M. House, August 17, 1931, LMH Papers; Carlson, *Roosevelt's Fight*, 171; Harris is quoted in the *New York Times*, October 14, 1931.

13. FDR to James J. Hoey, September 11, 1931, *Roosevelt Letters, Volume Three*, 73; Howe to Cordell Hull, September 5, 1931, Hull Papers; FDR memorandum regarding the platform is quoted in Freidel, *The Triumph*, 230.

14. Breckinridge Long to William Gibbs McAdoo, January 25, 1932, WGM Papers; Sam Rayburn's letter to Louis Carpenter is quoted in Martin, *Ballots and Bandwagons*, 289; Robert W. Woolley to Edward M. House, January 9, 1932, House Papers.

CHAPTER 4: PRIMARY COLORS

1. FDR to Fred W. McLean, January 22, 1932; *Public Papers and Addresses of Franklin D. Roosevelt: Volume One, The Genesis of the New Deal*, 623–624.

2. Frank R. Kent, "How Strong Is Roosevelt?" *Scribner's*, April 1932; *New York Times*, February 8, 1932.

3. Robert Jackson memorandum of January 26, 1932, meeting with Alfred E. Smith, JAF Papers; Farley to Robert Jackson, March 10, 1932, New Hampshire preconvention file, DNC.

4. Wayne Gard, "Alfalfa Bill," *New Republic*, February 17, 1932; Archibald Edwards, "Wild Bill Murray," *Forum*, February 1932; George Milburn, "Murray—Possible but Not Likely," *Nation*, April 6, 1932.

5. Murray's letter to his brother is quoted in Carlson, *Roosevelt's Fight*, 311; FDR to W. E. Chilton, February 20, 1932, West Virginia preconvention file, DNC; Burton K. Wheeler's North Dakota radio address is quoted in Keith L. Bryant Jr., *Alfalfa Bill Murray*, 229.

6. John F. Sullivan to FDR, March 31, 1932, JAF Papers; Jackson memorandum on the Maine Democratic Convention, JAF Papers; Farley, *Behind the Ballots*, 99.

7. *New York Times*, April 7, 1932.

8. Rollins, *Roosevelt and Howe*, 326; Woolley to House, April 26, 1932, House Papers; Jackson to FDR, February 2, 1932, New Hampshire preconvention file, DNC.

9. Woolley to House April 27, 1932, House Papers; Farley is quoted in Martin, *Ballots and Bandwagons*, 299; Howe to Stephen Bonsal, May 2, 1932, District of Columbia preconvention file, DNC.

10. Howe to Daniels, May 2, 1932, LMH Papers.

11. Justus Wardell to FDR, November 16, 1931, preconvention file, California, DNC; McAdoo endorsement of Garner, February 18, 1932, WGM Papers; the taunting reference to FDR is quoted in Freidel, *The Triumph*, 287.

12. Farley to George Martin, May 7, 1932, JAF Papers; FDR to Josephus Daniels, May 5, 1932, Daniels Papers.

13. Edward M. House to Robert W. Woolley, May 5, 1932, House Papers; Joseph P. Lash, *From the Diaries of Felix Frankfurter*, 42.

CHAPTER 5: CITIZEN HEARST

1. "Hearst," *Time*, May 1, 1933; Ken Murray, *The Golden Days of San Simeon*; Ben Procter, *William Randolph Hearst: The Early Years*, 41–49.

2. W. A. Swanberg, *Citizen Hearst*, 76, 80–82, 108, 158; E. L. Godkin is quoted in Charles Willis Thompson, "Hearst: A Modern Monte Cristo," *New York Times Book Review*, May 27, 1928.

3. David Nasaw, *The Chief: The Life of William Randolph Hearst*, 151, 155; Swanberg, *Citizen Hearst*, 182–183; Procter, *The Early Years*, 153.

4. Oliver Carlson and Ernest Sutherland Bates, *Hearst: Lord of San Simeon,* 112–113; Nasaw, *The Chief,* 148.

5. Lindsay Chaney and Michael Cieply, *The Hearsts: Family and Empire,* 35.

6. Procter, *Early Years,* 183–186; Nasaw, *The Chief,* 186–187; Carlson and Sutherland, *Lord of San Simeon,* 120–121, 130; Swanberg, *Citizen Hearst,* 217–219, 239; Edmond D. Coblentz, *William Randolph Hearst: A Portrait in His Own Words,* 37.

7. Thompson, "A Modern Monte Cristo:" Nasaw, *The Chief,* 207, 210–211; *Guide to U.S. Elections,* 422–423.

8. Coblentz, *William Randolph Hearst,* 30; Carlson and Bates, *Lord of San Simeon,* 190–192.

9. Swanberg, *Citizen Hearst,* 329–331; Carlson and Bates, *Lord of San Simeon,* 207–208.

10. FDR to Alfred E. Smith, August 13, 1922, quoted in Emily Smith Warner, *The Happy Warrior: The Story of My Father Alfred E. Smith,* 133; Freidel, *The Ordeal,* 116–119; Swanberg, *Citizen Hearst,* 346–347.

11. Coblentz, *William Randolph Hearst,* 118–119.

12. Ibid., 128.

13. *New York Times,* January 3, 1952; Coblentz, *William Randolph Hearst,* 40, 115.

14. Ibid., 120–121; FDR's 1920 comments about the League of Nations are quoted in Carlson, *Roosevelt's Fight,* 259.

15. Rollins, *Roosevelt and Howe,* 322; Freidel, *The Triumph,* 250–252.

16. Edward M. House to FDR, February 10, 1932, House Papers; Woolley to House, February 9, 1932, RWW Papers; Woolley to FDR, February 12, 1932 and FDR to Woolley, February 25, 1932, House Papers.

17. Coblentz, *William Randolph Hearst,* 122–123.

18. *Brooklyn Eagle,* June 28, 1932.

CHAPTER 6: BUGLE CALL

1. Pershing is quoted in *Time,* November 14, 1927; Frank R. Kent, "Newton D. Baker," *Forum,* September 1931; Frank E. Vandiver, *Black Jack: The Life and Times of John J. Pershing,* 869.

2. Ibid., 695; Baker to Mark S. Watson, April 25, 1931, NDB Papers; C. H. Cramer, *Newton D. Baker: A Biography,* 209.

3. George Creel, "Newton D. Baker's Measure," *Collier's,* March 19, 1932; Henry F. Pringle, "Dark Horse of Democracy," *Outlook,* January 13, 1932; Frank R. Kent, "Newton D. Baker," *Scribner's; New York Times,* June 29, 1924; Walter Johnson, *The Papers of Adlai E. Stevenson: Beginnings of Education, Volume 1,* 149; Oswald Garrison Villard, "Newton D. Baker—Just Another Politician," *Nation,* April 13, 1932.

4. Baker to Walter Lippmann, May 26, 1932, NDB Papers.

5. Frederick Palmer to Judge John H. Clarke, December 16, 1930, NDB Papers; Baker to Ralph Hayes, April 27, 1931; Cramer, *Newton D. Baker,* 236; *Baltimore Evening Sun,* June 24, 1932.

6. Woolley to House, October 6, 1931, House Papers; John Dos Passos, *Mr. Wilson's War,* 373.

7. Robert W. Bingham to William E. Dodd, August 12, 1932, Dodd Papers; Claude G. Bowers to FDR, June 7, 1931, governor's personal file.

8. FDR to Josephus Daniels, May 14, 1932, Daniels Papers.

9. Baker to Hayes, January 18, 1932, NDB Papers; Baker to Lippmann, November 28, 1931, NDB Papers.

10. Freidel, *The Apprenticeship,* 253–254; Freidel, *The Ordeal,* 127–129; FDR's speech to the

American Legion is quoted in Maurice A. Hallgren, "Franklin D. Roosevelt," *Nation,* June 1, 1932.

11. Hayes to Baker, November 17, 1931 and January 20, 1932, NDB Papers.

12. *New York Times,* January 27, 1932; Broun is quoted in Cramer, *Newton D. Baker,* 239; Villard, "Just Another Politician"; *Brooklyn Eagle,* February 7, 1932; Baker to Hayes, February 22, 1932, NDB Papers.

13. Walter Lippmann, *Interpretations: 1931–1932,* 259–263, 303–305.

14. Lippmann to Baker, December 18, 1931, NDB Papers; Baker to Lippmann, December 21, 1931, NDB Papers.

15. Lippmann to Baker, September 10 and 28, 1932, November 24, 1932, NDB Papers; and Baker to Lippmann, October 8, 1931, NDB Papers.

16. Hayes to Baker, April 1, 1932, NDB Papers; Baker to Hayes, April 5, 1932, NDB Papers; Bruce Barton to Roy Howard, April 14, 1932, NDB Papers.

17. Baker's letter to Hayes is quoted in Cramer, *Newton D. Baker,* 244–245.

18. Hayes to Louis Wiley, March 31, 1932, NDB Papers; Hayes to Jesse Straus, April 28, 1932, NDB Papers; and Hayes to Baker, May 12, 1932, NDB Papers.

19. Lippmann to House, April 27, 1932, House Papers; House to Lippmann, April 30, 1932, House Papers; Lippmann to House, May 4, 1932, House Papers.

20. Hayes to Roy Howard, June 3, 1932, NDB Papers.

CHAPTER 7: LONE STAR

1. *Chicago Herald and Examiner,* January 6, 1932; Lionel V. Patenaude, *Texas, Politics and the New Deal,* 8; Bascom N. Timmons, *Garner of Texas: A Personal History,* 153, 157.

2. Carlson, *Roosevelt's Fight,* 241; Rayburn's letter to Oscar Callaway is quoted in D. B. Hardeman and Donald C. Bacon, *Rayburn: A Biography,* 135–136; Timmons, *Garner of Texas,* 154.

3. Woolley to House, February 23, 1932, RWW Papers; Donald McCoy profile of Garner, *Dictionary of American Biography;* Paul Y. Anderson, "Texas Jack Garner," *Nation,* April 20, 1932.

4. Claude Bowers column, *New York Journal,* March 31, 1932; Garner interview, *U.S. News and World Report,* November 21, 1958; Marquis James, *Mr. Garner of Texas,* 28.

5. Ovie C. Fisher, *Cactus Jack,* 17–18; James, *Mr. Garner of Texas,* 30–31.

6. Farley, *Behind the Ballots,* 92.

7. James, *Mr. Garner of Texas,* Garner obituary in *New York Times,* November 7, 1967; 1958 *U.S. News* interview; Fisher, *Cactus Jack,* 79; Clinton W. Gilbert, "John Nance Garner," *Forum,* May 1932.

8. Moley, *27 Masters of Politics,* 69; James, *Mr. Garner of Texas,* 43–44, 66, 78–80.

9. Carlson, *Roosevelt's Fight,* 368; Sam Rayburn to Lewis T. Carpenter, January 11, 1932, quoted in H. G. Dulaney and Edward Hake Philips, *Speak Mr. Speaker,* 43; Shouse comment in John Nance Garner file, Moley Papers; House to Woolley, February 17, 1932, House Papers.

10. Tom Connally, *My Name Is Tom Connally,* 139; Garner interview, *U.S. News and World Report,* March 8, 1957; Sterling comment in Garner file, Moley Papers.

11. Hardeman and Bacon, *Rayburn,* 134; Carlson, *Roosevelt's Fight,* 242.

12. November 1958 *U.S. News* interview; *Chicago Herald-Examiner* editorial; Anderson, "Texas Jack Garner"; Owen P. White, "Garner on Parade," *Collier's,* May 28, 1932.

13. James, *Mr. Garner of Texas*, 125–126; Arthur Krock, "In the Nation," *New York Times*, March 30, 1932.
14. *Time*, June 6, 1932; March 1957 *U.S. News* interview.
15. *Houston Post*, June 27, 1932; David Burner, *Herbert Hoover: A Public Life*, 276.
16. Wellington Brink, "John Nance Garner," *Holland's*, May 1932; *New York Times*, June 22, 1932.
17. Timmons, *Garner of Texas*, 160; Hardeman and Bacon, *Rayburn*, 137–138.

CHAPTER 8: THE VIRGINIAN

1. *Pittsburgh Post-Gazette* and *Chicago American*, June 21, 1932.
2. Woolley to House, January 4, 1932, RWW Papers.
3. Gerald W. Johnson, "Senator Byrd of Virginia," *Life*, August 7, 1944; Ronald L. Heinemann, *Harry Byrd of Virginia*, 1–3, 12–15.
4. Ibid., 6–10, 15–17. Steve Neal profile of Byrd, *Dictionary of American Biography*.
5. Alden Hatch, *The Byrds of Virginia*, 414–421.
6. H. I. Brock, "Governor Byrd Conducts a Revolution," *New York Times Magazine*, March 4, 1928; Virginius Dabney, *Virginia: The New Dominion*, 481–488.
7. "Renaissance in Richmond," *Time*, October 15, 1928.
8. FDR's letter to Richard E. Byrd is quoted in Freidel, *The Triumph*, 214; FDR to Mrs. Richard E. Byrd, December 17, 1928, *Roosevelt Letter, Volume Three*, 24.
9. Heinemann, *Harry Byrd of Virginia*, 106.
10. Harry F. Byrd to FDR, February 27, 1931, Virginia preconvention file, DNC; FDR to Harry F. Byrd, March 2, 1931, Virginia preconvention file, DNC.
11. Farley, *Behind the Ballots*, 75; Undated memorandum from a "Washington newspaperman" to Frank C. Walker, Virginia preconvention file, DNC; Heineman, *Harry Byrd of Virginia*, 143–145; William E. Dodd to Richard Crane, July 13, 1932, Dodd Papers; House to Woolley, April 1, 1932, House Papers.
12. Virginia General Assembly resolution endorsing Byrd for the Democratic presidential nomination and text of Byrd's Jefferson Day Dinner speech, Byrd file, Moley Papers.
13. Heinemann, 145; Harry Flood Byrd, "Now or Never," *Collier's*, July 2, 1932; Harry F. Byrd, Jr., interview with author; Farley, *Behind the Ballots*, 136.

CHAPTER 9: EAST SIDE WEST SIDE

1. William Shannon, *The American Irish*, 155; Alfred E. Smith, *Up to Now*, 41–49; Christian Gauss, "How Governor Smith Educated Himself," *Saturday Evening Post*, February 27, 1932.
2. *Chicago Daily News*, *Chicago American*, June 22, 1932; *New York Herald-Tribune*, *New York Times*, *Brooklyn Eagle*, *Chicago Herald and Examiner*, *Chicago Tribune*, June 23, 1932; Frank R. Kent, "Smith and the Boys," *Baltimore Sun*, June 23, 1932.
3. Thomas L. Stokes, *Chip Off My Shoulder*, 314–315; Clark Howell to FDR, December 2, 1931, *Roosevelt Letters, Volume Three*, 74–76.
4. Robert A. Caro, *The Power Broker*, 284–285; Cordell Hull, *Memoirs of Cordell Hull, Volume One*, 143; Oscar Handlin, *Al Smith and His America*, 140.
5. Frances Perkins, *The Roosevelt I Knew*, 47; Matthew and Hannah Josephson, *Al Smith: Hero of the Cities*, 400.
6. Flynn, *You're the Boss*, 74–75.

7. Perkins, *The Roosevelt I Knew*, 53; Smith, *Up to Now*, 288; *New York Times*, October 1, 1930.

8. Hull, *Memoirs, Volume One*, 143; Freidel, *The Triumph*, 233.

9. Frank R. Kent, "The Roosevelt-Smith Affair," *Scribner's*, March 1932; Freidel, *The Triumph*, 237; Flynn, *You're the Boss*, 86.

10. Warner, *The Happy Warrior*, 251.

11. Charles C. Marshall, "An Open Letter to the Honorable Alfred E. Smith," *Atlantic*, April 1927; Smith response, *Atlantic*, May 1927; Pat Harrison comments quoted in Adolphus Ragan to Howe, March 26, 1931, Mississippi preconvention file, DNC; Barkley response to Straus poll, Kentucky preconvention file, DNC; Walter M. Pierce to FDR, December 16, 1928, Oregon preconvention file, DNC.

12. Alva Johnston, "Alfred E. Smith," *Forum*, December 1931; Mullen, *Western Democrat*, 260–261.

13. Elizabeth Israels Perry, *Belle Moskowitz: Feminine Politics and the Exercise of Power in the Age of Alfred E. Smith*, 211; Moskowitz to Felix Frankfurter, March 1, 1932, Frankfurter Papers; Caro, *Power Broker*, 321.

14. Frank R. Kent, "Pinned on Him," *Baltimore Sun*, July 17, 1932; Ely is quoted in *Time*, June 27, 1932.

CHAPTER 10: DOLLAR BILL

1. *Chicago Herald-Examiner*, June 24, 1932; *San Jose Mercury Herald*, June 4, 1932; William Gibbs McAdoo to Bernard M. Baruch, May 21, 1932, WGM Papers.

2. *Baltimore Sun*, June 23, 1932; Arthur S. Link, *Wilson: Road to the White House*, 451; McAdoo to W. E. Woodward, February 18, 1932; WGM Papers.

3. Warner, *Happy Warrior*, 252–253; Daniel C. Roper, *Fifty Years in Public Life*, 259; FDR to Homer Cummings, January 25, 1932, Connecticut preconvention file, DNC; Breckinridge Long to Key Pittman, Pittman Papers, July 5, 1932.

4. Farley diary, October 15, 1933, JAF Papers; Jordan A. Schwarz, *The New Dealers: Power Politics in the Age of Roosevelt*, 30; Clinton W. Gilbert, "The Man Who Never Forgets," *Collier's*, November 12, 1932; Roper, *Fifty Years*, 459–460.

5. McAdoo to George Fort Milton, January 19, 1932, WGM Papers; McAdoo to Baruch, March 16, 1932; WGM Papers; Jouett Shouse memorandum, "The Chicago Convention of 1932," Shouse Papers.

6. McAdoo to House, March 6 and 18, 1931, WGM Papers.

7. Thomas Storke, *California Editor*, 300; George Creel, *Rebel at Large*, 270; McAdoo to House, January 10, 1931, WGM Papers.

8. McAdoo to R.W. Lewis, January 26, 1932, WGM Papers; McAdoo to Brice Claggett, January 23, 1932; WGM Papers; House to McAdoo, January 17, 1931, WGM Papers.

9. McAdoo, *Crowded Years*, 528–529; Otis L. Graham, Jr., McAdoo profile, *Dictionary of American Biography, Supplement Three*, 479–482.

10. Mark Sullivan, *Our Times: Over Here, 1914–1918*, 462–463; Dos Passos, *Mr. Wilson's War*, 373.

11. Schwarz, *New Dealers*, 25–26.

12. David Burner, *The Politics of Provincialism*, 107–109; Freidel, *The Ordeal*, 140, 165–166; Mark Sullivan column about McAdoo's testimony, WGM Papers.

13. McAdoo to Daniel Roper, WGM Papers; Frank R. Kent, "The McAdoo-Smith Story," *Baltimore Sun*, November 18, 1932.

CHAPTER 11: RITCHIE OF MARYLAND

1. Mark S. Watson, "Albert C. Ritchie," *Forum*, August 1931; Robert B. Ennis telegram to Ritchie reported in *Baltimore Sun*, June 20, 1932; *New York Times*, June 28, 1932.
2. *Chicago American, Chicago Daily News, Chicago Daily Times*, June 24, 1932; *New York Times*, June 25, 1932; interview with Bernard Carey.
3. Stokes, *Chip Off My Shoulder*, 319–320; *Baltimore Sun*, June 25, 1932.
4. Mark S. Watson, "Albert Cabell Ritchie," *Dictionary of American Biography, Supplement Two*, 559–560; *Chicago Tribune*, November 29, 1931; Raymond Tucker, *Mirrors of 1932*, 170; Woolley to House, September 18, 1931, RWW Papers.
5. Gerald W. Johnson, "Ritchie and No Regrets," *Nation*, March 9, 1932; Frank R. Kent, "Ritchie of Maryland," *Scribner's*, October 1927.
6. "Ritchie of Maryland," *Time* cover article, May 24, 1926; George Creel, "State's Rights' Ritchie," *Collier's*, January 30, 1932; Albert C. Ritchie, "Too Much Government," *Plain Talk*, February 1928.
7. Straus poll, *New York Times*, March 30, 1931; Frank R. Kent, "Ritchie in Chicago," *Baltimore Sun*, July 7, 1932.
8. Ritchie endorsement, *New York Daily News*, June 17, 1932; *New York Times, Baltimore Evening Sun*, June 22, 1932.
9. Farley diary, Chicago Democratic convention, JAF Papers; Farley, *Behind the Ballots*, 116; Watson, "Albert C. Ritchie," *Forum*, August 1931.

CHAPTER 12: DEEP RIVER

1. Earl Dickerson testimony before Resolutions Committee, *Chicago Daily News*, June 24, 1932; W. A. Low and Virgil A. Clift, *Encyclopedia of Black America*.
2. Background on Black Chicago in Timuel D. Black, Jr., *Bridges of Memory: Chicago's First Wave of Black Migration;* Dempsey Travis, *Autobiography of Black Chicago;* Harold Gosnell, *Negro Politicians;* A. M. Burroughs versus Stoner Lunch Room, Municipal Court, May 15, 1932.
3. Gunnar Mydral, *An American Dilemma*, 455, 480–488; Ralph J. Bunche, *The Political Status of the Negro in the Age of FDR*, 151–155; Horace Mann Bond, "A Negro Looks at His South," *Harper's*, June 1931; Nancy J. Weiss, *Farewell to the Party of Lincoln*, 21; Patricia Sullivan, *Days of Hope: Race and Democracy in the New Deal Era*, 13–15.
4. Howard Sitkoff, *A New Deal for Blacks*, 7–8; Dabney, *Virginia: The New Dominion*, 430, 436; John Egerton, *Speak Now Against the Day*, 27–28; NAACP race relations plank for 1932 Democratic convention, NAACP Papers.
5. Kenneth Robert Janken, *White: The Biography of Walter White*, 199–202; Walter White, *Rope and Faggot*, 277–240; NAACP race relations plank, NAACP Papers.
6. Earl Dickerson to Walter White, June 25, 1932, NAACP Papers.
7. Walter White, *A Man Called White*, 3–12; 99–101.
8. Janken, *White*, 137–145.
9. W. E. B. DuBois, "Herbert Hoover," *The Crisis*, November 1932; David A. Bositis, "Blacks and the Republican National Convention," Joint Center for Political and Economic Studies, 1996.
10. "Democratic Opportunity," *Chicago Defender*, June 25, 1932; Morris J. MacGregor, Jr., *Integration of the Armed Forces*, 7, 46–47; Bryant, *Alfalfa Bill Murray*.

11. Freidel, *The Triumph*, 280; Rollins, *Roosevelt and Howe*, 269, 316; Pat Harrison is quoted in Bunche, *Political Status of the Negro*, 434–435.

12. Geoffrey Ward, *A First Class Temperament*, 173–174, 460; MacGregor, *Integration of the Armed Forces*, 4–5; Sitkoff, *A New Deal for Blacks*, 40–41; Kenneth O'Reilly, *Nixon's Piano*, 110–111; Richard Wormser, *The Rise and Fall of Jim Crow*, 145.

13. Freidel, *The Apprenticeship*, 334; Roy Wilkins with Tom Mathews, *Standing Fast*, 127; Richard Thayer Goldberg, *The Making of Franklin D. Roosevelt*, 146–149.

14. *Chicago Defender*, July 2, 1932; Donald Johnson, *National Party Platforms, Volume One*, 333; White to Edward Levinson, July 1, 1932, NAACP Papers.

CHAPTER 13: EYE OF THE TIGER

1. John C. O'Brien, "Tammany Braves Keep War Whoops in Restraint as They Travel to Battle Scene," *New York Herald Tribune*, June 26, 1932; S. J. Woolf, "The Big Chief of the Tammany Wigwam," *New York Times Magazine*, June 26, 1932. Published reports speculated that Curry would support Ritchie, Baker, Garner, Smith, Owen Young, or, as a favorite son, Senator Royal Copeland of New York.

2. Farley diary, March 14, 1932, JAF Papers.

3. M. R. Werner, *Tammany Hall*, 10–36; Oliver Allen, *The Tiger*, 1–26.

4. "William Marcy Tweed," *Dictionary of American Biography;* Denis T. Lynch, *Boss Tweed;* Werner, *Tammany Hall*, 104–105.

5. "Charles Francis Murphy," *Dictionary of American Biography;* Alfred Connable and Edward Silberfarb, *Tigers of Tammany*, 232–268.

6. "John Francis Curry," *Time* cover article, March 23, 1931; "John F. Curry: The Man Who Makes the Tiger Smile," *Literary Digest*, May 11, 1929; Connable and Silberfarb, *Tigers of Tammany*, 277–278; Woolf, "Big Chief of Tammany"; Herbert Mitgang, *Once Upon a Time in New York*, 136.

7. Flynn, *You're the Boss*, 55.

8. Gottfried, *Boss Cermak*, 299; Elliot A. Rosen, *Hoover, Roosevelt, and the Brains Trust*, 223–224.

9. Freidel, *The Apprenticeship*, 102–103, 130–131; Moley, *27 Masters of Politics*, 34.

10. FDR's 1911 interview is reprinted in Don Wharton, *Roosevelt Omnibus*, 28; Freidel, *The Apprenticeship*, 144–145, 183–189, 338; Freidel, *The Triumph*, 73–74.

11. Henry F. Pringle, "Franklin D. Roosevelt: Perched on the Bandwagon," *Nation*, April 27, 1932.

12. "Samuel Seabury," *Dictionary of American Biography;* Mitgang, *Once Upon a Time in New York*, 125–132; Caro, *Power Broker*, 324–325, 350–352; *New York Times*, February 25, 1932.

13. Moley, *After Seven Years*, 2; Franklin D. Roosevelt, *Public Papers of Franklin D. Roosevelt, 48th Governor of the State of New York: 1932*, 290–293.

14. Mitgang, *Once Upon a Time in New York*, 150–153; *New York Times, New York Herald Tribune*, June 23, 1932.

15. Lippmann, *Interpretations, 1931–1932*, 250.

16. "Samuel Seabury," *Time* cover article, August 17, 1931; Walter Chambers, "Samuel Seabury: Presidential Possibilities," *Forum*, November 1931; "Seabury's Political Bomb," *Literary Digest*, March 12, 1932; Samuel Seabury, "Battling for Honest Government," *Review of Reviews*, July 1932; Howe to FDR, undated memorandum regarding Seabury's presidential ambitions, LMH Papers; Moley, *27 Masters of Politics*, 207–208; *New York Times*, June 19, 1932.

17. FDR to Edward M. House, June 4, 1932, *Roosevelt Letters, Volume Three*, 87; Kenneth S. Davis, *Invincible Summer: An Intimate Portrait of the Roosevelts*, 257–258.

18. Moley, *27 Masters of Politics*, 209; Woolf, "Big Chief of the Tammany Wigwam."

CHAPTER 14: GRAND ILLUSION

1. Ferrell, *FDR's Quiet Confidant*, 69; Alva Johnston, "Boss Hague, the Bandwagon, and Beer," *New Yorker*, July 16, 1932.

2. Mullen, *Western Democrat*, 262; Alfred E. Smith, "Common Sense in Conventions and Campaigning," *Saturday Evening Post*, June 11, 1932; Mrs. Jesse W. Nicholson is quoted in *Time*, April 27, 1931.

3. John Gunther, *Roosevelt in Retrospect*, 238–239; David Halberstam, *The Powers That Be*, 10–11; Hugh Gregory Gallagher, *FDR's Splendid Deception*, 59–67.

4. FDR to George W. Marble, May 15, 1929, governor's personal file; FDR to editor of the *Butte Standard*, December 29, 1931, *Roosevelt Letters, Volume Three*, 79–80; Alan Brinkley, "Franklin D. Roosevelt," *American National Biography;* Dr. Lauro S. Halstead, *Managing Post-Polio*, 11–12.

5. Eleanor Roosevelt, *Autobiography of Eleanor Roosevelt*, 111; Freidel, *The Ordeal*, 103–113; Goldberg, *The Making of Franklin D. Roosevelt*, 43–55; Caro, *Power Broker*, 285.

6. Freidel, *The Ordeal*, 193–197; Gunther, *Roosevelt in Retrospect*, 232–235; Jane Smith, *Patenting the Sun*, 57–62; Gallagher, *FDR's Splendid Deception*, 34–46; Goldberg, *The Making of Franklin D. Roosevelt*, 95–102.

7. Richard Harrity and Ralph G. Martin, *The Human Side of FDR*, 13; Perkins, *The Roosevelt I Knew*, 29; Gunther, *Roosevelt in Retrospect*, 238; James Roosevelt and Sidney Shallett, *Affectionately, FDR*, 154.

8. Freidel, *The Triumph*, 157–158; Arthur Krock, *Memoirs: Sixty Years on the Firing Line*, 158–159; Gunther, *Roosevelt in Retrospect*, 266–267.

9. Robert H. Ferrell, *Ill-Advised: Presidential Health and Public Trust;* FDR to Hamilton Miles, May 4, 1931, quoted in Freidel, *The Triumph*, 210.

10. Earle Looker, "Is Franklin D. Roosevelt Physically Fit to Be President?" *Liberty*, July 25, 1931; Allen Churchill, *The Liberty Years 1924–1950*, 142–146.

11. Farley to FDR, July 17, 1931, JAF Papers; Rollins, *Roosevelt and Howe*, 313; FDR to V. Y. Dallman, November 28, 1931, Illinois preconvention file, DNC.

12. Woolley to House, March 21, 1932, and House to Woolley, March 22 and 28, 1932, House Papers; Wharton, *Roosevelt Omnibus*, 7.

13. Eleanor Roosevelt, *This I Remember*, 61; Timothy Walch and Dwight M. Miller, *Herbert Hoover and Franklin D. Roosevelt: A Documentary History*, 210.

14. Woolley to House, May 17, 1932, House Papers; Bryant, *Alfalfa Bill Murray*, 234–235.

15. Farley, *Behind the Ballots*, 115; Gilbert C. Fite, *Richard B. Russell Jr., Senator from Georgia*, 111; Krock, *Memoirs*, 158.

CHAPTER 15: HYDE PARK

1. Beatrice Fredriksen, *Our Local Heritage: A Short History of the Town of Hyde Park*, 5–14; Franklin D. Mares, *Springwood*, 6–10; James Roosevelt and Shalett, *Affectionately, FDR*, 44–49.

2. Farley diary, June 6, 1932, JAF Papers.
3. Ibid., May 3, 1932; Farley, *Behind the Ballots*, 100; Frank R. Kent, "A Parade of Senators," *New Republic*, December 16, 1931; Woolley to House, April 9, 1932, House Papers.
4. J. Leonard Bates, *Senator Thomas J. Walsh of Montana*, 187, 291; Farley diary, February 15, 1932, JAF Papers.
5. Mares, *Springwood*, 15; Agenda for Hyde Park meeting, Howe Papers.
6. Freidel, *The Triumph*, 293; Rosen, *Hoover, Roosevelt, and the Brains Trust*, 238; *New York Times*, May 15, 1932.
7. Ray Tucker, "Tom Walsh: The Saintly Senator," in Tucker and Frederick R. Barkley, *Sons of the Wild Jackass*, 123–147; L. C. Speers, "Walsh of Montana," *New York Times Magazine*, March 11, 1928; William Hard, "Dry Tom Walsh," *Review of Reviews*, April 1928; Farley, *Behind the Ballots*, 106; *New York Herald Tribune*, June 6, 1932.
8. Bates, *Senator Thomas J. Walsh of Montana*, 311.
9. FDR to Justus S. Wardell, December 22, 1932, California preconvention file, DNC; Farley, *Behind the Ballots*, 108–109; Thomas J. Walsh to Kenneth Romney, May 19, 1932, Walsh Papers.
10. Farley diary, June 6, 1932, JAF Papers.
11. Freidel, *The Triumph*, 293; Farley diary, October 15, 1933, JAF Papers.
12. FDR to Claude G. Bowers, August 23, 1929, governor's personal file; Merrill Peterson, *The Jefferson Image in the American Mind*, 350–354.
13. Farley diary, June 6, 1932, JAF Papers; Claude Bowers, *My Story*, 239–242.
14. Ibid., 240; Shouse, "The Chicago Convention."

CHAPTER 16: MAGIC NUMBER

1. Edward Hungerford, "Modernizing a Famous Landmark," *Hotel Management*, April 1924; Farley, *Behind the Ballots*, 109–110.
2. Frank R. Kent, "The Second Ballot," *Baltimore Sun*, June 24, 1932; E. J. Kahn, Jr., *The World of Swope: A Biography of Herbert Bayard Swope*, 366.
3. Kent, *The Democratic Party: A History*, 116–119.
4. Ibid., 136, 141; "The Two-Thirds Rule of the Democratic National Convention," Hull Papers; Champ Clark, *My Quarter Century of American Politics*, 405.
5. FDR's 1924 comments on the two-thirds rule were quoted in the *New York Times*, June 26, 1932.
6. Farley, *Behind the Ballots*, 116.
7. *New York Times*, June 24, 1932; Josephus Daniels column, *Raleigh News and Observer*, June 26, 1932; Dewson is quoted in Martin, *Ballots and Bandwagons*, 314.
8. Farley, *Behind the Ballots*, 117; Flynn, *You're the Boss*, 90.
9. James A. Hagerty, "Move to Alter Rule Surprised Governor," *New York Times*, June 25, 1932; Smith is quoted in Carlson, *Roosevelt's Fight*, 432.
10. *Boston Globe, Chicago Herald and Examiner, New York Times, New York Herald Tribune, Chicago Tribune, Houston Post, Atlanta Constitution*, June 26, 1932.
11. Farley statement on two-thirds rule, JAF Papers.
12. *Brooklyn Eagle, New York Herald Tribune, New York Times*, June 27, 1932; Flynn, *You're the Boss*, 90; W. A. Gunter open letter, NDB Papers.
13. "John Sharp Williams," *Dictionary of American Biography;* W. J. Cash, *Mind of the South*, 302; Williams telegram to James Reed is quoted in the *New York Times*, June 26, 1932.

14. FDR to Farley, June 27, 1932, JAF Papers; Farley, *Behind the Ballots*, 117; *New York Times*, June 27 and 28, 1932.

15. Hague is quoted in the *New York Times*, June 28, 1932; Farley Chicago convention diary, JAF Papers; Flynn, *You're the Boss*, 90; Samuel I. Rosenman, *Working with Roosevelt*, 68.

16. *New York Herald Tribune, New York Times*, June 28, 1932.

CHAPTER 17: RAINBOW

1. Farley, *Behind the Ballots*, 97.

2. O. P. Newman, "J. Hamilton Lewis: Behind a Pink Beaver," *Collier's*, January 3, 1931; Peel and Donnelly, *The 1932 Campaign*, 34–35; Lewis cover portrait, *Life*, June 14, 1937; Rodney Dutcher, "Lewis of Illinois," *Austin American*, June 24, 1932; Trohan, *Political Animals*, 49.

3. Irving Dilliard, "James Hamilton Lewis," *Dictionary of American Biography, Supplement Two*, 381–383; *Biographical Directory of the United States Congress: Bicentennial Edition;* Johnson, *Papers of Adlai E. Stevenson, Volume 1*, 318–319.

4. William H. Stuart, *20 Incredible Years*, 436–437; Trohan, *Political Animals*, 50.

5. *Guide to U.S. Elections*, 423, 490.

6. Alva Johnston, "Political Showmen," *Forum*, July 1932.

7. W. A. S. Douglas, "Kindling Wood Peddler," *American Mercury*, July 1933; Gottfried, *Boss Cermak*, 298.

8. Howe's letter to Daniel C. Roper is quoted in Martin, *Ballots and Bandwagons*, 271–272; Farley, *Behind the Ballots*, 120; Trohan, *Political Animals*, 48.

9. Farley diary, June 1932, JAF Papers; Farley, *Behind the Ballots*, 111; Gottfried, *Boss Cermak*, 301.

10. *Chicago Herald and Examiner, New York Times*, June 26, 1932; Will Rogers column, *Boston Globe*, June 27, 1932.

11. Farley, *Behind the Ballots*, 121.

CHAPTER 18: TODDLIN' TOWN

1. Memorandum on arrival of delegates, Howe Papers; Edward M. Burke and R. Craig Sautter, *Inside the Wigwam: Chicago Presidential Conventions*, 277–278; Lowell Thomas, *History as You Heard It*, 24.

2. William G. Shepherd, "Fair for Tomorrow," *Collier's*, September 17, 1932; Karl M. Kahn, "60 Army Planes Roar Welcome to Amelia," *Chicago American*, June 24, 1932; Saul Bellow, *It All Adds Up*, 21.

3. Jane Addams was featured in the *Houston Post*, June 25 and on June 28, 1932, in the *Chicago Tribune* and *Christian Science Monitor;* Darrow is quoted in the *New York Herald Tribune*, June 24, 1932; and Hutchins in the *Chicago Daily News*, June 24, 1932.

4. *Chicago Daily News*, June 27, 1932, and March 4, 1978.

5. Peterson, *Barbarians in Our Midst*, 158; Mullen, *Western Democrat*, 265.

6. McAdoo to Hotel Stevens manager, May 27, 1932, WGM Papers; *Chicago Daily News*, June 25, 1932.

7. Donald Honig, *Chicago Cubs: An Ilustrated History*, 88–91; Hayner and McNamee, *The Stadium*, 5; *Chicago Daily News*, June 27, 1932.

8. Kenan Heise, *Chaos, Creativity, and Culture*, 65–67, 75–76; Pauline Kael, *5001 Nights at the Movies*, 225–226, Gerald Nachman, *Raised on Radio*.

9. Mary Borden, "Chicago Revisited," *Harper's*, April 1932.

10. John Dos Passos, "Out of the Red with Roosevelt," *New Republic*, July 13, 1932; Mauritz A. Hallgren, "Help Wanted for Chicago," *Nation*, May 11, 1932.

11. Stephen Salsbury, "Samuel Insull," *American National Biography;* Marquis Childs, "Samuel Insull's Spectacular Smashup," *St. Louis Post-Dispatch Magazine*, July 3, 1932; John T. Flynn, "Up and Down with Samuel Insull," *Collier's*, December 3, 1932; *Chicago American*, June 6, 1932.

12. F. Cyril James, *The Growth of Chicago Banks: The Modern Age*, 1032–1036; *Chicago Tribune*, June 26, 1932.

13. Edward A. Goedeken, "Charles Gates Dawes," *American National Biography;* James, *The Modern Age*, 1037–1038.

14. Jesse H. Jones, *Fifty Billion Dollars: My Thirteen Years with the RFC*, 72–81.

15. Gottfried, *Boss Cermak*, 278; *Chicago Daily News*, *Chicago Tribune*, June 20 and 21, 1932.

16. *Official Proceedings*, 7–8; Stiles, *The Man Behind Roosevelt*, 108.

CHAPTER 19: KINGFISH

1. "Huey Long Gets an Offer to Run for the Presidency," *New York Herald Tribune*, June 19, 1932; William Ivy Hair, *The Kingfish and His Realm*, 242.

2. William E. Leuchtenburg, "FDR and the Kingfish," *American Heritage*, October–November, 1985; "Incredible Kingfish," *Time*, October 3, 1932.

3. Louis Cochran, "Louisiana Kingfish," *American Mercury*, July 1932; Krock, *Memoirs*, 173; T. Harry Williams, *Huey Long*, 471–478; Floyd C. Watkins, John T. Hiers, and Mary Louise Weaks, *Talking with Robert Penn Warren*, 57–58.

4. Williams, *Huey Long*, 554–563.

5. A. J. Liebling, *The Earl of Louisiana*, 8; Marquis Childs, *I Write from Washington*, 16–17.

6. Peel and Donnelly, *The 1932 Campaign*, 79; Williams, *Huey Long*, 572; *Time*, October 3, 1932; Burton K. Wheeler with Paul F. Healy, *Yankee from the West*, 285.

7. Flynn, *You're the Boss*, 95–96; *Chicago American*, June 21, 1932; Turner Catledge, *My Life and the Times*, 111.

8. Farley, *Behind the Ballots*, 124–125; Arthur Krock, *The Consent of the Governed and Other Deceits*, 187; Williams, *Huey Long*, 571, 576; *New Orleans Times-Picayune*, June 16, 1932.

9. *New York Herald Tribune*, June 28, 1932; Harry F. Byrd, Jr., "Conventions I Have Known," *Look*, July 19, 1960; Byrd interview with author.

10. Huey Long, *Every Man a King*, 304–305; *New York Times*, June 26, 1932.

11. *Brooklyn Eagle*, June 24, 1932.

12. Wheeler and Healy, *Yankee from the West*, 285–286.

13. Williams, *Huey Long*, 574–575; *Chicago American*, June 21, 1932.

14. Ferrell, *FDR's Quiet Confidant*, 73.

15. *New York Herald Tribune*, June 28, 1932; Farley, *Behind the Ballots*, 124.

16. Huey Long to John J. Raskob, June 22, 1932, *Official Proceedings*, 516–518; Long, *Every Man a King*, 307–311.

17. *Official Proceedings*, 549–572.

18. Ibid., 573–575; Farley, *Behind the Ballots*, 124; Mullen, *Western Democrat*, 264.

19. *New Orleans Times-Picayune*, June 28, 1932; H. L. Mencken, *Making a President*, 112.

20. Farley, *Behind the Ballots*, 124.

21. Joseph May, "Scott W. Lucas," *Dictionary of American Biography, Supplement Eight*, 391–392;

Biographical Directory of the United States Congress; Official Proceedings, 53–54, 58–60; Wheeler and Healy, *Yankee from the West*, 286.

22. Williams, *Huey Long*, 579–580; *Official Proceedings*, 61–64.

23. Will Rogers column, *New York Times*, June 29, 1932; Farley convention diary, JAF Papers.

CHAPTER 20: ROLL OUT THE BARREL

1. Lawrence W. Levine, *Defender of the Faith: William Jennings Bryan: The Last Decade*, 116, 124–125.

2. Kent, *Democratic Party: A History*, 345.

3. Freidel, *The Apprenticeship*, 127–128; Freidel, *The Ordeal*, 56, 162.

4. Ibid., 161–162; FDR to James C. Bonright, March 11, 1930, *Roosevelt Letters, Volume Three*, 52–53.

5. Carl Sifakis, *The Mafia Encyclopedia* [New York: Facts on File], 266–267; Freidel, *The Triumph*, 144–146.

6. Ray Tucker, *The Mirrors of 1932*, 246.

7. Woolley to House, February 23, 1932, House Papers; Josephus Daniels to Cordell Hull, March 7, 1932, and Hull reply, February 29, 1932, Daniels Papers.

8. "The Great Prohibition Poll's Final Report," *Literary Digest*, April 30, 1932; Stanley High, "A Dry Warns the Drys," *Harper's*, June 1932.

9. Winston Churchill, "The Shattered Cause of Temperance," *Collier's*, August 13, 1932; *New York Herald Tribune*, June 7, 1932.

10. *Baltimore Sun*, June 11, 1932; Dewey is quoted in Richard Oulahan, *The Man Who . . . The Story of the 1932 Democratic National Convention*, 102.

11. *New York Times*, June 16, 1932; *New York Herald Tribune*, June 16, 1932; Breckinridge Long to House, June 11, 1932, House Papers.

12. *New York Herald Tribune*, June 28 and 29, 1932; *New York Times*, June 28, 1932.

13. Woolley to FDR, June 20, 1932, RWW Papers; Hull, *Memoirs*, 151; Hull to H. B. McGinness, June 11, 1932, Hull Papers; Alben Barkley, *That Reminds Me*, 141–142; Transcript of Barkley interview, Truman Library.

14. Barkley's call for repeal, *Official Proceedings*, 36–37; *Boston Globe, Chicago Herald and Examiner, Chicago Tribune, New York Times, New York Herald Tribune, Baltimore Sun*, June 28, 1932.

15. Farley, *Behind the Ballots*, 128; Hull, *Memoirs*, 152.

16. *New York Times*, June 30, 1932.

17. Hull speech, *Official Proceedings*, 156–161.

18. Mencken, *Making a President*, 142; Bowers, *My Story*, 245.

19. Smith's speech, *Official Proceedings*, 162–164.

20. Warner, *Happy Warrior*, 258; *New York Times*, June 30, 1932.

CHAPTER 21: STALEMATE

1. Mullen, *Western Democrat*, 268.

2. Ferrell, *FDR's Quiet Confidant*, 70; *Christian Science Monitor*, July 1, 1932; Douglas, "Kindling Wood Peddler," *American Mercury; Chicago Daily News*, June 30, 1932.

3. *Official Proceedings*, 207–211; 218–222; Max Freedman, *Roosevelt and Frankfurter*, 75.

4. *New York Times, New York Herald Tribune, Brooklyn Daily Eagle*, July 1, 1932.

5. Flynn, *You're the Boss*, 91, 100.

6. *Chicago Daily News, New York Times*, July 1, 1932.

7. *Official Proceedings*, 214–218; *Boston Globe, New York Herald Tribune*, July 1, 1932; William Allen White column, *New York Times*, July 1, 1932.

8. *Official Proceedings*, 223–224; *New York Herald Tribune, Chicago Daily News*, July 1, 1932; *Baltimore Sun*, June 30, 1932.

9. Farley, *Behind the Ballots*, 130–131, 138.

10. *Official Proceedings*, 227–230; Farley convention diary, JAF Papers; Farley, *Jim Farley's Story*, 19; Heinemann, *Harry Byrd of Virginia*, 151; Rosen, *Hoover, Roosevelt, and the Brains Trust*, 255.

11. Breckinridge Long to Key Pittman, July 5, 1932, Pittman Papers; James Roosevelt column, *Boston Herald*, June 29, 1932; Farley convention diary, JAF Papers.

12. *Official Proceedings*, 244–245; Farley, *Behind the Ballots*, 139.

13. Rosenman, *Working with Roosevelt*, 69–70.

14. Farley, *Behind the Ballots*, 139–140.

15. Paul Y. Anderson column, *St. Louis Post-Dispatch*, July 1, 1932; Traylor controversy is described in the *Chicago Daily Times*, June 30, 1932; Rosen, *Hoover, Roosevelt, and the Brains Trust*, 255.

16. Will Rogers, *Autobiography*, 285; Farley, *Behind the Ballots*, 140; *Official Proceedings*, 239.

17. Connally, *My Name Is Tom Connally*, 141.

18. *Official Proceedings*, 287; Farley, *Behind the Ballots*, 141; *Baltimore Evening Sun*, July 1, 1932.

19. Mullen, *Western Democrat*, 271–272; *Official Proceedings*, 290–292.

20. Ibid., 294–297; Flynn, *You're the Boss*, 94.

21. Farley, *Behind the Ballots*, 142–143; Flynn, *You're the Boss*, 91–92.

22. Farley, *Jim Farley's Story*, 21; Mullen, *Western Democrat*, 272–273.

23. Carter H. Harrison, *Growing Up with Chicago*, 320–322; Douglas, "Kindling Peddler," *American Mercury;* Farley, *Behind the Ballots*, 142.

24. Mullen, *Western Democrat*, 275–276, Farley, *Behind the Ballots*, 143.

25. George Allen, *Presidents Who Have Known Me*, 55; Farley, *Behind the Ballots*, 143; Martha Swain, *Pat Harrison: The New Deal Years*, 28.

26. Flynn, *You're the Boss*, 100–101.

27. Ferrell, *FDR's Quiet Confidant*, 77; Farley, *Behind the Ballots*, 146.

28. Lippmann column, *New York Herald Tribune*, June 30, 1932.

29. *New York Herald Tribune*, July 1, 1932; Davis, *Invincible Summer*, 105; Moley, *After Seven Years*, 29–30.

30. Ibid., 30; Baker to John Stewart Bryan, NDB Papers, August 6, 1932.

31. FDR telegram, *New York Times*, July 1, 1932.

CHAPTER 22: SWITCH

1. Ross Gregory, "Joseph Patrick Kennedy," *American National Biography;* Joseph P. Kennedy, *I'm for Roosevelt*, 3, 15–17; David E. Koskoff, *Joseph P. Kennedy: A Life*, 43.; Doris Kearns Goodin, *The Kennedys and the Fitzgeralds*, 428.

2. Krock, *Memoirs*, 330; Koskoff, *Joseph P. Kennedy*, 44–45; Goodwin, *The Kennedys and the Fitzgeralds*, 429; Richard J. Whalen, *The Founding Father: The Story of Joseph P. Kennedy*, 124; Michael R. Beschloss, *Kennedy and Roosevelt*, 72; Krock, *Consent of the Governed*, 90–91.

3. Coblentz, *William Randolph Hearst*, 132–133.
4. Davis, *Invincible Summer*, 104; Farley, *Behind the Ballots*, 144.
5. Allen, *Presidents Who Have Known Me*, 55–56; Farley, convention diary, JAF Papers; Farley, *Behind the Ballots*, 144–145.
6. Ibid., 132–133; Pittman and Hawes telegram to Tom Connally, Connally Papers.
7. Connally, *My Name Is Tom Connally*, 142–143; Mullen, *Western Democrat*, 275.
8. Storke, *California Editor*, 315–317.
9. Woolley to House, July 8, 1932, House Papers; Breckinridge Long to Pittman, July 5, 1932, Pittman Papers; Russell M. Posner, "California's Role in the Nomination of Franklin D. Roosevelt," *California Historical Quarterly*, 1960; Coblentz, *William Randolph Hearst*, 122.
10. Ibid., 134–135; Timmons, *Garner of Texas*, 165–166.
11. Hardeman and Bacon, *Rayburn*, 141–142.
12. Sam Rayburn to McAdoo, February 23, 1938, WGM Papers; Hardeman and Bacon, *Rayburn*, 142.
13. McAdoo to Rayburn, April 28, 1939, WGM Papers; Clinton Gilbert, "The Man Who Never Forgets," *Collier's*, November 12, 1932.
14. Hardeman and Bacon, *Rayburn*, 142–143; *Fort Worth Star Telegram*, July 3, 1932.
15. Brice Claggett memorandum on McAdoo's convention role, February 22, 1933; WGM Papers; Rosen, *Hoover, Roosevelt, and the Brains Trust*, 261; Baruch, *Public Years*, 241.
16. *New York Times*, July 3, 1932.
17. Roper, *Fifty Years of Public Life*, 259–260.
18. Frank R. Kent, "Revenge Goaded McAdoo," *Baltimore Sun*, July 3, 1932.
19. Storke, *California Editor*, 321–325.
20. Warner, *Happy Warrior*, 261; Kent column, *Baltimore Sun*, November 18, 1932.
21. Timmons, *Garner of Texas*, 165.
22. Mencken, *Making a President*, 166; William Allen White to Ralph Hayes, July 18, 1932, NDB Papers; Shouse memorandum, "The 1932 Chicago Convention," Shouse Papers.
23. Farley, *Behind the Ballots*, 150–151; Moley, *After Seven Years*, 30.
24. Stiles, *Man Behind Roosevelt*, 188; Stokes, *Chip Off My Shoulder*, 322.
25. Storke, *California Editor*, 327–328; Moley, *After Seven Years*, 30.
26. McAdoo to Rayburn, April 28, 1939, WGM Papers; Storke, *California Editor*, 328.
27. Clinton W. Gilbert, "The Man Who Never Forgets"; Mencken, *Making a President*, 163; *Official Proceedings*, 325; Mullen, *Western Democrat*, 279.
28. *Official Proceedings*, 325–327.
29. Ibid., 327; Gottfried, *Boss Cermak*, 419; *New York Times*, July 2, 1932.
30. Farley, *Behind the Ballots*, 151; *Official Proceedings*, 329; Shouse to Baker, July 7, 1932.
31. Lippmann, *Interpretations, 1931–1932*, 312–314; Basil O'Connor to FDR, July 7, 1932, governor's personal file.

CHAPTER 23: WINGS

1. Arthur M. Schlesinger, Jr., *The Age of Roosevelt: Crisis of the Old Order*, 312; Rosenman, *Working with Roosevelt*, 74.
2. Thomas Petzinger, Jr., *Hard Landing*, 8.
3. Transcript of Goodrich Murphy interview, Plautt Papers; Rosenman, *Working with Roosevelt*, 74.

4. Tully, *FDR My Boss*, 51–52; Rosenman, *Working with Roosevelt*, 72.

5. Murphy interview; *New York Times*, July 3, 1932; R. G. Grant, *Flight: 100 Years of Aviation*, 140–141.

6. Tully, *FDR My Boss*, 52; Murphy interview.

7. Max Pollet memorandum of FDR's flight, July 13, 1932, Plautt Papers.

8. Transcript of FDR's telephone conversation with Felix Frankfurter is in Freedman, *Roosevelt and Frankfurter*, 74–76.

9. Bowers, *My Story*, 246; Pollet memorandum; Rosenman, *Working with Roosevelt*, 75.

10. *Cleveland Plain Dealer, New York Times*, July 3, 1932; Bowers, *My Story*, 246.

11. Farley, *Behind the Ballots*, 153; Tully, *FDR My Boss*, 50–51; Ferrell, *FDR's Quiet Confidant*, 77.

12. Farley, *Behind the Ballots*, 152–153; Hardeman and Bacon, *Rayburn*, 137.

13. Ibid., 138; Flynn, *You're the Boss*, 104–105.

14. Garner interview, *U.S. News and World Report*, March 8, 1957.

15. *Official Proceedings*, 338–339, 347, 355–356; *Chicago Herald and Examiner*, July 3, 1932.

16. Pollet memorandum; Tully, *FDR My Boss*, 52; Rosenman, *Working with Roosevelt*, 75.

17. *Official Proceedings*, 365–366.

18. *New York Times*, July 3, 1932; Rogers, *Autobiography*, 285.

19. *Official Proceedings*, 366–367; *Chicago Herald and Examiner, New York Herald Tribune, New York Times, Chicago Tribune*, July 3, 1932.

20. Stiles, *Man Behind Roosevelt*, 190–192.

21. Moley, *After Seven Years*, 33; Rosenman, *Working with Roosevelt*, 76; James Roosevelt, *Affectionately, FDR*, 225–226.

22. *Chicago Herald and Examiner, New York Times*, July 3, 1932.

23. Rosenman, *Working with Roosevelt*, 77–78.

24. Richard L. Strout, "Roosevelt's Own Appearance Highlight of the Convention," *Christian Science Monitor*, July 6, 1932; Stokes, *Chip Off My Shoulder*, 324; Halberstam, *The Powers That Be*, 15.

25. *Public Papers and Addresses: The Genesis of the New Deal*, 647–659.

BIBLIOGRAPHY

MANUSCRIPTS

Joseph Alsop Papers, Library of Congress

Newton D. Baker Papers, Library of Congress

Alben W. Barkley Papers, University of Kentucky Library

Bernard Baruch Papers, Mudd Manuscript Library, Princeton University

Robert W. Bingham Papers, Library of Congress

Claude Bowers Papers, Lilly Library, Indiana University

Raymond Clapper Papers, Library of Congress

Tom Connally Papers, Library of Congress

Josephus Daniels Papers, Library of Congress

Joseph E. Davies Papers, Library of Congress

John W. Davis Papers, Yale University

Democratic National Committee Papers, Franklin D. Roosevelt Library

William Dodd Papers, Library of Congress

James A. Farley Papers, Library of Congress

Felix Frankfurter Papers, Library of Congress

Frank Freidel Papers, Franklin D. Roosevelt Library

Truman K. Gibson, Jr., Papers, Library of Congress

Gilbert M. Hitchcock Papers, Library of Congress

Herbert C. Hoover Papers, Herbert Hoover Library

Edward M. House Papers, Yale University

Roy Howard Papers, Library of Congress

Louis McHenry Howe Papers, Franklin D. Roosevelt Library

Cordell Hull Papers, Library of Congress

Harold L. Ickes Papers, Library of Congress

Breckinridge Long Papers, Library of Congress

William Gibbs McAdoo Papers, Library of Congress

Raymond L. Moley Papers, Hoover Institution Library, Stanford University

NAACP Papers, Library of Congress

Key Pittman Papers, Library of Congress

Ed Plaut Papers, Franklin D. Roosevelt Library

John J. Raskob Papers, Hagley Museum and Library

Albert C. Ritchie Scrapbooks, Maryland Historical Society

Franklin D. Roosevelt Papers, Franklin D. Roosevelt Library

Samuel I. Rosenman Papers, Franklin D. Roosevelt Library

Charles G. Ross Papers, Harry S. Truman Library

Jouett Shouse Papers, University of Kentucky

Richard L. Strout Papers, Library of Congress

Mark Sullivan Papers, Library of Congress

Frank C. Walker Papers, Hesburgh Library, University of Notre Dame

Thomas J. Walsh Papers, Library of Congress

William Allen White Papers, Library of Congress

Robert W. Woolley Papers, Library of Congress

AUTHOR INTERVIEWS

Senator Harry F. Byrd, Jr.

Bernard Carey, former chairman, Chicago Board of Trade

Truman K. Gibson, Jr.

Irv Kupcinet

Former Congressman Dan Rostenkowski

Walter Trohan

ORAL HISTORIES

Alben W. Barkley, Transcripts of interviews with Sidney Shalett, Truman Library

Josephus Daniels, Memorandum of interview with Frank Freidel, FDRL

James A. Farley, Freidel interview, FDRL

Eleanor Roosevelt, Freidel interview, FDRL

Samuel I. Rosenman, Columbia University Oral History Project

BOOKS

Adams, Rosemary K. *A Wild Kind of Boldness: The Chicago History Reader.* Grand Rapids: Chicago Historical Society/William B. Eerdmans, 1998.

Allen, Frederick Lewis. *Only Yesterday: An Informal History of the 1920s.* New York: Harper & Brothers, 1931.

Allen, George E. *Presidents Who Have Known Me.* New York: Simon & Schuster, 1950.

Allen, Oliver. *The Tiger: The Rise and Fall of Tammany Hall.* Reading, Mass.: Addison-Wesley, 1993.

Alsop, Joseph. *FDR: A Centenary Remembrance.* New York: Viking, 1982.

Alsop, Joseph, and Robert Kintner. *Men Around the President.* Garden City, N.Y.: Doubleday, Doran, 1939.

Asbury, Herbert. *Gem of the Prairie, an Informal History of the Chicago Underworld.* New York: Knopf, 1940.

Badger, Anthony J. *The New Deal: The Depression Years, 1933–1940.* Chicago: Ivan Dee, 1989.

Barkley, Alben W. *That Reminds Me: The Autobiography of the Veep.* New York: Doubleday, 1954.

Barone, Michael. *Our Country: The Shaping of America from Roosevelt to Reagan.* New York: Free Press, 1990.

Baruch, Bernard M. *Baruch: The Public Years.* New York: Holt, 1960.

Bates, J. Leonard. *Senator Thomas J. Walsh of Montana.* Urbana: University of Illinois Press, 1999.

Beatty, Jack. *The Rascal King: The Life and Times of James Michael Curley.* Reading, Mass.: Addison-Wesley, 1992.

Bellow, Saul. *It All Adds Up: From the Dim Past to the Uncertain Future.* New York: Viking, 1994.

Bellush, Benjamin. *Franklin D. Roosevelt as Governor of New York.* New York: Columbia University Press, 1955.

Beschloss, Michael R. *Kennedy and Roosevelt: The Uneasy Alliance.* New York: Norton, 1980.

Black, Conrad. *Franklin Delano Roosevelt: Champion of Freedom.* New York: Public Affairs, 2003.

Black, Timuel D., Jr. *Bridges of Memory: Chicago's First Wave of Black Migration.* Evanston, Ill.: Northwestern University Press, 2003.

Blum, John Morton. *Roosevelt & Morgenthau.* Boston: Houghton Mifflin, 1970.

————. *Public Philosopher: Selected Letters of Walter Lippmann.* New York: Ticknor & Fields, 1985.

Bowers, Claude. *My Life: The Memoirs of Claude Bowers.* New York: Simon & Schuster, 1962.

Brinkley, Alan. *Voices of Protest: Huey Long, Father Coughlin, and the Great Depression.* New York: Knopf, 1982.

Broun, Heywood. *It Seems to Me: 1925–1935.* New York: Harcourt, 1935.

————. *Collected Edition of Heywood Broun.* Freeport, N.Y.: Books for Libraries Press, 1969.

Bryant, Keith L., Jr. *Alfalfa Bill Murray.* Norman: University of Oklahoma Press, 1968.

Bunche, Ralph J. *The Political Status of the Negro in the Age of FDR.* Chicago: University of Chicago Press, 1973.

Burke, Edward M., and R. Craig Sautter. *Inside the Wigwam: Chicago Presidential Conventions 1860–1996.* Chicago: Wild Onion/Loyola Press, 1996.

Burner, David. *The Politics of Provincialism: The Democratic Party in Transition, 1918–1932.* New York: Knopf, 1970.

Burns, James MacGregor. *Roosevelt: The Lion and the Fox.* New York: Harcourt, 1956.

————. *Roosevelt: Soldier of Freedom.* New York: Harcourt, 1970.

————. *The American Experiment: The Workshop of Democracy.* New York: Knopf, 1985.

————. *The American Experiment: The Crosswinds of Freedom.* New York: Knopf, 1989.

Byrnes, James F. *All in One Lifetime.* New York: Harper, 1958.

Carlson, Earland Irving. *Franklin D. Roosevelt's Fight for the Presidential Nomination, 1928–1932.* Urbana: University of Illinois dissertation, 1955.

Carlson, Oliver and Ernest Sutherland Bates. *Hearst: Lord of San Simeon.* New York: Viking, 1936.

Caro, Robert A. *The Power Broker: Robert Moses and the Fall of New York.* New York: Knopf, 1974.

————. *The Years of Lyndon B. Johnson: The Path to Power.* New York: Knopf, 1982.

Carter, John Franklin [The Unofficial Observer]. *The New Dealers.* New York: Literary Guild, 1934.

Cash, W. J. *The Mind of the South.* New York: Knopf, 1941.

Catledge, Turner. *My Life and the Times.* New York: Harper & Row, 1971.

Chaney, Lindsay and Michael Cieply. *The Hearsts: Family and Empire*. New York: Simon & Schuster, 1981.

Chidsey, Donald Barr. *On and Off the Wagon*. New York: Cowles, 1969.

Childs, Marquis. *I Write from Washington*. New York: Harper, 1942.

Ciccone, F. Richard. *Daley: Power and Presidential Politics*. Chicago: Contemporary Books, 1996.

———. *Chicago and the American Century*. Chicago: Contemporary Books, 1999.

Clapper, Raymond. *Watching the World*. New York: Whittlesey House, 1944.

Clark, Champ. *My Quarter Century of American Politics*. Two volumes. New York: Harper & Brothers, 1920.

Coben, Stanley. *A. Mitchell Palmer: Politician*. New York: Columbia University Press, 1963.

Coblentz, Edmond D. *William Randolph Hearst: A Portrait in His Own Words*. New York: Simon & Schuster, 1952.

Coffey, Thomas M. *The Long Thirst: Prohibition in America 1920–1933*. London: Hamish Hamilton, 1976.

Connable, Alfred, and Edward Silberfarb. *Tigers of Tammany Hall: Nine Men Who Ran New York:* New York: Holt, Rinehart & Winston, 1967.

Connally, Tom. *My Name Is Tom Connally*. New York: Crowell, 1954.

Cook, Blanche Wiesen. *Eleanor Roosevelt. Volume 1, 1884–1933*. New York: Viking Penguin, 1992.

Cox, James M. *Journey Through My Years: An Autobiography*. New York: Simon & Schuster, 1946.

Cramer, C. H. *Newton D. Baker: A Biography*. Cleveland: World, 1961.

Creel, George. *Rebel at Large: Recollections of Fifty Crowded Years*. New York: Putnam, 1947.

Cross, Wilbur L. *Connecticut Yankee: An Autobiography*. New Haven: Yale University Press, 1943.

Curley, James Michael. *I'd Do It Again*. Englewood Cliffs, N.J.: Prentice-Hall, 1957.

Dabney, Virginius. *Liberalism in the South*. Chapel Hill: University of North Carolina Press, 1932.

———. *Dry Messiah: The Life of Bishop Cannon*. New York: Knopf, 1949.

———. *Virginia: The New Dominion*. Garden City, N.Y.: Doubleday, 1971.

Daniels, Jonathan. *The Time Between the Wars*. Garden City, N.Y.: Doubleday, 1966.

Davis, Kenneth S. *Invincible Summer: An Intimate Portrait of the Roosevelts*. New York: Atheneum, 1974.

———. *FDR: The New York Years, 1928–1933*. New York: Random House, 1986.

Dedmon, Emmett. *Fabulous Chicago: A Great City's History and People*. New York: Atheneum, 1981.

Democratic National Committee. *Official Report of the Proceedings of the 1932 Democratic National Convention*. Washington D.C., 1932.

Dorsett, Lyle W. *Franklin D. Roosevelt and the City Bosses.* Port Washington, N.Y.: Kennikat Press, 1977.

Dos Passos, John. *Mr. Wilson's War.* Garden City, N.Y.: Doubleday, 1962.

Drell, Adrienne. *20th Century Chicago.* Chicago: *Chicago Sun-Times*, 1999.

Du Bois, W. E. B. *The Souls of Black Folk.* New York: Everyman's Library edition/Knopf, 1993.

Dulaney, H. G., and Edward Hake Phillips. *Speak Mr. Speaker.* Bonham, Tex.: Sam Rayburn Foundation, 1978.

Egerton, John. *Speak Now Against the Day: The Generation Before the Civil Rights Movement in the South.* New York: Knopf, 1994.

Eisenstein, Louis, and Elliot Rosenberg. *A Stripe of Tammany's Tiger.* New York: Speller, 1966.

Farley, James A. *Behind the Ballots.* New York: Harcourt Brace, 1938.

———. *Jim Farley's Story: The Roosevelt Years.* New York: Whittlesey House, 1948.

Ferrell, Robert H. *Woodrow Wilson and World War I.* New York: Harper & Row, 1985.

———. *Ill-Advised: Presidential Health and Public Trust.* Columbia: University of Missouri Press, 1992.

———. *FDR's Quiet Confidant: The Autobiography of Frank C. Walker.* Niwot: University Press of Colorado, 1997.

———. *The Dying President: Franklin D. Roosevelt 1944–1945.* Columbia: University of Missouri Press, 1998.

———. *Truman and Pendergast.* Columbia: University of Missouri Press, 1999.

Fields, Alonzo. *My 21 Years in the White House.* New York: Coward-McCann, 1961.

Finan, Christopher M. *Alfred E. Smith: The Happy Warrior.* New York: Hill & Wang, 2002.

Fisher, Ovie C. *Cactus Jack.* Waco, Tex.: 1978.

Fite, Gilbert C. *Richard B. Russell, Jr., Senator from Georgia.* Chapel Hill: University of North Carolina Press, 1991.

Flynn, Edward J. *You're the Boss: My Story of a Life in Practical Politics.* New York: Viking, 1947.

Fowler, Gene. *Beau James: The Life and Times of Jimmy Walker.* New York: Viking, 1949.

Fredriksen, Beatrice. *Our Local Heritage: A Short History of the Town of Hyde Park.* Hyde Park: Hyde Park Historical Association, 1962.

Freedman, Max. *Roosevelt and Frankfurter: Their Correspondence, 1928–1945.* Boston, 1967.

Freidel, Frank. *Franklin D. Roosevelt: The Apprenticeship.* Boston: Little, Brown, 1952.

———. *Franklin D. Roosevelt: The Ordeal.* Boston: Little, Brown, 1954.

———. *Franklin D. Roosevelt: The Triumph.* Boston: Little, Brown, 1956.

———. *FDR and the South.* Baton Rouge: Louisiana State University Press, 1967.

Gallagher, Hugh Gregory. *FDR's Splendid Deception*. New York: Dodd, Mead, 1985.

Garraty, John A. *The Great Depression*. Garden City, N.Y.: Anchor Press/Doubleday, 1987.

Gerard, James W. *My First Eighty-Three Years in America*. Garden City, N.Y.: Doubleday, 1951.

Goldberg, Richard Thayer. *The Making of Franklin D. Roosevelt: Triumph Over Disability*. Cambridge, Mass.: Abt Books, 1981.

Goodwin, Doris Kearns. *No Ordinary Time: Franklin and Eleanor Roosevelt: The Home Front in World War II*. New York: Simon & Schuster, 1994.

Gosnell, Harold F. *Negro Politicians*. Chicago: University of Chicago Press, 1930.

————. *Machine Politics: Chicago Model*. Chicago: University of Chicago Press, 1937.

————. *Champion Campaigner: Franklin D. Roosevelt*. New York: Macmillan, 1952.

Gottfried, Alex. *Boss Cermak of Chicago: A Study of Political Leadership*. Seattle: University of Washington Press, 1962.

Graham, Frank. *Al Smith: American*. New York: Putnam, 1945.

Graham, Otis L., Jr. *An Encore for Reform: The Old Progressives and the New Deal*. New York: Oxford University Press, 1967.

Graham, Otis L., Jr. with Meghan Robinson Wander. *Franklin D. Roosevelt: His Life and Times: An Encyclopedic View*. Boston: G.K. Hall, 1985.

Grant, R. G. *Flight: 100 Years of Aviation*. New York: DK Publishing, 2002.

Gunther, John. *Roosevelt in Retrospect: A Profile in History*. New York: Harper, 1950.

Hair, William Ivy. *The Kingfish and His Realm*. Baton Rouge: Louisiana State University Press, 1991.

Halberstam, David. *The Powers That Be*. New York: Knopf, 1979.

Halstead, Lauro S. *Managing Post-Polio*. Arlington, Va.: ABI Publications, 1998.

Hamby, Alonzo L. *The New Deal: Analysis & Interpretation*. New York: Weybright and Talley, 1969.

Handlin, Oscar. *Al Smith and His America*. Boston: Little, Brown, 1958.

Hapgood, Norman, and Henry Moskowitz. *Up From the City Streets: A Biographical Study of Alfred E. Smith*. New York: Grosset & Dunlap.

Harbaugh, William H. *Lawyer's Lawyer: The Life of John W. Davis*. New York: Oxford University Press, 1973.

Hardeman, D. B., and Donald C. Bacon. *Rayburn: A Biography*. Austin: Texas Monthly Press, 1987.

Harrison, Carter H. *Growing Up with Chicago*. Chicago: Seymour, 1944.

Harrity, Richard, and Ralph G. Martin. *The Human Side of FDR*. New York: Duell, Sloan & Pearce, 1960.

Hatch, Alden. *The Byrds of Virginia*. Holt, 1969.

Hayner, Don, and Tom McNamee. *The Stadium*. Chicago: Performance Media, 1993.

Hearst, William Randolph, Jr., and Jack Casserly. *The Hearsts: Father and Son.* Niwot, Colo.: Roberts Rinehart, 1991.

Heinemann, Ronald L. *Harry Byrd of Virginia.* Charlottesville: University of Virginia Press, 1996.

Heise, Kenan. *Chaos, Creativity, and Culture: A Sampling of Chicago in the Twentieth Century.* Salt Lake City: Gibbs-Smith, 1998.

Hines, Gordon. *Alfalfa Bill.* Oklahoma City: Oklahoma Books, 1932.

Hofstadter, Richard. *The American Political Tradition and the Men Who Made It.* New York: Knopf, 1948.

Holli, Melvin G. *The Wizard of Washington: Emil Hurja, Franklin Roosevelt, and the Birth of Public Opinion Polling.* New York: Palgrave, 2002.

Holli, Melvin G., and Paul M. Green. *The Mayors.* Carbondale: Southern Illinois University Press, 1987.

Hull, Cordell. *The Memoirs of Cordell Hull.* Two volumes. New York: Macmillan, 1948.

James, F. Cyril. *The Growth of Chicago Banks: The Modern Age, 1897–1938.* New York: Harper, 1938.

James, Marquis. *Mr. Garner of Texas.* Indianapolis: Bobbs-Merrill, 1939.

Janken, Kenneth Robert. *White: The Biography of Walter White, Mr. NAACP.* New York: The New Press, 2003.

Jenkins, Alan. *The Thirties.* New York: Stein & Day, 1976.

Johnson, Walter. *The Papers of Adlai E. Stevenson: Beginnings of Education, 1900–1941, Volume 1.* Boston: Little, Brown, 1972.

Jones, Jesse H. *Fifty Billion Dollars: My Thirteen Years with the RFC.* New York: Macmillan, 1951.

Josephson, Matthew, and Hannah Josephson. *Al Smith: Hero of the Cities.* Boston: Houghton Mifflin, 1969.

Kennedy, David M. *Freedom from Fear: The American People in Depression and War, 1929–1945.* New York: Oxford University Press, 1999.

Kennedy, Joseph P. *I'm for Roosevelt.* New York: Reynal & Hitchcock, 1936.

Kent, Frank R. *The Democratic Party: A History.* New York: The Century Co., 1928.

Kilpatrick, Carroll. *Roosevelt and Daniels: A Friendship in Politics.* Chapel Hill: University of North Carolina Press, 1952.

Koskoff, David. *Joseph P. Kennedy: A Life and Times.* Englewood Cliffs, N.J.: Prentice Hall, 1974.

Krock, Arthur. *In the Nation: 1932–1966.* New York: McGraw-Hill, 1966.

———. *Memoirs: Sixty Years on the Firing Line.* New York: Funk & Wagnalls, 1968.

———. *The Consent of the Governed and Other Deceits.* Boston: Little, Brown, 1971.

Larsen, Lawrence H., and Nancy J. Hulston. *Pendergast.* Columbia: University of Missouri Press, 1997.

Lash, Joseph. *Eleanor and Franklin: The Story of Their Relationship Based on Eleanor Roosevelt's Private Papers*. New York: Norton, 1971.

———. *From the Diaries of Felix Frankfurter*. New York: Norton, 1975.

———. *Dealers and Dreamers*. Garden City, N.Y.: Doubleday, 1988.

Leuchtenburg, William E. *The Perils of Prosperity, 1914–1932*. Chicago: University of Chicago Press, 1958.

———. *Franklin D. Roosevelt and the New Deal, 1932–1940*. New York: Harper & Row, 1963.

———. *In the Shadow of FDR: From Harry Truman to Ronald Reagan*. Ithaca, N.Y.: Cornell University Press, 1983.

———. *The FDR Years*. New York: Columbia University Press, 1995.

Levine, Lawrence W. *Defender of the Faith: William Jennings Bryan: The Last Decade 1915–1925*. New York: Oxford University Press, 1965.

Lewis, David Levering. *W.E.B. DuBois: The Biography of a Race, 1865–1919*. New York: Holt, 1993.

———. *W.E.B. DuBois: The Fight for Equality and the American Century*. New York: Holt, 2000.

Lewis, Lloyd, and Henry Justin Smith. *Chicago: The History of a Reputation*. New York: Harcourt, 1929.

Liebling, A. J. *The Earl of Louisiana*. Baton Rouge: Louisiana State University Press, 1970.

Lindley, Ernest L. *Franklin D. Roosevelt: A Career in Progressive Democracy*. New York: Blue Ribbon Books, 1931.

———. *The Roosevelt Revolution*. New York: Viking, 1933.

Link, Arthur S. *Wilson*. Five volumes. Princeton University Press, 1947–1965.

Lippmann, Walter. *Men of Destiny*. New York: Macmillan, 1927.

———. *Interpretations: 1931–1932*. New York: Macmillan, 1932.

Long, Huey. *Every Man a King*. New Orleans: National Book Company, 1933.

Lowe, David. *Lost Chicago*. Boston: Houghton Mifflin, 1975.

McAdoo, William Gibbs. *Crowded Years: The Reminiscences of William G. McAdoo*. Boston: Houghton Mifflin, 1931.

MacGregor, Morris J., Jr. *Integration of the Armed Forces, 1940–1965*. Washington: Center of Military History, U.S. Army, 1981.

McKean, Dayton David. *The Boss: The Hague Machine in Action*. Boston: Houghton Mifflin, 1940.

Mares, Franklin D. *Springwood*. Hyde Park: Roosevelt-Vanderbilt Historical Association.

Martin, Ralph G. *Ballots & Bandwagons*. Chicago: Rand McNally, 1964.

Mayer, Harold M., and Richard C. Wade. *Chicago: Growth of a Metropolis*. Chicago: University of Chicago Press, 1969.

Mencken, H. L. *Making a President: A Footnote to the Saga of Democracy*. New York: Knopf, 1932.

Michelson, Charles. *The Ghost Talks*. New York: Putnam, 1944.

Miller, Donald L. *City of the Century: The Epic of Chicago and the Making of America*. New York: Simon & Schuster, 1996.

Miller, Nathan. *FDR: An Intimate History*. Garden City, N.Y.: Doubleday, 1983.

Mitgang, Herbert. *Once Upon a Time in New York: Jimmy Walker, Franklin Roosevelt, and the Last Great Battle of the Jazz Age*. New York: Free Press, 2000.

Moley, Raymond. *After Seven Years*. New York: Harper, 1939.

———. *27 Masters of Politics*. New York: Funk & Wagnalls, 1949.

Mooney, Booth. *Roosevelt and Rayburn*. Philadelphia: Lippincott, 1971.

Morison, Samuel Eliot. *The Oxford History of the American People*. New York: Oxford University Press, 1965.

Moscow, Warren. *Politics in the Empire State*. New York: Knopf, 1948.

Mullen, Arthur. *Western Democrat*. New York: Wilfred Funk, 1940.

Murray, George. *The Legacy of Al Capone*. New York: Putnam, 1975.

Murray, Ken. *The Golden Days of San Simeon*. Garden City, N.Y.: Doubleday, 1971.

Murray, Robert K. *The 103rd Ballot*. New York: Harper & Row, 1976.

Myrdal, Gunnar. *An American Dilemma: The Negro Problem and Modern Democracy*. 20th Anniversary edition. New York: Harper & Row, 1964.

Nasaw, David. *The Chief: The Life of William Randolph Hearst*. Boston: Houghton Mifflin, 2000.

Neal, Steve. *Dark Horse: A Biography of Wendell Willkie*. Garden City, N.Y.: Doubleday, 1984.

O'Connor, Richard. *The First Hurrah: A Biography of Alfred E. Smith*. New York: Putnam, 1970.

O'Reilly, Kenneth. *Nixon's Piano: Presidents and Racial Politics from Washington to Clinton*. New York: Free Press, 1995.

Oulahan, Richard. *The Man Who . . . The Story of the 1932 Democratic National Convention*. New York: Dial, 1971.

Patenaude, Lionel V. *Texans, Politics and the New Deal*. New York: Garland, 1983.

Peel, Roy V., and Thomas C. Donnelly. *The 1932 Campaign: An Analysis*. New York: Da Capo, 1973.

Perkins, Frances. *The Roosevelt I Knew*. New York: Viking, 1946.

Perry, Elisabeth Israels. *Belle Moskowitz: Feminine Politics and the Exercise of Power in the Age of Alfred E. Smith*. New York: Oxford University Press, 1987.

Peterson, Merrill. *The Jefferson Image in the American Mind*. New York: Oxford University Press, 1960.

Peterson, Virgil W. *Barbarians in Our Midst: A History of Chicago Crime and Politics*. Boston: Atlantic, Little, Brown, 1952.

Petzinger, Thomas Jr. *Hard Landing*. New York: Times Business/Random House, 1995.

Philips, Harlan B. *Felix Frankfurter Reminisces*. New York: Reynal & Company, 1960.

Procter, Ben. *William Randolph Hearst: The Early Years*. New York: Oxford University Press, 1998.

Robertson, David. *Sly and Able: A Political Biography of James F. Byrnes*. New York: Norton, 1994.

Rogers, Will. *The Autobiography of Will Rogers: Selected and Edited by Donald Day*. Boston: Houghton Mifflin, 1949.

Rollins, Alfred B., Jr. *Roosevelt and Howe*. New York: Knopf, 1962.

Roosevelt, Eleanor. *This I Remember*. New York: Harper, 1949.

———. *The Autobiography of Eleanor Roosevelt*. New York: Harper, 1961.

Roosevelt, Elliott. *FDR: His Personal Letters*. Three volumes. New York: Duell, Sloan and Pearce, 1947–1950.

Roosevelt, Franklin D. *Public Papers of Franklin D. Roosevelt, 48th Governor of New York*. Four volumes. Albany: State of New York, 1930–1939.

———. *Public Papers and Addresses of Franklin D. Roosevelt: Volume One: The Genesis of the New Deal, 1928–1932*. Edited by Samuel I. Rosenman. New York: Random House, 1938.

Roosevelt, James, and Sidney Shalett. *Affectionately, FDR*. New York: Harcourt, Brace, 1959.

Roosevelt, James, with Bill Libby. *My Parents: A Differing View*. Chicago, Playboy Press, 1975.

Roper, Daniel. *Fifty Years in Public Life*. Durham, N.C.: Duke University Press, 1941.

Rosen, Elliot A. *Hoover, Roosevelt, and the Brains Trust*. New York: Columbia University Press, 1977.

Rosenman, Samuel I. *Working with Roosevelt*. New York: Harper, 1952.

Russell, Francis. *The President Makers: From Mark Hanna to Joseph P. Kennedy*. Boston: Little, Brown, 1976.

Schlesinger, Arthur M., Jr. *The Age of Roosevelt: The Crisis of the Old Order, 1919–1933*. Boston: Houghton Mifflin, 1957.

———. *The Age of Roosevelt: The Coming of the New Deal*. Boston: Houghton Mifflin, 1958.

———. *The Age of Roosevelt: The Politics of Upheaval*. Boston: Houghton Mifflin, 1960.

Shannon, William V. *The American Irish: A Political and Social Portrait*. New York: Macmillan, 1963.

Sitkoff, Harvard. *A New Deal for Blacks*. New York: Oxford University Press, 1978.

Slayton, Robert A. *The Empire Statesman: The Rise and Redemption of Al Smith*. New York: Free Press, 2001.

Smith, Alfred E. *Campaign Addresses of 1928*. Washington: Democratic National Committee, 1929.

———. *Up to Now: An Autobiography*. Garden City, N.Y.: Garden City, 1929.

Smith, Gene. *The Shattered Dream*. New York: Morrow, 1970.

Smith, Jane S. *Patenting the Sun: Polio and the Salk Vaccine*. New York: Morrow, 1990.

Smith, Red. *To Absent Friends*. New York: Atheneum, 1982.

Smith, Richard Norton. *An Uncommon Man: The Triumph of Herbert Hoover*. New York: Simon & Schuster, 1984.

Steel, Ronald. *Walter Lippmann and the American Century*. Boston: Atlantic–Little, Brown, 1980.

Steinberg, Alfred. *The Bosses*. New York: Macmillan, 1972.

Stiles, Lela. *The Man Behind Roosevelt: The Story of Louis McHenry Howe*. Cleveland: World, 1954.

Stokes, Thomas L. *Chip Off My Shoulder*. Princeton: Princeton University Press, 1940.

Stone, Irving. *They Also Ran: The Story of the Men Who Were Defeated for the Presidency*. Garden City, N.Y.: Doubleday, 1944.

Storke, Thomas M. *California Editor*. Los Angeles: Westernlore Press, 1958.

Stuart, William H. *The 20 Incredible Years*. Chicago: Donohue, 1935.

Sullivan, Mark. *Our Times: The War Begins, 1909–1914*. New York: Scribner's, 1932.

———. *Our Times: Over Here, 1914–1918*. New York: Scribner's, 1933.

———. *Our Times: The Twenties*. New York: Scribner's, 1935.

Sullivan, Patricia. *Days of Hope: Race and Democracy in the New Deal Era*. Chapel Hill: University of North Carolina Press, 1996.

Swain, Martha H. *Pat Harrison: The New Deal Years*. Jackson: University Press of Mississippi, 1978.

Swanberg, W. A. *Citizen Hearst*. New York: Scribner's, 1961.

Thomas, Lowell. *History as You Heard It*. Garden City, N.Y.: Doubleday, 1957.

Timmons, Bascom N. *Garner of Texas*. New York: Harper, 1948.

Trohan, Walter. *Political Animals*. Garden City, N.Y.: Doubleday, 1975.

Tucker, Raymond. *The Mirrors of 1932*. New York: Brewer, Warren & Putnam, 1931.

Tugwell, Rexford Guy. *The Democratic Roosevelt*. Garden City, N.Y.: Doubleday, 1957.

Tully, Grace. *FDR: My Boss*. New York: Scribner's, 1949.

Van Devander, Charles. *The Big Bosses*. New York: Howell-Soskin, 1944.

Vandiver, Frank E. *Black Jack: The Life and Times of John J. Pershing*. Two volumes. College Station: Texas A&M University Press, 1977.

Walch, Timothy, and Dwight M. Miller. *Herbert Hoover and Franklin D. Roosevelt: A Documentary History*. Westport, Conn.: Greenwood, 1998.

Walsh, George. *Gentleman Jimmy Walker: Mayor of the Jazz Age*. New York: Praeger, 1974.

Ward, Geoffrey C. *Before the Trumpet: Young Franklin Roosevelt 1882–1905*. New York: Harper & Row, 1985.

———. *A First-Class Temperament: The Emergence of Franklin Roosevelt*. New York: Harper & Row, 1989.

Warner, Emily Smith with Hawthorne Daniel. *The Happy Warrior: The Story of My Father, Alfred E. Smith*. Garden City, N.Y.: Doubleday, 1956.

Warren, Robert Penn. *All the King's Men*. New York: Harcourt, Brace, 1946.

Watkins, T. H. *Righteous Pilgrim: The Life and Times of Harold L. Ickes*. New York: Holt, 1990.

Weiss, Nancy J. *Farewell to the Party of Lincoln: Black Politics in the Age of FDR*. Princeton: Princeton University Press, 1983.

Werner, M. R. *Tammany Hall*. Garden City, N.Y.: Doubleday, 1928.

Whalen, Richard J. *The Founding Father: The Story of Joseph P. Kennedy*. New York: New American Library, 1964.

Wharton, Don. *The Roosevelt Omnibus*. New York: Knopf, 1934.

Wheeler, Burton K. with Paul F. Healy. *Yankee from the West*. Garden City, N.Y.: Doubleday, 1962.

White, Walter. *Rope and Faggot: A Biography of Judge Lynch*. New York: Knopf, 1929.

———. *A Man Called White: The Autobiography of Walter White*. New York: Viking, 1948.

Wilkins, Roy with Tom Mathews. *Standing Fast: The Autobiography of Roy Wilkins*. New York: Viking, 1982.

Williams, T. Harry. *Huey Long*. New York: Knopf, 1969.

Woodward, C. Vann. *The Strange Career of Jim Crow*. New York: Oxford University Press, 1974.

Wormser, Richard. *The Rise and Fall of Jim Crow*. New York: St. Martin's, 2003.

NEWSPAPERS

Arkansas Democrat

Atlanta Constitution

Austin American

Baltimore Evening Sun

Baltimore Sun

Boston Globe

Boston Herald

Boston Post

Brooklyn Eagle

Chicago American

Chicago Daily News

Chicago Daily Times

Chicago Defender

Chicago Herald-Examiner

Chicago Tribune

Christian Science Monitor

Cleveland Plain Dealer

Cleveland Press

Fort Worth Star-Telegram

Houston Post

Jackson Daily News

Kansas City Star

Los Angeles Times

Louisville Courier-Journal

Nashville Tennessean

New Orleans Times-Picayune

New York Evening Post

New York Herald-Tribune

New York Journal

New York Times

New York World-Telegram

Newark News

Philadelphia Evening Bulletin

Philadelphia Inquirer

Philadelphia Public Ledger

Philadelphia Record

Raleigh News and Observer

Richmond News-Leader

St. Louis Post-Dispatch

San Francisco Chronicle

San Francisco Examiner

Washington Evening Star

Washington Post

Washington Times-Herald

MAGAZINES, 1931–1932 EDITIONS

American Mercury

Atlantic

Collier's

The Crisis

Forum

Harper's

Liberty

Literary Digest

Nation

New Republic

New Yorker

Review of Reviews

Saturday Evening Post

Scribner's

Time

Vanity Fair

ACKNOWLEDGMENTS

I AM GRATEFUL to the archival staff of the Franklin D. Roosevelt Library at Hyde Park, New York, for helping me navigate through its vast collections. Raymond Teichman, supervisory archivist, and his longtime colleague Robert Parks were of invaluable assistance. Many thanks to Brian Hickey, grandson of James A. Farley, for alerting me to the existence of his grandfather's diary that was an essential source for this book. David Wigdor, assistant chief of the Manuscript Division at the Library of Congress, has been enormously helpful over the last four years. Thanks also to Elizabeth Safly, reference librarian at the Harry S. Truman Library at Independence, Missouri; Marjorie G. McMinch, reference archivist at the Hagley Museum and Library in Wilmington, Delaware; Tad Benicoff, special collections assistant at the Seeley G. Mudd Library, Princeton University; Jeff Suchanek and the special collections staff at the University of Kentucky Library; archivists Christine Weideman and Nancy F. Lyon of the Yale University Library; Yvonne Brooks of the Library of Congress; and Patricia

Palmer, Maureen Rehmer, Nell Ingalls, Lance Anderson, Gary Yurgil, Diane Brooks, and Ann Marie Siudzinksi of the Hinsdale Public Library's reference department.

Former New York governor Mario M. Cuomo, former U.S. senator Paul Simon, former Illinois state senator Jeremiah E. Joyce, and Loop lawyer Wayne W. Whalen were generous in sharing their insights and making suggestions that broadened the scope of this work. I also want to thank friends and colleagues Rudy Abramson, Ken Bode, Robert W. Merry, Gloria Steinem, and Curtis Wilkie for their interest in this work and helping in so many ways.

I am grateful to former senator Harry F. Byrd of Virginia and Walter Trohan of the *Chicago Tribune* for sharing their memories of the 1932 Democratic National Convention.

Thanks also to the historians Robert H. Ferrell, John A. Garraty, Alonzo L. Hamby, and Robert V. Remini for their wisdom and perspective on the history of the Democratic Party. I first became interested in the 1932 presidential election when I took a graduate history seminar more than three decades ago from Garraty at Columbia University.

My editor, Henry Ferris, shares my enthusiasm for the Age of Roosevelt, and his belief in this project has made it a reality. His hands-on editing has also made this a better book. Thanks also to his assistant Lisa Nager. I am also grateful to my agent Deborah Grosvenor for her encouragement and thoughtful suggestions.

At the *Chicago Sun-Times*, editor Michael Cooke, vice president of editorial John Cruickshank, and editorial page editor Steve Huntley have been helpful and generous in their support of this book.

Finally, I want to thank my wife, Susan, and our daughters, Erin and Shannon, for their love and constant support.

INDEX